THE OXFORD GRAMMAR OF
Classical Greek

James Morwood

OXFORD
UNIVERSITY PRESS

OXFORD
UNIVERSITY PRESS

Oxford   New York
Auckland   Bangkok   Buenos Aires
Cape Town   Chennai   Dar es Salaam   Delhi   Hong Kong   Istanbul
Karachi   Kolkata   Kuala Lumpur   Madrid   Melbourne   Mexico City   Mumbai
Nairobi   São Paulo   Shanghai   Singapore   Taipei   Tokyo   Toronto

Library of Congress Cataloging-in-Publication Data
is available at the Library of Congress
ISBN 0-19-521851-5

3 5 7 9 10 8 6 4 2
Printed in the United States of America
on acid-free paper

Contents

Appendices

Preface

This grammar is intended for those studying Greek in schools and universities as well as the ever-increasing number who learn it in adult education.

It is a grammar of Attic Greek (the dialect centred on Athens) from about 500 to 300 BC, but there is an appendix giving key information about the Homeric and Ionic dialects and New Testament Greek. As in the companion Latin grammar, I have aimed to cut down on the amount of accidence with which traditional grammars of classical languages have confronted their readers. I have given a large number of principal parts but divided them into two lists, the first for learning, the second for reference. Again as in the Latin grammar, to the analyses of the constructions I have added sentences from both Greek into English and English into Greek through which students can practise what they are learning. Vocabularies which cover these sentences are included. Greek names have generally been Latinized in my English, e.g. Crito for Kritōn, Cyrus for Kūros, and Thucydides for Thoukūdidēs.

I am very conscious that the demands of pedagogical clarity have at times led me to take liberties with philological truth. I am also aware that my decision not to adjust the original words in any of the numerous quotations has made the Greek in this grammar less smoothly regular than that in any of its predecessors. The justification for this is that I wanted to centre the grammar around true unvarnished Attic.

Acknowledgements

Any compiler of a grammar will inevitably owe a great deal to his predecessors. I am delighted to acknowledge my very considerable debt to two important American Greek grammars, those by William W. Goodwin (Macmillan, 1894; Thomas Nelson & Sons, 1992) and Herbert Weir Smyth (Harvard University, 1920; revised by Gordon M. Messing, 1956). These are too detailed for the tyro Greekist but remain classics in their field. The latter has proved especially valuable to me, and it will provide the answers to most questions left unanswered in this book. Raphael Kühner and

Bernhard Gerth's monumental *Ausführliche Grammatik der griechischen Sprache* (Hanover, 1898–1904) is the fullest work of reference.

I am equally delighted to express my appreciation of the generous help given me by the following: Michael Atkinson, Christopher Collard, E. J. Kenney, David Langslow, John Penney, Philomen Probert and John Taylor (who wrote the section on New Testament Greek). Rachel Chapman, James Clackson and Andrew Hobson have made important contributions, as has W. Sidney Allen. (The essay on the history of the pronunciation of Greek is in fact a simple précis of material in Allen's *Vox Graeca*.) Jason Zerdin has been the most vigilant and constructive of proof-readers. To my grateful acknowledgement of how much I owe to all of them, I must add that I take full responsibility for any errors which my obstinacy or carelessness has allowed to remain.

Richard Ashdowne has been my amanuensis since the start of this project. He has seen to the production of the manuscript and has proved more than equal to the challenge set him by the scribblings with which I littered the successive revisions. He has been a constant source not only of support but of helpful counsel too. I thank him warmly.

I dedicate this book to the Joint Association of Classical Teachers' Greek Summer School at Bryanston, an institution which has played an incalculable rôle in ensuring the survival of Greek studies in the UK.

Wadham College,
Oxford

James Morwood,
Grocyn Lecturer,
Faculty of Literae Humaniores,
University of Oxford

Glossary of grammatical terms

accent   a mark (acute, grave or circumflex) placed above a vowel or the second letter of a diphthong to indicate the musical pitch at which the accented syllable was pronounced.

accidence   the area of grammar dealing with endings.

accusative   the usual case of a direct object; many prepositions take the accusative.

active   the form of a verb most commonly used when the subject of the sentence performs the action (e.g. we do = ποιοῦμεν) or has his/her/its/their state described (e.g. we are kind = εὔφρονές ἐσμεν).

adjective   a word describing, identifying or saying something about a noun, with which it agrees in gender, number and case: the *big* book = τὸ *μέγα* βιβλίον; the book is *big* = τὸ βιβλίον (ἐστὶ) *μέγα*.

adverb   a word which describes or changes the meaning of a verb, an adjective or another adverb: he walks *slowly* = *βραδέως* βαδίζει.

agent   the person who causes an action: it was done by *this man* = ὑπὸ *τούτου* ἐπράχθη.

agree with   have the same gender, case and number as.

antecedent   the noun, pronoun or clause to which a relative pronoun refers back.

aorist tense   the tense of a verb which refers to something that happened in the past: I *did* this = τοῦτο *ἐποίησα*. Distinguish between this past tense and the imperfect ('I was doing'), the perfect ('I have done') and the pluperfect ('I had done').

apodosis   the main clause of a conditional sentence, i.e. not the 'if ...' or 'unless ...' clause but the clause giving the result.

apposition   the placing of a word, phrase or clause in parallel with another word, phrase or clause to give further information about the latter: George Washington, *the President*, spoke eloquently.

aspect   the term referring to the distinction between two ways in which a verb can convey time (the time and the type of time) – see p. 61.

augment   something added at the beginning of verbs to denote a past tense. If the verb begins with a consonant, this is the letter ἐ-: for example, ἔπαυον is the imperfect of παύω.

cardinals   see *numerals*.

case   the form of a noun, pronoun, adjective or article that shows the part it plays in a sentence; there are six cases: nominative, genitive, dative, accusative, vocative, and locative.

clause   a section of a sentence in which there are at least a subject and a verb.

common   either masculine or feminine in gender, according to meaning: man = *ὁ* ἄνθρωπος; woman = *ἡ* ἄνθρωπος.

comparative   the form of an adjective or adverb that makes it mean 'more', 'rather' or 'too': more wise (wiser), rather wise, too wise = σοφώτερος.

complement   a word or phrase which describes the subject of the verb and completes the description; it is used with verbs such as 'I am' and 'I become' which cannot take an object: my mother is *intelligent* = ἡ μήτηρ *σοφή* ἐστιν; my mother became *priestess* = ἡ μήτηρ *ἱέρεια* ἐγένετο.

compound verb   a verb formed by adding a prefix to a simple verb: I *over*shoot = *ὑπερ*βάλλω.

concessive clause   a clause usually beginning in English with the word 'although' or 'though'.

conditional clause   a clause usually beginning in English with the words 'if', 'if not' or 'unless'.

conjugate   give the different forms of the verb: παύω, παύεις, παύει, παύομεν, παύετε, παύουσι; ἔπαυον, ἔπαυες, ἔπαυε, etc.

conjunction	a word used to join clauses, phrases or words together: men *and* women = ἄνδρες **καὶ** γυναῖκες.
consonant	a sound, or letter representing a sound, that is used together with a vowel, such as β, γ, δ; cf. *vowel*.
construction	the way in which a clause is constructed grammatically.
contraction	the process by which two vowels or a vowel and a diphthong standing next to each other in adjacent syllables are united into a single vowel or diphthong, e.g. χρύσε-ος (golden) contracts to χρῡσοῦς and τῑμά-εις (you honour) contracts to τῑμᾷς.
dative	the case of an indirect object; among the many meanings of the dative are 'to', 'for', 'with' and 'by'; many prepositions take the dative.
declension	there are a number of patterns according to which Greek nouns change their endings; we call these declensions.
decline	go through (or, more literally, down) the different cases of a noun, adjective or pronoun, in order.
definite article	in English, 'the'; in Greek, ὁ, ἡ, τό.
deictic	deictic (noun: **deixis**) is used of words or expressions which 'point' (= δείκνῡμι) to some feature of a situation. Pronouns (e.g., οὗτος, οὑτοσί, ἐκεῖνος (this, this ... here, that), etc.) and words of place (ἐνθάδε, ἐκεῖ (here, there), etc.) and time (νῦν, τότε (now, then), etc.) tell us such things about a situation as who is involved in it, and where it takes place.
deliberative	showing that a thought process about a possible action is going on: What am I to do?
deponent	the passive form of a verb when that form is active in meaning.
diaeresis	two dots (¨) placed over the second of two adjacent vowels which are to be pronounced separately: βοΐ (to an ox).
dialect	this term refers to the different forms of Greek used in different areas of the Greek world. The chief dialects that occur in literature are Aeolic, Doric, Ionic and Attic.
diminutive	a word formed from another to express diminished size, e.g. 'hillock' from 'hill' – τὸ παιδίον (little child) from παῖς (child).

diphthong   the union of two vowels pronounced as one syllable (or, more properly, one vowel followed by a glide into a second vowel).

direct object   see *object (direct)*.

direct speech   the words actually used by a speaker.

dual   in Greek, nouns or adjectives representing two people or things, and verbs with two people or things as their subject, can adopt a special form which is known as the dual (see pp. 232–3).

enclitic   a short word which cannot stand alone but has to follow another word, onto which it throws back its accent (see p. 224). 'Enclitic' means 'leaning on'.

ending   a letter or letters added to the stem (or modification of the stem) of verbs, nouns and adjectives, in order to mark tense, case, etc. Compare the way in which an English noun changes in the plural: dish, dish*es*.

feminine   one of the three Greek genders: γραῦς (old woman) and ναῦς (ship) are both feminine nouns; they take the feminine form of the article, ἡ.

finite verb   a verb with a personal ending, as opposed to infinitives and participles.

future perfect tense   the tense of a verb that refers to something in the future at a stage after it has happened: I *shall have* ceased = *πεπαύσομαι*. In Greek this is a rare form – many verbs do not possess it – and it appears in the middle or passive (indistinguishable from each other in appearance).

gender   the class in which a noun or pronoun is placed in a grammatical grouping; in Greek, these classes are masculine, feminine, neuter and common (i.e. masculine or feminine according to meaning).

genitive   the case that shows possession; among its many meanings, the dominant one is 'of'; in Greek it is also the case of separation; many prepositions take the genitive.

gerund   a verbal noun. Greek uses the neuter singular of the definite article followed by the infinitive to supply this: the art of *fighting* = ἡ *τοῦ μάχεσθαι* τέχνη.

gerundive   a verbal adjective which expresses the idea of obligation: this is (*requiring-*)*to-be-done* (*i.e.*, this *must* be done) = τοῦτο **ποιητέον** ἐστίν.

imperative   the parts of the verb that express a command: *do* this! = τοῦτο **ποίει**.

imperfect tense   the tense which expresses continuous or repeated or incomplete action in the past: I *was* considering = ἐνόμιζ*ον*.

impersonal verb   a verb introduced in English by the word 'it' (e.g., 'it is raining'), and in Greek used impersonally in the 3rd person singular: *it is necessary* for me = **χρή** με.

indefinite article   in English, 'a' or 'an'; there is no indefinite article in Greek, though enclitic τις can serve as an equivalent: *a* (*certain*) woman = γυνή **τις**.

indefinite construction   the English word 'ever' added to the end of another word brings out the force of this construction. Compare 'Pericles, who says that, is mad' (specific) with 'Who*ever* says that is mad' (indefinite).

indicative   usually refers to a verb when it makes a statement or asks a question: τοῦτο εἶπεν = he said this. With reference to Greek, the word usually indicates that the verb is not in the imperative, subjunctive, optative, infinitive or participle.

indirect command   the reporting of an actual (direct) command, e.g. Do this! (direct speech, direct command): She instructed him *to do this* (indirect command).

indirect object   the noun or pronoun indirectly affected by the verb, at which the direct object is aimed: I gave *him* the book = τὸ βιβλίον **αὐτῷ** ἔδωκα.

indirect question   the reporting of an actual (direct) question, e.g. What are you doing? (direct speech, direct question): I asked her *what she was doing* (indirect question).

indirect statement   the reporting of someone's words, e.g. I have done this (direct statement): He said *that he had done this* (indirect statement).

infinitive   the form of a verb that means 'to do something': to teach = διδάσκειν. In Greek, infinitives vary according to tense and voice.

inflection   see *ending*.

interjection a sound, word or phrase standing outside the grammatical structure of the sentence and expressing an emotion such as distress, joy or disgust: alas! = οἴμοι.

intransitive verb a verb which does not take a direct object, e.g. 'go', 'come'.

irregular verb a verb that does not follow the set pattern of παύω (the regular verb in this Grammar) and either belongs to a small class of verbs or has its own individual forms.

jussive giving an order.

locative the case which tells us where something is happening: οἴκοι = at home; Ἀθήνησι = in Athens.

macron a line above a vowel indicating that it is long, e.g. ᾱ ῑ ῡ.

main clause the clause which is the basic grammatical unit of a sentence. 'Although I love her, she still avoids me.' 'She still avoids me' makes sense on its own, while 'although I love her' does not. Thus 'she still avoids me' is the main clause, and 'although I love her' is a subordinate clause.

masculine one of the three Greek genders: ἀνήρ (man) and λόγος (word) are both masculine nouns; they take the masculine form of the definite article, ὁ.

middle a term applying to certain Greek verb forms. The middle often has a reflexive quality: παύομαι = I stop *myself*, i.e. I cease; φέρομαι = I carry off *for myself*, I win. However, a number of verbs have a middle form but an entirely active meaning, e.g. ἥδομαι = I rejoice.

mood the grammatical form of a verb which shows whether it is in the indicative, subjunctive, optative or imperative.

negative expressing denial, refusal or prohibition. In English, the words 'no' or 'not' are generally used.

neuter one of the three Greek genders: γάλα (milk) and δῶρον (gift) are both neuter nouns; they take the neuter form of the definite article, τό.

nominative the case of the subject of a sentence or (usually) of the complement of a verb: *the king* is angry = *ὁ βασιλεὺς* ὀργίζεται.

noun a word that names or denotes a person or thing: ὄνομα = name *or* noun, βιβλίον = book, ὀργή = anger.

number the state of being either singular or plural or dual.

numerals numbers; these are either cardinals (1, 2, 3, etc.), ordinals (1st, 2nd, 3rd, etc.) or adverbs (once, twice, three times, etc.).

object (direct) a noun or its equivalent acted upon by a transitive verb: the dog bites *the boy* = ὁ κύων *τὸν παῖδα* δάκνει.

optative a Greek mood of the verb which does not express statements but such concepts as 'would', 'might', 'if only!' It is also used in the indefinite construction and in certain subordinate clauses. It is more remote than the subjunctive in either likelihood or time. (The pronunciations 'óptative' and 'optátive' are both current, with the UK having a preference for the latter.)

ordinals see *numerals*.

parse to give a full grammatical description of a word: for verbs this means to give the person, number, tense, mood, voice and meaning, e.g., φιλεῖς is the second person singular present indicative active of φιλέω, 'I love'.

particle Greek particles, short words which never change, can connect clauses and qualify – and colour – words, phrases or clauses.

participle an adjective formed from a verb (it can still take an object). In Greek, participles are either present (a *loving* woman = γυνὴ φιλοῦσα), future (*about to love* her husband = φιλήσουσα τὸν ἄνδρα), aorist (*after loving* her husband = φιλήσασα τὸν ἄνδρα) or perfect (*after having died, i.e. being dead* = τεθνηκυῖα).

part of speech a grammatical term identifying the function of a word: noun, adjective, pronoun, verb, adverb, preposition, conjunction, interjection.

passive when the verb is in the passive form, the subject of the verb does not perform the action but experiences it: the king *was loved* = ὁ βασιλεὺς *ἐφιλήθη*. In Greek, a significant number of middle verbs use the passive form in the aorist (see p. 66).

perfect tense the tense of a verb that refers to a completed action, the effects of which still continue in the present; in English the word 'have' or 'has' is generally used: he *has written* a letter (and it is now written) = *γέγραφεν* ἐπιστολήν. The Greek perfect may often be translated by the present: τέθνηκε = he has died, *i.e.* he is dead.

person a term identifying the subject of a verb: 1st person – I (singular), we (plural); 2nd person – you (both singular and plural); 3rd person – he, she, it (singular), they (plural); dual – both of you (2nd person), both of them (3rd person). (Adjective: **personal**.)

personal pronoun a pronoun that refers to a person, e.g. I, you = ἐγώ, σύ.

phrase a self-contained group of words which does not contain a finite verb: I walked *through the city*.

pluperfect tense the tense that means 'had', referring to a past state resulting from a completed action: the flower *had bloomed* (and was then in flower) = τὸ ἄνθος *ἠνθήκει*.

plural of nouns and other parts of speech, referring to more than one: the ships = αἱ νῆες.

positive not negative; (of adjectives) not comparative or superlative.

possessive pronoun a pronoun, in an adjectival form, that shows possession, belonging to someone or something: my, mine = ἐμός, ἐμή, ἐμόν.

prefix a syllable or word added to the beginning of another word: I *over*shoot = *ὑπερ*βάλλω.

preposition a word that stands (almost always) in front of a noun or pronoun to produce an adverbial phrase. It expresses a spatial, temporal or logical meaning. In Greek it is followed by the accusative, genitive or dative: *according to* the laws = *κατὰ* τοὺς νόμους.

present tense the tense of a verb that refers to something happening now: I am playing, I play = παίζω.

principal parts the forms of a verb that must be learnt to give access to all its parts.

pronoun a word that stands instead of a noun (person or thing), e.g. 'it' used in place of 'the tree': this, that = οὗτος, αὕτη, τοῦτο; ἐκεῖνος, ἐκείνη, ἐκεῖνο. See also *personal pronoun*.

protasis the 'if ...' or 'unless ...' clause of a conditional sentence.

reduplication the process by which verbs begining with a single consonant (but not ῥ) form a prefix in the perfect, pluperfect and future perfect by adding that letter followed by an ε at the beginning: παύω, *πέπαυκα*, *ἐπεπαύκη*, *πεπαύσομαι*.

reflexive pronoun a word referring back to the subject of the main verb and indicating that the action of the verb is performed on its subject: he killed *himself* = ἀπέκτεινεν *ἑαυτόν*. The reflexive pronoun never appears in the nominative.

regular verb a verb that follows παύω in its forms.

relative pronoun a pronoun that introduces a subordinate clause, identifying the person or thing mentioned in the main clause: the man *who* loves me = ὁ ἀνὴρ *ὃς* φιλεῖ ἐμέ.

sentence a group of words with a subject and a verb, that can stand on its own to make a statement, ask a question, give a command or express a wish.

sequence of tenses and moods the principle according to which the use of a certain tense in the main clause determines whether the subjunctive or the optative should be used in a subordinate clause.

singular of nouns and other parts of speech, referring to just one: the tree = τὸ δένδρον.

stem the part of a noun, adjective or verb to which endings are added: *λόγ-* is the stem of *λόγος* = word; *παυ-* is the stem of *παύω* = I stop; *παύσ-* is the stem of *παύσω* = I shall stop.

subject in a clause or sentence, the noun or pronoun that causes the action of the verb or has his/her/its/their state described: *the queen* killed the king = *ἡ βασίλεια* ἀπέκτεινε τὸν βασιλέᾱ.

subjunctive a verb form that is used, among many other functions, to express doubt, unlikelihood or possibility; it is less remote than the optative in either likelihood or time. Words such as 'may', 'might' and 'should' can indicate a subjunctive in English (see p. 61).

subordinate clause
a clause which depends on another clause (usually the main clause) of the sentence in which it stands. In the sentence, 'He is an author who is easy to understand', the clause 'who is easy to understand' describes the author. The clause would not make sense on its own. Thus it is subordinate.

superlative
the form of an adjective or adverb that makes it mean 'most' or 'very': *most* small (small*est*), *very* small = μῑκρότατος.

syllable
part of a word that forms a spoken unit, usually a vowel sound with consonants before and/or after: συμ-βάλ-λω (I throw together); σύ-νο-δος (meeting).

syntax
the area of grammar dealing with constructions.

tense
the form of a verb that shows when the action takes place: present, future, perfect, etc. (The word 'tense' is related to French *temps* (= time).)

terminations
the endings of nouns, adjectives and verbs that show their case, number, gender, tense, person etc.

tragedy
the tragic plays of the three great Attic poets of the fifth century BC, Aeschylus, Sophocles and Euripides.

transitive verb
a verb used with a direct object either expressed or understood, e.g. 'pick apples' or 'pick till you are tired' (but not 'he picked at his lunch' – here 'picked' is intransitive).

verb
a word that describes an action: I *arrived* at Athens = *ἀφῑκόμην* εἰς τὰς Ἀθήνᾱς.

vocative
the case by which one addresses or calls to someone: *Demosthenes*, come here! = ὦ *Δημόσθενες*, ἐλθὲ δεῦρο.

voice
the set of forms of a verb that show the relation of the subject to the action, i.e. (in Greek) active, middle or passive.

vowel
a sound, or letter representing a sound, that can be spoken by itself: α, ε, η, ι, ο, ω, υ.

Abbreviations

acc.	accusative		**indef.**	indefinite
act.	active		**infin.**	infinitive
aor.	aorist		**intr.**	intransitive
c.	common (i.e, masculine or feminine as appropriate)		**m.**	masculine
			mid.	middle
			n.	neuter
cf.	*confer* (Latin for 'compare')		**N.B.**	*NOTA BENE* (Latin for 'note well')
dat.	dative		**nom.**	nominative
def.	definite		**opt.**	optative
e.g.	*exempli gratia* (Latin: 'for [the sake of an] example')		**p(p).**	page(s)
			pass.	passive
etc.	*et cetera* (Latin for 'and so on')		**pf.**	perfect
			pl.	plural
f.	feminine		**plpf.**	pluperfect
fut.	future		**pp.**	pages
gen.	genitive		**pple.**	participle
i.e.	*id est* (Latin for 'that is', introducing an explanation)		**sg.**	singular
			subj.	subjunctive
			tr.	transitive
impf.	imperfect		**usu.**	usually

The Greek alphabet and its pronunciation

Greek letter	written as		English equivalent	Recommended pronunciation[1] (standard southern British English)
	small	capital		
alpha	α	A	a	short: as in <u>a</u>wake, Italian <u>a</u>mare long: as in f<u>a</u>ther, Italian am<u>a</u>re
beta	β	B	b	as English <u>b</u>
gamma	γ	Γ	g	as in go before κ, χ, ξ, γ: as in i<u>n</u>k, ly<u>n</u>x, fi<u>n</u>ger
delta	δ	Δ	d	as French <u>d</u> (with tongue on teeth, not gums)
epsilon	ε	E	e	short, as in p<u>e</u>t
zeta	ζ	Z	sd	as in wi<u>sd</u>om
eta	η	H	ē	long, as in <u>ai</u>r
theta	θ	Θ	th	as in <u>t</u>op (emphatically pronounced); later, as in <u>th</u>in
iota	ι	I	i	short: as in l<u>i</u>t, French v<u>i</u>tesse long: as in b<u>ea</u>d

[short iota is often written under η, ω or long ā, i.e. ῃ, ῳ, ᾳ (iota subscript) – see under Diphthongs, below]

kappa	κ	K	c	hard c: as in s<u>k</u>ill; contrast khi
lambda	λ	Λ	l	as in <u>l</u>eap
mu	μ	M	m	as in <u>m</u>et
nu	ν	N	n	as in <u>n</u>et
xi	ξ	Ξ	x	as in bo<u>x</u>

---

[1] Where two recommendations are given for pronunciation, the first is a less accurate approximation than the second.

Greek letter	written as		English equivalent	Recommended pronunciation (standard southern British English)
	small	capital		
omicron	o	O	o	short, as in p<u>o</u>t, German G<u>o</u>tt
pi	π	Π	p	as in s<u>p</u>ot; contrast phi
rho	ρ	P	r	Scottish rolled <u>r</u>
sigma	σ, ς	Σ	s	as in <u>s</u>ing, le<u>ss</u>on

[ς is used at the end of a word, σ elsewhere, e.g. ὅστις. Many Greek texts print a so-called lunate sigma, c, capital C (in the shape of the crescent moon), which is used in all positions, e.g. ὅϲτιϲ.]

tau	τ	T	t	as English <u>t</u> in s<u>t</u>op(with tongue on teeth not gums); contrast theta
upsilon	υ	Y	u, y	short: as in French l<u>u</u>ne, German M<u>ü</u>ller long: as in French r<u>u</u>se, German M<u>ü</u>hle
phi	φ	Φ	ph	as in p<u>o</u>t (emphatically pronounced); later, as in <u>f</u>oot
khi	χ	X	ch	as in <u>k</u>ill (emphatically pronounced); later, as in Scottish lo<u>ch</u>
psi	ψ	Ψ	ps	as in la<u>ps</u>e
omega	ω	Ω	ō	as in s<u>aw</u>

Throughout this Grammar, where α, ι or υ are long, they are marked by a macron (i.e. ᾱ, ῑ, ῡ), unless they are already shown to be long either by an iota subscript beneath them (i.e. ᾳ) or by a circumflex above them (except that, when ι or υ forms part of a diphthong, a circumflex does not indicate that the ι or υ is long but that the diphthong as a whole is long).

| Diphthongs

ᾳ (ᾱ with iota subscript)	as long ᾱ (more correctly with ι sounded at the end)
αι	as in h<u>igh</u>
αυ	as in h<u>ow</u>
ει	as in fianc<u>ée</u>, German B<u>ee</u>t
ευ	as in Cockney b<u>el</u>t

ῃ (η with iota subscript)	as η (more correctly with ι sounded at the end)
ηυ	as ευ, but with the first part longer
οι	as in boy, coin
ου	as in pool, French rouge
υι	close to French huit
ῳ (ω with iota subscript)	as ω (more correctly with ι sounded at the end)

Breathings and accents (see below for both) are written over the second letter of a diphthong, e.g. οἶδα (I know). Where one of the above combinations is pronounced as two separate vowels, breathings are written over the first letter, e.g. ἄϊδρις (ignorant), while the accent is written over the vowel to which it belongs. Note also the diaeresis (¨).

In many modern texts the iota subscript will not be found. The iota will be placed at the same level as the other letters (e.g. ωι, not ῳ). This was in fact the practice in classical times. The iota subscript was a later invention.

| Double consonants

When double consonants are used, the sound is correspondingly lengthened, e.g.

νν	unnamed (compare unaimed)
ππ	hip-pocket
σσ	disservice
ττ	rat-trap

The exception is γγ which is pronounced as in linger, i.e. as if νγ. Similarly, γκ γχ are pronounced with an 'n' as in encore and anchor. Note also that in many words Attic has ττ where other dialects (including Ionic) have σσ: thus θάλαττα (the sea) is Attic, cf. θάλασσα.

| Moveable ν

In the accidence tables in this Grammar you will see that some forms are given which end in (ν). This is the so-called **moveable nu**, which is generally added at the end of a word when the next word begins with a vowel. It can be added to words ending in -σι, to the 3 sg. (of verbs) in -ε and to ἐστι (= is). Compare the following:

πᾶσι δίδωσι ταῦτα	he gives these things to everybody
πᾶσιν ἔδωκεν αὐτά	he gave these very things to everybody

☑ Moveable nu can also be added at the end of a sentence, e.g.

πᾶσι ταῦτα ἔδωκεν.	he gave these things to everybody

| Breathings

Words which begin with a vowel have a breathing mark over the first (in the case of a diphthong, over the second) letter. This will either be:

    ῾   the 'rough' breathing, denoting the sound 'h'; or
    ᾽   the 'smooth' breathing, denoting the absence of the sound 'h'

Note that all words beginning with ρ and υ take a rough breathing, e.g. ῥόδον (rose) and ὕδωρ (water), hence, e.g., 'rheumatism' and 'hydraulics'.

    Some examples:

    ἡ, αὕτη, αὐτή, ὁ ῥήτωρ (speaker)

Note the position of the breathing with capital letters: Ἡρόδοτος, Αἰσχύλος.

| Crasis

In Greek, some combinations of words which occurred frequently together could coalesce to form a single word by a process called **crasis** (κρᾶσις = mixing), if the first ended in a vowel and the second began with one. This is similar to the English contraction in words like 'won't', 'shan't', 'I'm' and 'I'd'. In Greek it is usually indicated by a smooth breathing on the first vowel sound of the word even though it begins with a consonant. Some common examples (with their full forms) are:

καλοὶ κἀγαθοί	καλοὶ καὶ ἀγαθοί	good and fine men
ταὐτά	τὰ αὐτά	the same things
χὠ	καὶ ὁ	and the, and he
ὦνδρες	ὦ ἄνδρες	O men!

In recognising crasis, it is worth remembering that χ or θ may represent a combination of κ or τ with the rough breathing.

| Accents

Greek words have pitch accents, not stresses. These accents, ´ (acute),
` (grave) and ˆ (circumflex), denote the musical pitch at which the
accented syllable was pronounced. The acute (´) denotes high pitch, the
grave (`) lower pitch and the circumflex (ˆ, originally written as a grave
and an acute combined, ´`) high pitch falling to low.

This is difficult for English speakers — whose language is stressed —
to reproduce. Modern Greeks in fact use the accents to denote stress, not
pitch — in fact, the change from the pitch to the stress accent took place in
antiquity, probably before the end of the fourth century AD —, and
English-speaking learners may wish to follow their example.

In the UK, USA and Holland, there is a strong tradition of stressing Greek
according to the rules for Latin (for which, see p. 1 of the companion Latin
Grammar). This follows the mistaken arguments of a Dutch medical doctor
named Henning in the 17th century, and cannot be recommended in spite
of its widespread use.

The tradition of writing accents appears to have started at Alexandria
around 200 BC and is generally accredited to Aristophanes of Byzantium.
Initially its use seems to have been intermittent and mainly to clarify
ambiguities — in which respect it can still prove helpful.

Accents are marked throughout this Grammar, and we outline various
ways in which they are of use in the understanding of Greek on p. 218.
However, those who do not wish to master the expertise of accentuation
surely need feel no shame. It did not exist at the high period of Attic
literature. Those who wish to go ahead are referred to the appendix on
accentuation on pp. 222–6.

| Punctuation

There was virtually no punctuation in fifth- and fourth-century Athens.
Nor were there any gaps between words. It seems good sense, however, to
adopt the conventions developed later in these areas.

Note, therefore, the following punctuation marks:

.	full stop, as in English
,	comma, as in English
·	colon or semi-colon (placed on a level with the top of the small letters)
;	question mark (?)

| Practice exercises

Write the following Greek words in English letters:

δρᾶμα, ἱπποπόταμος (-ος = -us), Ζεύς, Παρθενών, λύγξ, Γοργών, ἠχώ, Ἀφροδίτη, Βάκχος, πρῶτον.

Write the following English words in Greek:

acropolis (c = κ), rhododendron, dogma, symposium (-um = -ov), charactēr, asbestos, Sphinx, Sōcratēs, Athēnē, Cyclōps.

Which animals do you imagine make the following noises in Greek?

αὖ αὖ, βῆ βῆ, βρεκεκεκέξ, κικκαβαῦ, κόκκῡ.[1]

We give here a fable of Aesop (336) so that you can practise your pronunciation:

χειμῶνος ὥρᾳ τὸν σῖτον βραχέντα οἱ μύρμηκες ἔψυχον. τέττιξ δὲ λῑμώττων ἤτει αὐτοὺς τροφήν. οἱ δὲ μύρμηκες εἶπον αὐτῷ· 'διὰ τί τὸ θέρος οὐ συνῆγες καὶ σὺ τροφήν;' ὁ δὲ εἶπεν· 'οὐκ ἐσχόλαζον, ἀλλ' ᾖδον μουσικῶς.' οἱ δὲ γελάσαντες εἶπον· 'ἀλλ' εἰ θέρους ὥραις ηὔλεις, χειμῶνος ὀρχοῦ.'

ὁ μῦθος δηλοῖ ὅτι οὐ δεῖ τινα ἀμελεῖν ἐν παντὶ πράγματι, ἵνα μὴ λῡπηθῇ καὶ κινδῡνεύσῃ.

In the winter season, the ants dried out their drenched grain. A grasshopper who was famished with hunger asked them for food. The ants said to him, 'Why didn't you collect food in the summer like us (*literally*, also)?' And he said, 'I did not have the time, but I sang away melodiously.' And they said with a laugh, 'Well then, if you made music in the summer months, (you can) dance in the winter!'

The story shows that one should not be negligent in any matter if one wants to avoid distress and danger.

---

[1] Some of these may defeat you. They are the calls of dogs, sheep, frogs, screech owls and cuckoos respectively.

| The history of the pronunciation of Greek

In 1267, Roger Bacon, the English philosopher and experimental scientist, observed that there were not five men in Latin Christendom acquainted with Greek grammar. And despite efforts to improve the situation, Petrarch could count only eight or nine Italians who knew Greek a hundred years later.

However, Italy did see a gradual growth in the teaching of Greek in the fourteenth and fifteenth centuries, a progress further speeded by the influx of Byzantine scholars after the fall of Constantinople to the Turks in 1453. Naturally enough, these scholars pronounced ancient Greek like their native tongue of modern Greek. Thus, in addition to the other distortions they inevitably inflicted upon the pronunciation of ancient Greek, they gave respectability to the considerable reduction of the rich variety of vowel sounds available to the classical language. ι, η, υ, ει, οι and υι were all pronounced as 'i', and the judgement of another English scholar of the following century, Roger Ascham — the author of 'The Scholemaster' — is understandable, however hyperbolically expressed: 'all sounds in Greek are now exactly the same, reduced, that is to say, to a like thin and slender character, and subjected to the authority of a single letter, the *iota*; so that all one can hear is a feeble piping like that of sparrows, or an unpleasant hissing like that of snakes.'

Long before Ascham's broadside, scholarly doubts had arisen about the current pronunciation of Greek. A Spanish humanist, Antonio of Lebrixa, led the way in 1486. In a further treatise of 1503, he argued, among other things, that η is a long vowel corresponding to ε as ω does to o, and that ζ is pronounced σδ. Further progress was made by the great Venetian printer Aldus Manutius, who was the first to cite the correct bleating pronunciation of βῆ βῆ, rejecting the current 'vee vee'.

Then in 1528 Erasmus' dialogue *De recta Latini Graecique sermonis pronuntiatione* ('Concerning the correct pronunciation of Latin and Greek') was published in Basle. This light-hearted conversation between a bear (the instructor) and a lion was a milestone on the journey towards the re-establishment of the classical pronunciation.

Though his work appeared to have liberated ancient Greek from the tyranny of its modern delivery, Erasmus himself did not in fact practise what he preached. The credit for practical application of the reformed pronunciation must go to two Cambridge scholars, John Cheke and

Thomas Smith, who in 1540 were elected Regius Professors of Greek and Civil Law respectively. Their attempts to establish the new pronunciation[1] were temporarily halted when the Chancellor of the University published in 1542 an edict specifically forbidding it — undergraduates, he claimed, were becoming insolent in making use of an exotic pronunciation and relishing the fact that their elders could not understand it. However, his edict was repealed in 1558. As W.S. Allen[2] remarks, 'with all their imperfections, the 16th-century reforms resulted in something like an approximation to what we now believe to have been the classical Attic values ...'. The so-called Erasmian pronunciation now reached out from England to the continent.

But at the very time that English scholarship seemed to be leading the rest of Europe in this area, it suffered a major set-back. In the sixteenth century, the Middle English vowel system shifted to that of modern English (the so-called Great English Vowel Shift). This altered the nature of the English long vowels to which sixteenth-century scholars had, with remarkable accuracy, tied the Greek vowel sounds. The most notorious examples of what happened are the pronunciation of η as in m<u>ea</u>t, αι as in p<u>ay</u>, ει as in kal<u>ei</u>doscope, and ου as in g<u>ow</u>n.

And so by the end of the nineteenth century, a new set of reforms had to be instituted. The Cambridge University Press has played an honourable rôle in publishing the necessary documentation. First, there was *The Restored Pronunciation of Greek and Latin* by E.V. Arnold and R.S. Conway (1895, 4th revised edition 1908). Then there was *The Teaching of Classics* (1954). Finally there has been the influential work of W. Sidney Allen (*Vox Graeca*, 1968). We begin the new millennium with no excuse for failing to fall in line with philological scholarship in this important area.

[1] Not directly derived from Erasmus. Cheke and Smith did not, in fact, always agree among themselves: while Cheke pours scorn on 'af af' as the English equivalent of a Greek dog's αὖ αὖ, Smith cites the 'af af' bark of Maltese terriers.

[2] This essay is in fact a summary of pp. 125–34 of W. Sidney Allen's *Vox Graeca* (Cambridge, 2nd edition, 1974). The quotation is from p. 130.

Reference grammar

Nouns, adjectives and pronouns

Number and gender

In English grammar we are familiar with the concept of **number**, i.e. singular and plural:

> The **girl was** cleverer than the <u>boys</u> but <u>they were</u> not afraid of **her**.

Here the words in bold are in the singular, while the words underlined are in the plural.

We are also familiar with the concept of **gender**, i.e. masculine, feminine and neuter:

> The boy and the girl love the parrot but it feels no affection for them.

Here the boy is 'masculine' and the girl is 'feminine'. While the parrot will of course in reality be either male or female, it is here regarded as neither: hence the word 'it'. This is the 'neuter' gender.

The assignment of gender in Greek will strike English speakers as extremely arbitrary. Greek, for example, has a feminine as well as a neuter word for 'book', and feminine words for 'island', 'army' and 'cavalry'.

Cases

Greek is an **inflected** language, i.e. the endings of nouns, pronouns, adjectives and verbs change to reflect their relationship with other words in a sentence. English is largely uninflected, though some words do change according to their function.

> I am searching for a woman <u>whom</u> I admire, but I cannot find <u>her</u>.
> Is she avoiding <u>me</u>?

'Whom', 'her' and 'me' are the **accusative** (direct object forms) of 'who', 'she' and 'I'. (You can see how English tends to abolish inflection from the fact that most speakers nowadays would say 'who' and not 'whom', or omit the word altogether, in the first sentence.)

Verbs in tenses (see pp. 60–1) with personal endings are called **finite** verbs; they have **subjects** and often have **objects**. The subject carries out the action of the verb; the object is on the receiving end of the action of the verb. In the first sentence above, 'I' is the subject of the verb 'am searching for', and 'a woman' is the object. 'I' am doing the searching; 'a woman' is being searched for. The subject is in the **nominative** case; the object is in the **accusative** case.

Which words are the subjects and the objects in the following sentences?

> He is studying his grammar.
> The dog keeps distracting him.
> I am watching them.
> These people I am watching especially carefully.

In what case are the following?

> she, her, whom, us, me

Nominative and accusative are the names of two of the Greek **cases**. In Greek there are five main cases, and they all have names which are still used in English grammars.

In Greek the endings of nouns, pronouns and adjectives vary according to the case they are in as well as according to their number and gender.[1] Generally speaking, in modern English this happens only with some pronouns, as in the examples above.

The endings by which the cases are marked on most Greek nouns fall into a number of regular patterns. (The word 'case' comes from the Latin word meaning 'fall'.) We call these patterns **declensions**. It is customary to recognise three of these in Greek. To **decline** is to go through (or down) the different cases of a noun, adjective or pronoun in order.

---

[1] In the vocabulary lists in this grammar, nouns are given in their nom. and gen. singular (though the gen. is omitted in the case of regular nouns of the first and second declensions), while adjectives and pronouns are given in their nom. sg. masculine, feminine and neuter.

In Greek, adjectives are in the same number, gender and case as the nouns to which they refer. (This is called **agreement**.) The endings, however, may differ since the adjective may belong to a different declension from its noun.

1 | Nominative

The nominative is, as we have seen, the case of the subject of the verb:

ὁ Σωκράτης αἰνιγματωδῶς λέγει.
Socrates is speaking in riddles.

It is also used for the **complement** of the verb, when the verb's subject is in the nominative.

Σωκράτης φιλόσοφός ἐστιν.
Socrates is a philosopher.

☑ Neuter plural subjects are almost always followed by singular verbs:

τὰ οἰκήματα ᾠκοδομήθη.
The buildings were put up.

---

2 | Genitive

The basic meaning of the genitive case is 'of'. It is used mainly in these senses:

• the **possessive** genitive:

τὴν οἰκίᾱν τὴν Σίμωνος (Lysias 3.32)
the house of Simon

τίς ἔσθ' ὁ χῶρος; τοῦ θεῶν νομίζεται; (Sophocles, *Oedipus at Colonus* 38)
What is this place? Which of the gods is it considered to belong to?

Θουκῡδίδην τὸν Ὀλόρου (Thucydides 4.104.4)
Thucydides, the son of Olorus

• the **partitive** genitive:

τοὺς ... ἀπόρους τῶν πολιτῶν (Demosthenes 18.104)
the needy among (out of) the citizens

τὸν δὲ πεσόντα ποδῶν ἔλαβε. (Homer, *Iliad* 4.463)
But he held him by his feet as he fell.

- of <u>price</u>, <u>value</u> and <u>the penalty</u>:

  ἱερὰ … τριῶν ταλάντων (Lysias 30.20)
  offerings worth three talents

  ἀργυρίου … πρίασθαι ἢ ἀποδόσθαι ἵππον. (Plato, *Republic* 333b)
  to buy or sell a horse for money

  οὓς πάντες ᾔδεσαν … ἀπὸ συκοφαντίας ζῶντας … ὑπῆγον θανάτου
  (Xenophon, *Hellenica* 2.3.12)
  the people who everybody knew were living off malicious prosecutions,
  they impeached on a capital charge

- of <u>crimes</u>:

  δώρων ἐκρίθησαν (Lysias 27.3)
  they were tried for bribery

  But note that compounds of κατα- take the genitive of the person
  charged and the accusative of the crime: καταγιγνώσκω (I condemn),
  καταδικάζω (I judge against), καταψηφίζομαι (I vote against),
  κατακρίνω (I give sentence against) and κατηγορέω (I accuse).

  τούτου … δειλίαν καταψηφίζεσθαι (Lysias 14.11)
  to vote this man guilty of cowardice

- of <u>separation</u>, <u>lack</u>:

  οὐ πόνων ὑφίετο, οὐ κινδύνων ἀφίστατο, οὐ χρημάτων ἐφείδετο.
  (Xenophon, *Agesilaus* 7.1)
  He did not relax his efforts, stand aloof from dangers, or spare his
  money.

  πολλοῦ δεῖ οὕτως ἔχειν (Plato, *Apology* 35d)
  That is far from being the case. (πολλοῦ δεῖ = there is a lack of
  much, much is lacking)

  ἐνδεᾶ … κάλλους ἢ ἀρετῆς (Plato, *Republic* 381c)
  lacking in beauty or virtue

- of <u>comparison</u>:

  When ἤ (= than) is not used,[1] the object of comparison (i.e. the word
  after 'than' in English) is in the genitive.

---

[1] When ἤ is used, the people or things compared are in the same case:
φιλῶ γὰρ οὐ σὲ μᾶλλον ἢ δόμους ἐμούς. (Euripides, *Medea* 327)
For I do not love you more than my own house.

ἥττων ... ἀμαθὴς σοφοῦ, δειλὸς ἀνδρείου. (Plato, *Phaedrus* 239a)
An ignorant man is inferior to a wise man, a coward to a brave man.

- of <u>superiority:</u>

    Ἔρως τῶν θεῶν βασιλεύει. (Plato, *Symposium* 195c)
    Love is king of the gods.

- of <u>exclamation</u> (the thing exclaimed over):

    ὦ Ζεῦ βασιλεῦ, τῆς λεπτότητος τῶν φρενῶν. (Aristophanes, *Clouds* 153)
    O King Zeus, what (an example of) subtlety of intellect!

- 'the <u>rôle</u> of', 'the <u>nature</u> of':

    πενίαν φέρειν οὐ παντός, ἀλλ' ἀνδρὸς σοφοῦ. (Menander, *Sententiae* 463)
    To bear poverty is the mark not of everybody, but of the wise man.

    οὐδ' ἐμοιγε δοκεῖ δικαίου τοῦτ' εἶναι πολίτου. (Demosthenes 8.72)
    And this does not seem to me to be the duty of a just citizen.

- of <u>quality:</u>

    ἐόντα (= Attic ὄντα) ... τρόπου ἡσυχίου (Herodotus 1.107)
    being of a peaceful disposition

- of <u>degree:</u> εἰς τοῦτο, εἰς τοσοῦτο

    εἰς γὰρ τοῦτο θράσους καὶ ἀναιδείᾱς τοτ' ἀφίκετ[ο] (Demosthenes 21.194)
    for he reached such a pitch of boldness and shamelessness then

    ὁρᾶτε ... οἷ προελήλυθ' ἀσελγείᾱς. (Demosthenes 4.9)
    You see to what a pitch of brutality he has come.

- the genitive may be found after ἐν and εἰς where the place is omitted:

    ἐν Ἀρίφρονος (Plato, *Protagoras* 320a)
    at Ariphron's (house)

    εἰς διδασκάλου φοιτῶν (Plato, *Alcibiades 1* 109d)
    going to the school (*i.e.*, (to the house) of the teacher)

    εἰν (εἰς) Ἀΐδᾱο (Homer)
    in, to (the kingdom of) Hades

- verbs of *desire* (ἐπιθῡμέω, ἐράω) are followed by a genitive:

    (οἱ φαῦλοι) ἐρῶσι τῶν σωμάτων μᾶλλον ἢ τῶν ψῡχῶν. (Plato, *Symposium* 181b)
    Base men are in love with the bodies rather than the souls.

However, φιλέω (I love) and ποθέω (I long for) take the accusative.

The genitive is also used:

- with a number of prepositions (see pp. 56–9)
- in some expressions of time and space (see pp. 131–5)
- in the genitive absolute construction (see pp. 140–1)

The following verbs take the genitive:

- *share in, take hold of, touch, aim at, miss, begin*

μετέχω	I share in
(συλ)λαμβάνομαι	I take hold of
ἅπτομαι	I grasp, take hold of
ἀντέχομαι	I cling to
θιγγάνω	I touch, take hold of
ὀρέγομαι	I reach out for, grasp at, long for
ἁμαρτάνω	I miss, fail to win
σφάλλομαι	I am cheated of, foiled in
ἄρχω	I begin
τυγχάνω	I meet with

- *taste, smell, perceive, remember, desire* (see p. 14 above), *spare, care for, neglect, despise*

γεύομαι	I taste
ὀσφραίνομαι	I smell
ἀκούω	I hear (usually with the accusative of the thing heard but the genitive of the person heard from)
αἰσθάνομαι	I perceive
μέμνημαι	I remember (something about a thing *as opposed to* something as a whole)
φροντίζω	I take thought for
ἐπιλανθάνομαι	I forget
ἐπιθῡμέω	I desire
ἐράω	I desire, love
ἐφίεμαι	I long for, desire
φείδομαι	I spare, refrain from
ἐπιμέλομαι ἐπιμελέομαι	} I care for, take care of
ἀμελέω	I neglect
ὀλιγωρέω	I despise, pay no attention to
καταφρονέω	I despise, look down on

- *rule, command*

ἄρχω	I command, rule over
κρατέω	I get possession of, rule over
στρατηγέω	I am general of

The above list is by no means exhaustive and a number of these verbs can take the accusative too.

3 | Dative

The basic meanings of the dative case are 'to' and 'for'. It goes naturally with verbs of *giving* and the like ('dative' derives from the Latin word for 'give'). These verbs are regularly followed by a direct object in the accusative and an indirect object in the dative.

> ῥόδον ἔδωκα τῇ ἐμῇ ἀδελφῇ.
> I gave a rose (direct object) <u>to</u> my sister (indirect object).
> > *or* I gave my sister a rose.

Other uses of the dative include the following:

- the **possessive** dative:

> ἄλλοις μὲν γὰρ χρήματά ἐστι πολλὰ καὶ νῆες καὶ ἵπποι, ἡμῖν δὲ ξύμμαχοι ἀγαθοί. (Thucydides 1.86.3)
> For others have a lot of money and ships and horses, but we have good allies (*literally,* to others there is a lot of money ...).

- of <u>advantage</u> or <u>disadvantage</u>:

> πᾶς ἀνὴρ αὑτῷ πονεῖ. (Sophocles, *Ajax* 1366)
> Every man toils for himself.

> ἥδε ἡ ἡμέρα τοῖς Ἕλλησι μεγάλων κακῶν ἄρξει. (Thucydides 2.12.4)
> This day will be the beginning of great sorrows for the Greeks (*i.e.,* for their disadvantage).

- the '**ethic**' or 'polite' dative:

> τούτῳ πάνυ μοι προσέχετε τὸν νοῦν. (Demosthenes 18.178)
> Pay close attention to this, I beg you. (*i.e.,* Please pay ...)

Cf. 'Study me how to please the eye' (Shakespeare, *Love's Labour's Lost* I.i.80).

> ὦ μῆτερ, ὡς καλός μοι ὁ πάππος. (Xenophon, *Education of Cyrus* 1.3.2)
> Oh, mother, how handsome grandpa is (I've just realized)!

In the second example, the feeling conveyed is surprise.

- likeness and unlikeness:

  σκιαῖς ἐοικότες
  like shadows

- 'in':

  ἀνὴρ ἡλικίᾳ ... ἔτι τότε ὢν νέος (Thucydides 5.43.2)
  a man who was then still young in age

- 'with', 'by':

  ἔβαλλέ με λίθοις. (Lysias 3.8)
  He hit me with stones.

  νόσῳ ὕστερον ἀποθανόντα (Thucydides 8.84)
  having died later of (from) a disease

  If the agent (doer) of an action is a person, he or she is usually in the genitive after ὑπό (by, at the hands of). However, with the perfect and pluperfect passive, and after the verbal adjective in -τέος (see pp. 193–4), the agent can be in the dative:

  πολλαὶ θεραπεῖαι τοῖς ἰατροῖς εὕρηνται. (Isocrates 8.39)
  Many cures have been discovered by doctors.

- the measurement of difference:

  τῇ κεφαλῇ μείζονα (Plato, *Phaedo* 101a)
  taller by a head

  μακρῷ ἄριστος (Plato, *Laws* 729d)
  by far the best

- note the idiomatic use of the dative plural with αὐτός (usually without the article) in such expressions as:

  μίαν δὲ (ναῦν) αὐτοῖς ἀνδράσιν εἷλον ἤδη. (Thucydides 2.90)
  They had already taken one ship with its men and all.

  ἀποδόσθαι βούλομαι τὸν ὄνον ἄγων αὐτοῖσι τοῖς κανθηλίοις.
      (Aristophanes, *Wasps* 169–70)
  I want to take this donkey and sell it, pack-saddle and all.

- for the use of the dative in expressions of time and place,
  see pp. 131–3.

- the dative is used with a number of prepositions (see pp. 56–9).

The following verbs take the dative:

- *help, injure*
  βοηθέω   I help

ἀρέσκω	I please
εὐνοέω	I am friendly, favourable to
ὀργίζομαι	I am angry with
ἀπειλέω	I threaten
φθονέω	I feel ill-will towards, envy
μάχομαι	I fight
πολεμέω	I make war on, quarrel with
λῡσιτελεῖ μοι	it profits me, it is better for me
συμφέρει μοι	it is of advantage to me

But note that ὠφελέω (I help), μῑσέω (I hate) and βλάπτω (I hurt, hinder) take the accusative.

- *meet, yield*

ἀπαντάω	
ἐντυγχάνω	I meet
ἐπιτυγχάνω	
συγγίγνομαι	I associate with
πελάζω	I approach
εἴκω	I yield

- *obey, serve, trust, pardon, advise*

πείθομαι	I obey
δουλεύω	I serve, am subject to
πιστεύω	I trust
συγγιγνώσκω	I pardon
παραινέω	I advise

- *similarity, equality* and their opposites

ἔοικα	I am like
ὅμοιός εἰμι	
ἐνάντιός εἰμι	I am unlike, opposite to
πρέπει μοι	it is fitting for me

- note also χράομαι with the dative = I use, experience, treat, deal with, have sexual intercourse with.

4 | Accusative

The accusative is, as we have seen, the case of the (direct) object:

φιλῶ τὴν γραῦν.
I love the old woman.

Note:

- the 'cognate' accusative:
  Here the noun in the accusative is from the same origin as the verb
  ('cognate' means 'born together with'), e.g.

  ἄλλην πολλὴν φλυᾱρίᾱν φλυᾱροῦντα (Plato, *Apology* 19c)
  talking another lot of nonsense

  τί προσγελᾶτε τὸν πανύστατον γέλων; (Euripides, *Medea* 1041)
  Why do you smile the last smile you will ever smile?

- the accusative of respect:

  πόδας ὠκὺς Ἀχιλλεύς (Homer)
  swift-footed Achilles (*literally,* Achilles, swift as to (with respect to)
      his feet)

  διεφθαρμένον τὴν ἀκοήν (Herodotus 1.38)
  deaf (*literally,* destroyed/ruined as to his hearing)

  πλήγεντα τὴν κεφαλὴν πελέκει (Herodotus 6.38)
  struck on his head with an axe

Some verbs are followed by two accusatives, e.g.

- *make somebody something, regard someone as something*

  στρατηγὸν ... αὐτὸν ἀπέδειξε. (Xenophon, *Anabasis* 1.1.2)
  He appointed him general.

  τρεῖς τῶν ἐμῶν ἐχθρῶν νεκροὺς
  θήσω, πατέρα τε καὶ κόρην πόσιν τ' ἐμόν. (Euripides, *Medea* 374–5)
  I shall make corpses of three of my enemies, the father and the girl
      and my husband.

  οἱ ... κατάπτυστοι Θετταλοὶ καὶ ἀναίσθητοι Θηβαῖοι φίλον,
      εὐεργέτην, σωτῆρα τὸν Φίλιππον ἡγοῦντο. (Demosthenes 18.43)
  The contemptible Thessalians and stupid Thebans considered Philip
      their friend, their benefactor, their saviour.

- *ask, teach someone something; conceal, take something away from
  someone*

  οὐ τοῦτ' ἐρωτῶ σε. (Aristophanes, *Clouds* 641)

I am not asking you this.

τὴν θυγατέρα ἔκρυπτε τὸν θάνατον τοῦ ἀνδρός. (Lysias 32.7)
He concealed from his daughter her husband's death.

τούτων τὴν τῑμὴν ἀποστερεῖ με. (Demosthenes 28.13)
He robs me of the price of these things.

- *treat someone* [*well* or *badly*], *speak of someone* [*well* or *badly*]

  πολλὰ ἀγαθὰ ὑμᾶς ἐποίησεν. (Lysias 5.3)
  He did you much good.

  τότε δὴ ὁ Θεμιστοκλέης κεῖνόν τε καὶ τοὺς Κορινθίους πολλά τε καὶ κακὰ ἔλεγε. (Herodotus 8.61)
  Then Themistocles spoke many damning words about that man and the Corinthians.

The following are other uses of the accusative:

- It is used after a large number of prepositions (see pp. 56–9).
- It is used in many expressions of time, place and space (see pp. 131–5).
- For the 'accusative absolute', see pp. 141–2.

5 | Vocative

The vocative is the case by which one addresses or calls to someone. It is used with or without ὦ (O!):

ὦ Ζεῦ καὶ θεοί (Plato, *Protagoras* 310d)
O Zeus and you gods!

ἀκούεις, Αἰσχίνη; (Demosthenes 18.121)
Do you hear, Aeschines?

The vocative is generally identical or close in form to the nominative and so is not included in the tables in this Grammar. Where a separate form needs to be learnt, we have given it in a note.

Note the use of the nominative with a vocative force in these examples:

ὁ παῖς, ἀκολούθει δεῦρο (Aristophanes, *Frogs* 521)
Boy, follow me over here!

οὗτος, τί πάσχεις, ὦ κακόδαιμον Ξανθίᾱ; (Aristophanes, *Wasps* 1)
You there, what's your problem, you accursed Xanthias?

ὦ γενναῖος (Plato, *Phaedrus* 277c)
Oh, the noble man!

| The dual

In Greek, nouns representing a pair of people or things can adopt special forms, known as the **dual**. Adjectives and verbs may agree and thus be in the dual as well, or they may be in the plural. This number is not included in the accidence section of this Grammar, but it is explained in an appendix on pp. 232–3.

| Practice sentences

Translate into English or Greek as appropriate:

1 οὐκ ὀρθῶς εἰσηγῇ, εἰσηγούμενος τῆς τῶν πολλῶν δόξης δεῖν ἡμᾶς φροντίζειν. (Plato, *Crito* 48a)

2 Θησεύς τιν' ἡμάρτηκεν εἴς σ' ἁμαρτίᾶν; (Euripides, *Hippolytus* 319)

3 κείνους δὲ κλαίω ξυμφορᾷ κεχρημένους. (Euripides, *Medea* 347)

4 οἰκονόμου ἀγαθοῦ ἐστιν εὖ οἰκεῖν τὸν ἑαυτοῦ οἶκον. (Xenophon, *Oeconomicus* 1.2)

5 τυφλὸς τά τ' ὦτα τόν τε νοῦν τά τ' ὄμματ' εἶ. (Sophocles, *Oedipus Tyrannus* 371)

6 νίκης τε τετυχήκαμεν καὶ σωτηρίᾶς. (Xenophon, *Education of Cyrus* 4.1.2)

7 μετάδος φίλοισι σοῖσι (= σοῖς) σῆς εὐπρᾶξίᾶς. (Euripides, *Orestes* 450)

8 οἳ ὕστερον ἐλήφθησαν τῶν πολεμίων (this is not a genitive of comparison), ταὐτὰ (= the same things) ἤγγελλον. (Xenophon, *Anabasis* 1.7.13)

9 The slave gave the snake to Cleopatra by (*i.e.*, using) a trick.

10 I love you,Cleopatra, and am trying to save you.

11 I have been wounded by an enemy like you.

12 Since I am so wise (= of such wisdom), I love the boy's soul.

13 I, being a woman, am much wiser than all men.

14 Whose country have I come to, my companions?

15 The Greeks will make Cyrus king.

16 The queen heard the messenger but could not understand his words.

Accidence

The definite article

| | ὁ ἡ τό the | | |
	m.	f.	n.
singular			
nom.	ὁ	ἡ	τό
gen.	τοῦ	τῆς	τοῦ
dat.	τῷ	τῇ	τῷ
acc.	τόν	τήν	τό
plural			
nom.	οἱ	αἱ	τά
gen.	τῶν	τῶν	τῶν
dat.	τοῖς	ταῖς	τοῖς
acc.	τούς	τάς	τά

Note

The definite article provides a good guide to most of the endings of first and second declension nouns and adjectives.

Nouns

| First declension

Stems in -η, -α and -ᾱ

	honour, f.	sea, f.	land, f.	judge, m.	young man, m.
singular					
nom.	τῑμ-ή	θάλαττ-α	χώρ-ᾱ	κριτ-ής	νεᾱνί-ᾱς
gen.	τῑμ-ῆς	θαλάττ-ης	χώρ-ᾱς	κριτ-οῦ	νεᾱνί-ου
dat.	τῑμ-ῇ	θαλάττ-ῃ	χώρ-ᾳ	κριτ-ῇ	νεᾱνί-ᾳ
acc.	τῑμ-ήν	θάλαττ-αν	χώρ-ᾱν	κριτ-ήν	νεᾱνί-ᾱν
plural					
nom.	τῑμ-αί	θάλαττ-αι	χῶρ-αι	κριτ-αί	νεᾱνί-αι
gen.	τῑμ-ῶν	θαλαττ-ῶν	χωρ-ῶν	κριτ-ῶν	νεᾱνι-ῶν
dat.	τῑμ-αῖς	θαλάττ-αις	χώρ-αις	κριτ-αῖς	νεᾱνί-αις
acc.	τῑμ-ᾱς	θαλάττ-ᾱς	χώρ-ᾱς	κριτ-ᾱς	νεᾱνί-ᾱς

Note

1 -η in the nom. singular of feminine nouns is kept in all cases of the singular.
2 -α (usually long) in the nom. singular after ε, ι or ρ is kept in all cases of the singular.
3 -α (usually short) in the nom. singular after any other letter changes to η in the gen. and dat. only.
4 <u>All</u> first declension nouns have plural endings -αι, -ῶν, -αις, -ᾱς.
5 The vocative of first declension feminine nouns is the same as the nominative. Masculine nouns ending in -της and -ᾱς have vocative singulars in -τα and -ᾱ respectively, e.g. κριτά, νεᾱνίᾱ. Proper nouns endings in -άδης and -ίδης have vocatives in -άδη and -ίδη, e.g. Μιλτιάδη. The vocative plural is always identical with the nominative plural.
6 Most first declension nouns are feminine. Masculine nouns are obvious from their meaning and from the special form of their nom. and gen. singular.

| Second declension

Stems in -o

	word, m.	*gift*, n.	*mind*, m.	*bone*, n.
singular				
nom.	λόγ-ος	δῶρ-ον	νοῦς (νό-ος)	ὀστοῦν (ὀστέ-ον)
gen.	λόγ-ου	δώρ-ου	νοῦ (νό-ου)	ὀστοῦ (ὀστέ-ου)
dat.	λόγ-ῳ	δώρ-ῳ	νῷ (νό-ῳ)	ὀστῷ (ὀστέ-ῳ)
acc.	λόγ-ον	δῶρ-ον	νοῦν (νό-ον)	ὀστοῦν (ὀστέ-ον)
plural				
nom.	λόγ-οι	δῶρ-α	νοῖ (νό-οι)	ὀστᾶ (ὀστέ-α)
gen.	λόγ-ων	δώρ-ων	νῶν (νό-ων)	ὀστῶν (ὀστέ-ων)
dat.	λόγ-οις	δώρ-οις	νοῖς (νό-οις)	ὀστοῖς (ὀστέ-οις)
acc.	λόγ-ους	δῶρ-α	νοῦς (νό-ους)	ὀστᾶ (ὀστέ-α)

Note

1 Vocatives of second declension masculine nouns ending in -ος have the ending -ε in the singular, e.g. ὦ ἄνθρωπε.

2 In neuter nouns, the nominative, vocative and accusative are always the same and in the plural they end in -α.

3 Be careful to distinguish second declension nouns in -ος from third declension neuter nouns such as γένος (race), ὄρος (mountain), τεῖχος (wall), etc.

☑ A certain number of common feminine nouns decline like λόγος. These include:

ἡ βίβλος	book
ἡ γνάθος	jaw
ἡ ἤπειρος	mainland, terra firma
ἡ νῆσος	island
ἡ νόσος	disease
ἡ ὁδός	road, way
ἡ πλίνθος	brick
ἡ ψῆφος	pebble, vote

| Attic declension

Stems in -ω

temple, m.

singular

nom.	νε-ώς
gen.	νε-ώ
dat.	νε-ῴ
acc.	νε-ών

plural

nom.	νε-ῴ
gen.	νε-ών
dat.	νε-ῴς
acc.	νε-ώς

Note

1 In tragedy, the Doric form νᾱός (temple) is likely to be used.
2 Other words in this declension are λεώς, m. (people) and λαγώς, m. (hare).

| Third declension

Consonant stems (-κ, -ατ (neuter), -ντ)

	guard, m.	body, n.	old man, m.
singular			
nom.	φύλαξ	σῶμα	γέρων
gen.	φύλακ-ος	σώματ-ος	γέροντ-ος
dat.	φύλακ-ι	σώματ-ι	γέροντ-ι
acc.	φύλακ-α	σῶμα	γέροντ-α
plural			
nom.	φύλακ-ες	σώματ-α	γέροντ-ες
gen.	φυλάκ-ων	σωμάτ-ων	γερόντ-ων
dat.	φύλαξι(ν)	σώμασι(ν)	γέρουσι(ν)
acc.	φύλακ-ας	σώματ-α	γέροντ-ας

Consonant stems (-ρ, -δ)

	man, m.	father, m.	hope, f.
singular			
nom.	ἀνήρ	πατήρ	ἐλπίς
gen.	ἀνδρός	πατρός	ἐλπίδ-ος
dat.	ἀνδρί	πατρί	ἐλπίδ-ι
acc.	ἄνδρα	πατέρα	ἐλπίδ-α
plural			
nom.	ἄνδρες	πατέρες	ἐλπίδ-ες
gen.	ἀνδρῶν	πατέρων	ἐλπίδ-ων
dat.	ἀνδράσι(ν)	πατράσι(ν)	ἐλπίσι(ν)
acc.	ἄνδρας	πατέρας	ἐλπίδ-ας

Consonant stems (-ρ, -κ, -υ (ϝ))

	speaker, m.	woman, f.	Zeus, m.
singular			
nom.	ῥήτωρ	γυνή	Ζεύς
gen.	ῥήτορ-ος	γυναικ-ός	Δι-ός
dat.	ῥήτορ-ι	γυναικ-ί	Δι-ί
acc.	ῥήτορ-α	γυναῖκ-α	Δί-α
plural			
nom.	ῥήτορ-ες	γυναῖκ-ες	
gen.	ῥητόρ-ων	γυναικ-ῶν	
dat.	ῥήτορ-σι(ν)	γυναιξί(ν)	
acc.	ῥήτορ-ας	γυναῖκ-ας	

Note

1 In order to identify the <u>stem</u> of nouns of the third declension with consonant stems, it is important to learn their genitive singular. The stem can be found by taking off the final -ος of the genitive; and the following endings are added to the stem: in the singular, gen. -ος, dat. -ι, acc. -α; in the plural, nom. -ες, gen. -ων, dat. -σι (see next note), acc. -ας; neuter pl. nom. & acc. -α.

2 To accommodate the -σι ending of the dative plural, changes often have to be made for reasons of euphony. So from ἔρως, ἔρωτος (love) we have dat. pl. ἔρωσι (τ is omitted); and from λέων, λέοντος (lion) we have dat. pl. λέουσι (for λέοντσι, cf. γέρων, γέρουσι).

3 Note that the endings of γέρων are identical with the masculine forms of the present participle (see p. 38).

4 Vocative singulars (where different from the nominative): γέρον, ἄνερ, πάτερ, μῆτερ, ῥῆτορ, γύναι, Ζεῦ. Note the vowel shortening.

5 Note how πατήρ (and μήτηρ (mother) and θυγάτηρ (daughter)) have an epsilon before the ρ of their stem in the acc. singular and nom., gen. and acc. plural, but not in the gen. or dat. singular or the dat. plural.

6 Like ἐλπίς goes πούς, m. (foot): πούς, ποδός, ποδί, πόδα; πόδες, ποδῶν, ποσί(ν), πόδας.

7 (a) Ζεύς is classified as a noun with a consonant stem because originally there was a consonant called a digamma (ϝ) after the ε. This letter, pronounced like <u>w</u>, dropped out of the Attic alphabet.
(b) The following forms of Ζεύς are frequently met in tragedy: Ζην-ός (gen.), Ζην-ί (dat.), Ζῆν-α (acc.).

Stems in -ι, -υ, -ευ

	city, f.	city, n.	king, m.
singular			
nom.	πόλις	ἄστυ	βασιλεύς
gen.	πόλεως	ἄστεως	βασιλέως
dat.	πόλει	ἄστει	βασιλεῖ
acc.	πόλιν	ἄστυ	βασιλέᾱ
plural			
nom.	πόλεις	ἄστη	βασιλῆς (later βασιλεῖς)
gen.	πόλεων	ἄστεων	βασιλέων
dat.	πόλεσι(ν)	ἄστεσι(ν)	βασιλεῦσι(ν)
acc.	πόλεις	ἄστη	βασιλέᾱς

Stems in -ου, -αυ / Irregular stem

	ox, cow, c.	ship, f.	son, m.
singular			
nom.	βοῦς	ναῦς	υἱός
gen.	βο-ός	νε-ώς	υἱέος or υἱοῦ
dat.	βο-ί	νη-ί	υἱεῖ or υἱῷ
acc.	βοῦν	ναῦν	υἱόν
plural			
nom.	βό-ες	νῆ-ες	υἱεῖς or υἱοί
gen.	βο-ῶν	νε-ῶν	υἱέων or υἱῶν
dat.	βουσί(ν)	ναυσί(ν)	υἱέσι(ν) or υἱοῖς
acc.	βοῦς	ναῦς	υἱεῖς or υἱούς

Contracted forms

	race, n.	trireme, f.	Demosthenes, m.
singular			
nom.	γέν-ος	τριήρ-ης	Δημοσθέν-ης
gen.	γέν-ους (ε-ος)	τριήρ-ους (ε-ος)	Δημοσθέν-ους
dat.	γέν-ει (ε-ι)	τριήρ-ει (ε-ι)	Δημοσθέν-ει
acc.	γέν-ος	τριήρ-η (ε-α)	Δημοσθέν-η
plural			
nom.	γέν-η (ε-α)	τριήρ-εις (ε-ες)	
gen.	γεν-ῶν (ε-ων)	τριήρ-ων (ε-ων)	
dat.	γέν-εσι(ν)	τριήρ-εσι(ν)	
acc.	γέν-η (ε-α)	τριήρ-εις (ε-ας)	

Note

1 γένος and τριήρης observe the rules of <u>contraction</u>. The uncontracted endings are given in brackets but are not used in Attic.

2 It is extremely important to distinguish between the third declension neuter nouns ending in -ος and the second declension masculine nouns with the same ending.

3 Vocative singulars (where different from the nominative): πόλι, βασιλεῦ, βοῦ, ναῦ, υἱέ, Δημόσθενες.

4 With the declension of Demosthenes compare: Περικλῆς (Pericles), gen. Περικλέους, dat. Περικλεῖ, acc. Περικλέα, voc. Περίκλεις. Σωκράτης (Socrates) declines like Δημοσθένης.

Distinguish between these -ης names and the first declension names ending in -άδης and -ίδης. See p. 25, note 5.

5 With the declension of ναῦς compare: γραῦς, f. (old woman), singular: gen. γρᾱός, dat. γρᾱΐ, acc. γραῦν, voc. γραῦ; plural: nom. γρᾶες, gen. γρᾱῶν, dat. γραυσί(ν), acc. γραῦς, voc. γρᾶες.

6 Note:

αἰδώς, f. (shame), singular: gen. αἰδοῦς, dat. αἰδοῖ, acc. αἰδῶ, voc. αἰδώς.

πειθώ, f. (persuasion), singular: gen. πειθοῦς, dat. πειθοῖ, acc. πειθώ, voc. πειθοῖ.

ἥρως, m. (hero), singular: gen. ἥρωος, dat. ἥρωϊ or ἥρῳ, acc. ἥρωα or ἥρω, voc. ἥρως; plural: nom. ἥρωες or ἥρως, gen. ἡρώων, dat. ἥρωσι(ν), acc. ἥρωας or ἥρως, voc. ἥρωες or ἥρως.

ἕως, f. (dawn), follows the Attic declension (νεώς, p. 27) except that its accusative is ἕω (not ἕων). The Ionic declension of ἠώς, f. (dawn) will be met in Homer: gen. ἠοῦς, dat. ἠοῖ, acc. ἠῶ (like αἰδώς).

Adjectives

| First/second declension

Stems in -η and -o

σοφός *wise*

	m.	f.	n.
singular			
nom.	σοφ-ός	σοφ-ή	σοφ-όν
gen.	σοφ-οῦ	σοφ-ῆς	σοφ-οῦ
dat.	σοφ-ῷ	σοφ-ῇ	σοφ-ῷ
acc.	σοφ-όν	σοφ-ήν	σοφ-όν
plural			
nom.	σοφ-οί	σοφ-αί	σοφ-ά
gen.	σοφ-ῶν	σοφ-ῶν	σοφ-ῶν
dat.	σοφ-οῖς	σοφ-αῖς	σοφ-οῖς
acc.	σοφ-ούς	σοφ-άς	σοφ-ά

Stems in -ᾱ and -o

φίλιος *friendly*

	m.	f.	n.
singular			
nom.	φίλι-ος	φιλί-ᾱ	φίλι-ον
gen.	φιλί-ου	φιλί-ᾱς	φιλί-ου
dat.	φιλί-ῳ	φιλί-ᾳ	φιλί-ῳ
acc.	φίλι-ον	φιλί-ᾱν	φίλι-ον
plural			
nom.	φίλι-οι	φίλι-αι	φίλι-α
gen.	φιλί-ων	φιλί-ων	φιλί-ων
dat.	φιλί-οις	φιλί-αις	φιλί-οις
acc.	φιλί-ους	φιλί-ᾱς	φίλι-α

Note

1 All middle and passive participles ending in -μενος decline like σοφός.
2 If the ending -ος comes after an ε, ι or ρ, the feminine ends in -ᾱ.

Stems in -ε and -ο — contracted

χρύσεος *golden*

	m.	f.	n.
singular			
nom.	χρῡσ-οῦς (ε-ος)	χρῡσ-ῆ (έ-ᾱ)	χρῡσ-οῦν (ε-ον)
gen.	χρῡσ-οῦ	χρῡσ-ῆς	χρῡσ-οῦ
dat.	χρῡσ-ῷ	χρῡσ-ῇ	χρῡσ-ῷ
acc.	χρῡσ-οῦν	χρῡσ-ῆν	χρῡσ-οῦν
plural			
nom.	χρῡσ-οῖ	χρῡσ-αῖ	χρῡσ-ᾶ
gen.	χρῡσ-ῶν	χρῡσ-ῶν	χρῡσ-ῶν
dat.	χρῡσ-οῖς	χρῡσ-αῖς	χρῡσ-οῖς
acc.	χρῡσ-οῦς	χρῡσ-ᾶς	χρῡσ-ᾶ

Note

Most contracted adjectives ending in -όος follow the same pattern, e.g. ἁπλόος (single): ἁπλοῦς (ό-ος), ἁπλῆ (έ-ᾱ), ἁπλοῦν (ό-ον).

Stems in -ο (two terminations)

ἄδικος *unjust*

	m. & f.	n.
singular		
nom.	ἄδικ-ος	ἄδικ-ον
gen.	ἀδίκ-ου	
dat.	ἀδίκ-ῳ	
acc.	ἄδικ-ον	ἄδικ-ον
plural		
nom.	ἄδικ-οι	ἄδικ-α
gen.	ἀδίκ-ων	
dat.	ἀδίκ-οις	
acc.	ἀδίκ-ους	ἄδικ-α

Note

Compound adjectives (i.e. adjectives beginning with a preposition or some other prefix, including ἀ(ν)- (not)) do not usually have a separate feminine ending, e.g. ἄ-λογος (irrational), ἐπί-σημος (remarkable), εὔ-ξενος (hospitable), καλλί-νῑκος (gloriously triumphant). They are called **two-termination** adjectives.

| Attic declension

Stems in -ω (two terminations)

ἵλεως *gracious*

	m. & f.	n.
singular		
nom.	ἵλε-ως	ἵλε-ων
gen.	ἵλε-ω	
dat.	ἵλε-ῳ	
acc.	ἵλε-ων	ἵλε-ων
plural		
nom.	ἵλε-ῳ	ἵλε-α
gen.	ἵλε-ων	
dat.	ἵλε-ῳς	
acc.	ἵλε-ως	ἵλε-α

Note

1 In the poets, the form ἵλαος -ον (gracious) will be met.

2 πλέως (full) has three terminations, the feminine in -ᾱ.

| Irregular first/second declension adjectives

Irregular stem

μέγας *great*

	m.	f.	n.
singular			
nom.	μέγας	μεγάλ-η	μέγα
gen.	μεγάλ-ου	μεγάλ-ης	μεγάλ-ου
dat.	μεγάλ-ῳ	μεγάλ-ῃ	μεγάλ-ῳ
acc.	μέγαν	μεγάλ-ην	μέγα
plural			
nom.	μεγάλ-οι	μεγάλ-αι	μεγάλ-α
gen.	μεγάλ-ων	μεγάλ-ων	μεγάλ-ων
dat.	μεγάλ-οις	μεγάλ-αις	μεγάλ-οις
acc.	μεγάλ-ους	μεγάλ-ᾱς	μεγάλ-α

Note

The masculine vocative singular is μεγάλε.

Irregular stem

πολύς *much, many*

	m.	f.	n.
singular			
nom.	πολύς	πολλή	πολύ
gen.	πολλοῦ	πολλῆς	πολλοῦ
dat.	πολλῷ	πολλῇ	πολλῷ
acc.	πολύν	πολλήν	πολύ
plural			
nom.	πολλοί	πολλαί	πολλά
gen.	πολλῶν	πολλῶν	πολλῶν
dat.	πολλοῖς	πολλαῖς	πολλοῖς
acc.	πολλούς	πολλάς	πολλά

Note

Both πολύς and μέγας start in the masculine and neuter as third declension but change to the second in the genitive and dative, and accusative plural.

| Third declension

Stems in -εσ; stems in –ον uncontracted (two terminations)

	ἀληθής *true*		εὔφρων *kindly*	
	m. & f.	n.	m. & f.	n.
singular				
nom.	ἀληθ-ής	ἀληθ-ές	εὔφρων	εὖφρον
gen.	ἀληθ-οῦς		εὔφρον-ος	
dat.	ἀληθ-εῖ		εὔφρον-ι	
acc.	ἀληθ-ῆ	ἀληθ-ές	εὔφρον-α	εὖφρον
plural				
nom.	ἀληθ-εῖς	ἀληθ-ῆ	εὔφρον-ες	εὔφρον-α
gen.	ἀληθ-ῶν		εὐφρόν-ων	
dat.	ἀληθ-έσι(ν)		εὔφροσι(ν)	
acc.	ἀληθ-εῖς	ἀληθ-ῆ	εὔφρον-ας	εὔφρον-α

Note

1 The vocative singular forms are ἀληθές and εὖφρον.
2 Distinguish these from participles in -ων (p. 38).
3 Comparatives like μείζων have alternative (contracted) endings in the m. & f. acc. singular and the nom. and acc. plural. These shorter forms were more common in everyday speech than in literature.

Stems in -ον contracted (two terminations)

	μείζων *greater, bigger*		(alternative forms)	
	m. & f.	n.	m. & f.	n.
singular				
nom.	μείζων	μεῖζον		
gen.	μείζον-ος			
dat.	μείζον-ι			
acc.	μείζον-α	μεῖζον	μείζω	
plural				
nom.	μείζον-ες	μείζον-α	μείζους	μείζω
gen.	μειζόν-ων			
dat.	μείζοσι(ν)			
acc.	μείζον-ας	μείζον-α	μείζους	μείζω

| Mixed first/third declension

Stems in -υ

ἡδύς *sweet*

	m.	f.	n.
singular			
nom.	ἡδ-ύς	ἡδ-εῖα	ἡδ-ύ
gen.	ἡδ-έος	ἡδ-είᾱς	ἡδ-έος
dat.	ἡδ-εῖ	ἡδ-είᾳ	ἡδ-εῖ
acc.	ἡδ-ύν	ἡδ-εῖαν	ἡδ-ύ
plural			
nom.	ἡδ-εῖς	ἡδ-εῖαι	ἡδ-έα
gen.	ἡδ-έων	ἡδ-ειῶν	ἡδ-έων
dat.	ἡδ-έσι(ν)	ἡδ-είαις	ἡδ-έσι(ν)
acc.	ἡδ-εῖς	ἡδ-είᾱς	ἡδ-έα

Note
Distinguish this type from participles in -υς, e.g. nom. δεικνύς, δεικνῦσα, δεικνύν; gen. δεικνύντος, δεικνύσης, δεικνύντος, etc. (*present active participle of* δείκνῡμι / *show*).

Stems in -ν

τάλᾱς *unhappy*

	m.	f.	n.
singular			
nom.	τάλᾱς	τάλαιν-α	τάλαν
gen.	τάλαν-ος	ταλαίν-ης	τάλαν-ος
dat.	τάλαν-ι	ταλαίν-ῃ	τάλαν-ι
acc.	τάλαν-α	τάλαιν-αν	τάλαν
plural			
nom.	τάλαν-ες	τάλαιν-αι	τάλαν-α
gen.	ταλάν-ων	ταλαιν-ῶν	ταλάν-ων
dat.	τάλασι(ν)	ταλαίν-αις	τάλασι(ν)
acc.	τάλαν-ας	ταλαίν-ᾱς	τάλαν-α

Stems in -οντ

ἑκών *willing*

	m.	f.	n.
singular			
nom.	ἑκ-ών	ἑκ-οῦσα	ἑκ-όν
gen.	ἑκ-όντος	ἑκ-ούσης	ἑκ-όντος
dat.	ἑκ-όντι	ἑκ-ούσῃ	ἑκ-όντι
acc.	ἑκ-όντα	ἑκ-οῦσαν	ἑκ-όν
plural			
nom.	ἑκ-όντες	ἑκ-οῦσαι	ἑκ-όντα
gen.	ἑκ-όντων	ἑκ-ουσῶν	ἑκ-όντων
dat.	ἑκ-οῦσι(ν)	ἑκ-ούσαις	ἑκ-οῦσι(ν)
acc.	ἑκ-όντας	ἑκ-ούσᾱς	ἑκ-όντα

παύων *stopping* (*present active participle of* παύω *I stop*)

	m.	f.	n.
singular			
nom.	παύ-ων	παύ-ουσα	παῦ-ον
gen.	παύ-οντος	παυ-ούσης	παύ-οντος
dat.	παύ-οντι	παυ-ούσῃ	παύ-οντι
acc.	παύ-οντα	παύ-ουσαν	παῦ-ον
plural			
nom.	παύ-οντες	παύ-ουσαι	παύ-οντα
gen.	παυ-όντων	παυ-ουσῶν	παυ-όντων
dat.	παύ-ουσι(ν)	παυ-ούσαις	παύ-ουσι(ν)
acc.	παύ-οντας	παυ-ούσᾱς	παύ-οντα

Note

1 The present participle of εἰμί (I am) is ὤν, οὖσα, ὄν.

2 Declined exactly like παύων with the exception of the nom. sg. masculine are all participles in -ους, e.g. nom. διδούς, διδοῦσα, διδόν; gen. διδόντος, διδούσης, διδόντος (*present active participle of* δίδωμι *I give*).

Stems in -αντ

πᾶς *all, every*

	m.	f.	n.
singular			
nom.	πᾶς	πᾶσ-α	πᾶν
gen.	παντ-ός	πᾱσ-ης	παντ-ός
dat.	παντ-ί	πᾱσ-ῃ	παντ-ί
acc.	πάντ-α	πᾶσ-αν	πᾶν
plural			
nom.	πάντ-ες	πᾶσ-αι	πάντ-α
gen.	πάντ-ων	πᾱσ-ῶν	πάντ-ων
dat.	πᾶσι(ν)	πᾱσ-αις	πᾶσι(ν)
acc.	πάντ-ας	πᾱσ-ᾱς	πάντ-α

παύσᾱς *having stopped (aorist active participle of παύω I stop)*

	m.	f.	n.
singular			
nom.	παύσ-ᾱς	παύσ-ᾱσα	παῦσ-αν
gen.	παύσ-αντος	παυσ-άσης	παύσ-αντος
dat.	παύσ-αντι	παυσ-άσῃ	παύσ-αντι
acc.	παύσ-αντα	παύσ-ᾱσαν	παῦσ-αν
plural			
nom.	παύσ-αντες	παύσ-ᾱσαι	παύσ-αντα
gen.	παυσ-άντων	παυσ-ᾱσῶν	παυσ-άντων
dat.	παύσ-ᾱσι(ν)	παυσ-άσαις	παύσ-ᾱσι(ν)
acc.	παύσ-αντας	παυσ-άσᾱς	παύσ-αντα

Stems in -εντ

χαρίεις *graceful*

	m.	f.	n.
singular			
nom.	χαρίεις	χαρίεσσ-α	χαρίεν
gen.	χαρίεντ-ος	χαριέσσ-ης	χαρίεντ-ος
dat.	χαρίεντ-ι	χαριέσσ-ῃ	χαρίεντ-ι
acc.	χαρίεντ-α	χαρίεσσ-αν	χαρίεν
plural			
nom.	χαρίεντ-ες	χαρίεσσ-αι	χαρίεντ-α
gen.	χαριέντ-ων	χαριεσσ-ῶν	χαριέντ-ων
dat.	χαρίεσι(ν)	χαριέσσ-αις	χαρίεσι(ν)
acc.	χαρίεντ-ας	χαριέσσ-ᾱς	χαρίεντ-α

Note

This is a very rare class of adjectives in Attic. The voc. sg. masculine is χαρίεν.

παυσθείς *having been stopped*
(*aorist passive participle of* παύω *I stop*)

	m.	f.	n.
singular			
nom.	παυσθείς	παυσθεῖσ-α	παυσθέν
gen.	παυσθέντ-ος	παυσθείσ-ης	παυσθέντ-ος
dat.	παυσθέντ-ι	παυσθείσ-ῃ	παυσθέντ-ι
acc.	παυσθέντ-α	παυσθεῖσ-αν	παυσθέν
plural			
nom.	παυσθέντ-ες	παυσθεῖσ-αι	παυσθέντ-α
gen.	παυσθέντ-ων	παυσθεισ-ῶν	παυσθέντ-ων
dat.	παυσθεῖσι(ν)	παυσθείσ-αις	παυσθεῖσι(ν)
acc.	παυσθέντ-ας	παυσθείσ-ᾱς	παυσθέντ-α

Stems in -οτ

πεπαυκώς *having stopped* (*perfect active participle of* παύω / stop)

	m.	f.	n.
singular			
nom.	πεπαυκώς	πεπαυκυῖ-α	πεπαυκός
gen.	πεπαυκότ-ος	πεπαυκυί-ᾱς	πεπαυκότ-ος
dat.	πεπαυκότ-ι	πεπαυκυί-ᾳ	πεπαυκότ-ι
acc.	πεπαυκότ-α	πεπαυκυῖ-αν	πεπαυκός
plural			
nom.	πεπαυκότ-ες	πεπαυκυῖ-αι	πεπαυκότ-α
gen.	πεπαυκότ-ων	πεπαυκυι-ῶν	πεπαυκότ-ων
dat.	πεπαυκόσι(ν)	πεπαυκυί-αις	πεπαυκόσι(ν)
acc.	πεπαυκότ-ας	πεπαυκυί-ᾱς	πεπαυκότ-α

Comparison of adjectives

The **comparative** ('more ...') is most commonly formed by adding -τερος, -τέρᾱ, -τερον to the masculine stem.

The **superlative** ('most ...') is most commonly formed by adding -τατος, -τάτη, -τατον to the masculine stem.

When the adjective ends in -ος, the vowel before -τερος and -τατος etc. is o if the preceding syllable is heavy and ω if the preceding syllable is light. (A syllable is light if it contains a short vowel which is followed by no more than one consonant. Otherwise it is heavy.)[1]

		Comparative		**Superlative**	
δεινός	strange	δεινό-τερος	stranger	δεινό-τατος	strangest, very strange
σοφός	wise	σοφώ-τερος		σοφώ-τατος	

But note:

βαρύς	heavy	βαρύ-τερος		βαρύ-τατος
ἀληθής	true	ἀληθέσ-τερος		ἀληθέσ-τατος
μέλας	black	μελάν-τερος		μελάν-τατος

The following drop the omicron:

γεραιός	old	γεραί-τερος		γεραί-τατος
παλαιός	ancient	παλαί-τερος		παλαί-τατος

But ἀρχαῖος (ancient), ἀναγκαῖος (necessary), βέβαιος (firm), δίκαιος (just), σπουδαῖος (serious) follow the most common rule, e.g. ἀρχαιότερος, etc.

Note the following irregular formations in -αί-τερος and -αί-τατος:

ἥσυχος	quiet	ἡσυχαί-τερος	ἡσυχαί-τατος
πρῷος	early	πρωαί-τερος	πρωαί-τατος
μέσος	middle	μεσαί-τερος	μεσαί-τατος
ἴσος	equal	ἰσαί-τερος	ἰσαί-τατος
φίλος	friendly	φιλαί-τερος	φιλαί-τατος
		φίλ-τερος (poetic)	φίλ-τατος

[1] The two exceptions are κενός (empty) and στένος (narrow) which have their comparatives and superlatives κενότερος, κενότατος and στενότερος, στενότατος. See also **12** on p. 220.

Adjectives ending in -ων and some others have -έσ-τερος and -έσ-τατος:

εὔφρων	kindly	εὐφρονέσ-τερος	εὐφρονέσ-τατος
χαρίεις	graceful	χαριέσ-τερος	χαριέσ-τατος
εὔνους	kindly	εὐνούσ-τερος	εὐνούσ-τατος (οὐ = ο-έ)

A few very common words have comparative -ἰων (declining like μείζων) and superlative -ιστος (declining like σοφός):

ἡδύς	sweet	ἡδ-ἰων	ἥδ-ιστος
αἰσχρός	disgraceful	αἰσχ-ἰων	αἴσχ-ιστος
ἐχθρός	hostile	ἐχθ-ἰων	ἔχθ-ιστος
ἀλγεινός	painful	ἀλγ-ἰων	ἄλγ-ιστος

| Irregular comparisons

		Comparative	Superlative
ἀγαθός	good	ἀμείνων	ἄριστος (ability, excellence)
		βελτίων	βέλτιστος (virtue)
		κρείττων	κράτιστος (force, superiority)
κακός	bad	κακίων	κάκιστος
		χείρων *inferior*	χείριστος
		ἥττων *weaker, inferior*	ἥκιστα (adverb) *least*
καλός	beautiful	καλλίων	κάλλιστος
μέγας	great	μείζων	μέγιστος
μῑκρός	little	μῑκρότερος	μῑκρότατος
		μείων	
ὀλίγος	little		ὀλίγιστος
	few	ἐλάττων *smaller, fewer*	ἐλάχιστος
πολύς	much	πλείων, πλέων	πλεῖστος
ῥᾴδιος	easy	ῥᾴων	ῥᾷστος
ταχύς	fast	θάττων	τάχιστος

☑ Note the following which only have a comparative and superlative:

	πρότερος *former*	πρῶτος *first*
	ὕστερος *later*	ὕστατος *latest, last*
[πλησίος *near* (poetic)]	πλησιαίτερος *nearer*	πλησιαίτατος *nearest*

Adverbs

The adverbial ending of most adjectives is -ως, and so adverbs are usually derived from adjectives by adding -ως to the stem. As a rule of thumb, the form of adverbs can be found by changing the -ν of the genitive plural masculine to -ς, e.g.

δικαίως	justly
ἡδέως	sweetly
πάντως	wholly

Note the following neuters (either singular or plural) used as adverbs:

πολύ, πολλά	much
μέγα, μεγάλα	greatly (also μεγάλως)
μόνον	only

Note the following:

μάλα	very
σφόδρα	very much, exceedingly
τάχα	quickly, perhaps
ἄνω	above
κάτω	beneath, below
ἐγγύς	near
εὖ	well

Comparison of adverbs

The comparative of an adverb is regularly the neuter acc. <u>singular</u> of the comparative adjective, and its superlative is the neuter acc. <u>plural</u> of the superlative adjective:

		Comparative	Superlative
σοφῶς	wisely	σοφώτερον *more wisely*	σοφώτατα *most wisely*
ταχέως	quickly	θᾶττον *more quickly*	τάχιστα *very quickly*
Note also:			
μάλα	much	μᾶλλον *more*	μάλιστα *very much*
εὖ	well	ἄμεινον *better*	ἄριστα *very well*

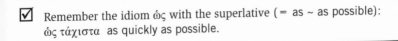

☑ Remember the idiom ὡς with the superlative (= as ~ as possible):
ὡς τάχιστα as quickly as possible.

Pronouns

| Personal pronouns

	I, we	you	self; him, her, it, them		
	(m. f. n.)	(m. f. n.)	m.	f.	n.
singular					
nom.	ἐγώ	σύ	αὐτός	αὐτή	αὐτό
gen.	ἐμοῦ, μου	σοῦ	αὐτοῦ	αὐτῆς	αὐτοῦ
dat.	ἐμοί, μοι	σοί	αὐτῷ	αὐτῇ	αὐτῷ
acc.	ἐμέ, με	σέ	αὐτόν	αὐτήν	αὐτό
plural					
nom.	ἡμεῖς	ὑμεῖς	αὐτοί	αὐταί	αὐτά
gen.	ἡμῶν	ὑμῶν	αὐτῶν	αὐτῶν	αὐτῶν
dat.	ἡμῖν	ὑμῖν	αὐτοῖς	αὐταῖς	αὐτοῖς
acc.	ἡμᾶς	ὑμᾶς	αὐτούς	αὐτάς	αὐτά

Note

In all cases, αὐτός can mean 'self'. In the accusative, genitive and dative, it can mean 'him', 'her', 'it' and 'them'. Preceded by the article, it means 'same'. See p. 145.

| Possessive pronouns

ἐμός -ή -όν   my
σός -ή -όν   your (singular)   } decline like σοφός
ἡμέτερος -ᾱ -ον   our
ὑμέτερος -ᾱ -ον   your (plural)   } decline like φίλιος
σφέτερος -ᾱ -ον   their own

To express possession in the third person, the genitive of αὐτός or (if reflexive) ἑαυτοῦ is used in the singular or plural. See pp. 147 & 149.

| Reflexive pronouns

The reflexive pronouns (here in the masculine) are: ἐμαυτοῦ (myself), σεαυτοῦ (yourself), ἑαυτοῦ, αὑτοῦ (himself), ἡμῶν αὐτῶν (ourselves), ὑμῶν αὐτῶν (yourselves), ἑαυτῶν, αὑτῶν (themselves). **Reflexive pronouns are never found in the nominative.**

	myself; ourselves		*himself, herself, itself; themselves*		
	m.	f.	m.	f.	n.
singular					
gen.	ἐμαυτοῦ	ἐμαυτῆς	ἑαυτοῦ	ἑαυτῆς	ἑαυτοῦ
dat.	ἐμαυτῷ	ἐμαυτῇ	ἑαυτῷ	ἑαυτῇ	ἑαυτῷ
acc.	ἐμαυτόν	ἐμαυτήν	ἑαυτόν	ἑαυτήν	ἑαυτό
plural					
gen.	ἡμῶν αὐτῶν	ἡμῶν αὐτῶν	ἑαυτῶν	ἑαυτῶν	ἑαυτῶν
dat.	ἡμῖν αὐτοῖς	ἡμῖν αὐταῖς	ἑαυτοῖς	ἑαυταῖς	ἑαυτοῖς
acc.	ἡμᾶς αὐτούς	ἡμᾶς αὐτάς	ἑαυτούς	ἑαυτάς	ἑαυτά

Note

Sometimes σεαυτοῦ (which declines like ἐμαυτοῦ) and frequently ἑαυτοῦ contract to σαυτοῦ and αὑτοῦ respectively.

| Reciprocal pronoun

	ἀλλήλων *each other, one another*		
	m.	f.	n.
plural			
gen.	ἀλλήλων	ἀλλήλων	ἀλλήλων
dat.	ἀλλήλοις	ἀλλήλαις	ἀλλήλοις
acc.	ἀλλήλους	ἀλλήλᾱς	ἄλληλα

| Interrogative and indefinite pronouns

	τίς who? what? which?		τις someone, anyone; some, any	
	m. & f.	n.	m. & f.	n.
singular				
nom.	τίς	τί	τις	τι
gen.	τίνος or τοῦ		τινός or του	
dat.	τίνι or τῷ		τινί or τῳ	
acc.	τίνα	τί	τινά	τι
plural				
nom.	τίνες	τίνα	τινές	τινά or ἄττα
gen.	τίνων		τινῶν	
dat.	τίσι(ν)		τισί(ν)	
acc.	τίνας	τίνα	τινάς	τινά or ἄττα

Note

When τίς is used in asking a question, it <u>always</u> has an accent on its first syllable. τις, the indefinite pronoun, is an enclitic and may or may not be accented, but it <u>never</u> has an accent on its first syllable (unless it gets it from another enclitic), and must follow another word. See p. 149.

| Deictic pronouns

The deictic pronouns οὗτος, ὅδε (i.e. ὁ + δε) and ἐκεῖνος, like αὐτός and ἄλλος, follow the definite article (see p. 24) and the relative pronoun (p. 50) in having the ending -ο (<u>not</u> -ον) in the nom. and acc. neuter singular.

	οὗτος *this*			ὅδε *this*		
	m.	f.	n.	m.	f.	n.
singular						
nom.	οὗτος	αὕτη	τοῦτο	ὅδε	ἥδε	τόδε
gen.	τούτου	ταύτης	τούτου	τοῦδε	τῆσδε	τοῦδε
dat.	τούτῳ	ταύτῃ	τούτῳ	τῷδε	τῇδε	τῷδε
acc.	τοῦτον	ταύτην	τοῦτο	τόνδε	τήνδε	τόδε
plural						
nom.	οὗτοι	αὗται	ταῦτα	οἵδε	αἵδε	τάδε
gen.	τούτων	τούτων	τούτων	τῶνδε	τῶνδε	τῶνδε
dat.	τούτοις	ταύταις	τούτοις	τοῖσδε	ταῖσδε	τοῖσδε
acc.	τούτους	ταύτᾱς	ταῦτα	τούσδε	τάσδε	τάδε

Note

1 Be careful not to confuse the following:

αὕτη, αὗται   from οὗτος (this, these)
αὐτή, αὐταί   from αὐτός (self)
αὐτή, αὐταί   from ὁ αὐτός (the same)

2 The gen. pl. feminine of οὗτος is *τούτων*.

	ἐκεῖνος *that*		
	m.	f.	n.
singular			
nom.	ἐκεῖνος	ἐκείνη	ἐκεῖνο
gen.	ἐκείνου	ἐκείνης	ἐκείνου
dat.	ἐκείνῳ	ἐκείνῃ	ἐκείνῳ
acc.	ἐκεῖνον	ἐκείνην	ἐκεῖνο
plural			
nom.	ἐκεῖνοι	ἐκεῖναι	ἐκεῖνα
gen.	ἐκείνων	ἐκείνων	ἐκείνων
dat.	ἐκείνοις	ἐκείναις	ἐκείνοις
acc.	ἐκείνους	ἐκείνᾱς	ἐκεῖνα

| Relative pronouns

Specific relative (see p. 127)

ὅς *who, which*		
m.	f.	n.

singular

nom.	ὅς	ἥ	ὅ
gen.	οὗ	ἧς	οὗ
dat.	ᾧ	ᾗ	ᾧ
acc.	ὅν	ἥν	ὅ

plural

nom.	οἵ	αἵ	ἅ
gen.	ὧν	ὧν	ὧν
dat.	οἷς	αἷς	οἷς
acc.	οὕς	ἅς	ἅ

Note

Notice the similarity of this pronoun to the definite article (p. 24). Observe that the relative pronoun <u>always</u> has an accent.

Indefinite relative (see p. 128)

ὅστις *whoever, anyone who; whatever, anything which*		
m.	f.	n.

singular

nom.	ὅστις	ἥτις	ὅτι (ὅ τι)
gen.	οὗτινος *or* ὅτου	ἧστινος	οὗτινος *or* ὅτου
dat.	ᾧτινι *or* ὅτῳ	ᾗτινι	ᾧτινι *or* ὅτῳ
acc.	ὅντινα	ἥντινα	ὅτι (ὅ τι)

plural

nom.	οἵτινες	αἵτινες	ἅτινα *or* ἅττα
gen.	ὧντινων *or* ὅτων	ὧντινων	ὧντινων *or* ὅτων
dat.	οἷστισι(ν) *or* ὅτοις	αἷστισι(ν)	οἷστισι(ν) *or* ὅτοις
acc.	οὕστινας	ἅστινας	ἅτινα *or* ἅττα

Note

1 Note that ὅστις = ὅς + τις.
2 ὅ τι can be used to avoid confusion with ὅτι = *that or because*.
3 The shorter alternative forms are rare in prose but almost always found in poetry.

Correlatives

| Correlative pronouns

Question word (direct and indirect question)	Indefinite	Deictic	Relative (specific)	Indefinite relative (also indirect question)
τίς; *who?* *which?* *what?*	τις *someone,* *anyone;* *some, any*	ὅδε *this (here)* οὗτος *this* ἐκεῖνος *that*	ὅς *who,* *which*	ὅστις *whoever,* *anyone who*
πότερος; *which of two?*		ἕτερος *the one* or *the other of two*	ὁπότερος *which of* *two*	ὁπότερος *whichever* *of two*
πόσος; *how much?* *how many?*	ποσός *of some* *quantity* *or number*	τόσος, τοσοῦτος, τοσόσδε *so much,* *so many*	ὅσος *as much as,* *as many as*	ὁπόσος *of whatever* *quantity* *or number*
ποῖος; *of what sort?*	ποιός *of some* *sort*	τοῖος, τοιόσδε, τοιοῦτος *such*	οἷος *of which* *sort*	ὁποῖος *of whatever* *sort*

Note
The forms τόσος and τοῖος are poetic.

| Correlative adverbs

Question word (direct and indirect question)	Indefinite	Deictic	Relative (specific)	Indefinite relative (also indirect question)
ποῦ; *where?*	που *somewhere, anywhere*	ἐνθάδε *here* ἐκεῖ *there*	οὗ *where*	ὅπου *where, wherever*
ποῖ; *to where?*	ποι *to any, some place*	δεῦρο *to here* ἐκεῖσε *to there*	οἷ *to where*	ὅποι *to where, to wherever*
πόθεν; *from where?*	ποθέν *from anywhere, from somewhere*	ἐνθένδε *from here* ἐκεῖθεν *from there*	ὅθεν *from where*	ὁπόθεν *from where, from wherever*
πότε; *when?*	ποτέ *at some time, ever*	τότε *then*	ὅτε *when*	ὁπότε *when, whenever*
πῶς; *how?*	πως *somehow*	ὧδε, οὕτω(ς) *thus, in this way*	ὡς *how*	ὅπως *how, however*

Numerals

Cardinals	Ordinals	Adverbs
one, two etc.	*first, second* etc.	*once, twice* etc.
1 εἷς, μία, ἕν	πρῶτ-ος, -η, -ον	ἅπαξ
2 δύο	δεύτερος	δίς
3 τρεῖς, τρία	τρίτος	τρίς
4 τέτταρες, τέτταρα	τέταρτος	τετράκις
5 πέντε	πέμπτος	πεντάκις
6 ἕξ	ἕκτος	ἑξάκις
7 ἑπτά	ἕβδομος	ἑπτάκις
8 ὀκτώ	ὄγδοος	ὀκτάκις
9 ἐννέα	ἔνατος	ἐνάκις
10 δέκα	δέκατος	δεκάκις
11 ἕνδεκα	ἑνδέκατος	ἑνδεκάκις
12 δώδεκα	δωδέκατος	δωδεκάκις
13 τρεῖς καὶ δέκα	τρίτος καὶ δέκατος	τρεισκαιδεκάκις
14 τέτταρες καὶ δέκα	τέταρτος καὶ δέκατος	τετταρεσκαιδεκάκις
15 πεντεκαίδεκα	πέμπτος καὶ δέκατος	πεντεκαιδεκάκις
16 ἑκκαίδεκα	ἕκτος καὶ δέκατος	ἑκκαιδεκάκις
17 ἑπτακαίδεκα	ἕβδομος καὶ δέκατος	ἑπτακαιδεκάκις
18 ὀκτωκαίδεκα	ὄγδοος καὶ δέκατος	ὀκτωκαιδεκάκις
19 ἐννεακαίδεκα	ἔνατος καὶ δέκατος	ἐννεακαιδεκάκις
20 εἴκοσι(ν)	εἰκοστός	εἰκοσάκις
23 εἴκοσι τρεῖς	εἰκοστὸς τρίτος	εἰκοσάκις τρίς
30 τριάκοντα	τριᾱκοστός	τριᾱκοντάκις
40 τετταράκοντα	τετταρακοστός	τετταρακοντάκις
50 πεντήκοντα	πεντηκοστός	πεντηκοντάκις
60 ἑξήκοντα	ἑξηκοστός	ἑξηκοντάκις
70 ἑβδομήκοντα	ἑβδομηκοστός	ἑβδομηκοντάκις
80 ὀγδοήκοντα	ὀγδοηκοστός	ὀγδοηκοντάκις
90 ἐνενήκοντα	ἐνενηκοστός	ἐνενηκοντάκις

	Cardinals	Ordinals	Adverbs
	one, two etc.	*first, second* etc.	*once, twice* etc.
100	ἑκατόν	ἑκατοστός	ἑκατοντάκις
200	διᾱκόσι-οι, -αι, -α	διᾱκοσιοστός	διᾱκοσιάκις
300	τριᾱκόσι-οι, -αι, -α	τριᾱκοσιοστός	τριᾱκοσιάκις
400	τετρακόσι-οι, -αι, -α	τετρακοσιοστός	τετρακοσιάκις
500	πεντακόσι-οι, -αι, -α	πεντακοσιοστός	πεντακοσιάκις
600	ἑξακόσι-οι, -αι, -α	ἑξακοσιοστός	ἑξακοσιάκις
700	ἑπτακόσι-οι, -αι, -α	ἑπτακοσιοστός	ἑπτακοσιάκις
800	ὀκτακόσι-οι, -αι, -α	ὀκτακοσιοστός	ὀκτακοσιάκις
900	ἐνακόσι-οι, -αι, -α	ἐνακοσιοστός	ἐνακοσιάκις
1,000	χῑλι-οι, -αι, -α	χῑλιοστός	χῑλιάκις
2,000	δισχῑλι-οι, -αι, -α	δισχῑλιοστός	δισχῑλιάκις
10,000	μῡρι-οι, -αι, -α	μῡριοστός	μῡριάκις

Note

1 The numbers one to four decline as follows:

	εἷς *one*			δύο *two*
	m.	f.	n.	m., f. & n.
nom.	εἷς	μία	ἕν	δύο
gen.	ἑνός	μιᾶς	ἑνός	δυοῖν (a dual form)
dat.	ἑνί	μιᾷ	ἑνί	δυοῖν (a dual form)
acc.	ἕνα	μίαν	ἕν	δύο

The negatives of εἷς are οὐδείς and μηδείς (no one) and they decline in the same way, i.e. οὐδ-είς, οὐδε-μία, οὐδ-έν.

	τρεῖς *three*		τέτταρες *four*	
	m. & f.	n.	m. & f.	n.
nom.	τρεῖς	τρία	τέτταρες	τέτταρα
gen.	τριῶν		τεττάρων	
dat.	τρισί(ν)		τέτταρσι(ν)	
acc.	τρεῖς	τρία	τέτταρας	τέτταρα

2 Cardinal numbers from 5 to 199 are indeclinable, except that in compound numbers (see below) εἷς, δύο, τρεῖς and τέτταρες are declined if they occur as distinct words; hundreds and thousands decline like the plural of φίλιος. Ordinals decline in full like σοφός, except δεύτερος which declines like φίλιος, because of its ρ before the -ος (see p. 32).

3 In compound numbers, the smaller and the larger number can come either way around if they are linked with καί. Thus 24 can be εἴκοσι καὶ τέτταρες or τέτταρες καὶ εἴκοσι (as in 'four-and-twenty'). If καί is not used, the larger number comes first: εἴκοσι τέτταρες (as in 'twenty-four').

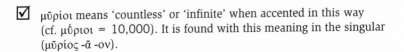

☑ μῡρίοι means 'countless' or 'infinite' when accented in this way (cf. μύριοι = 10,000). It is found with this meaning in the singular (μῡρίος -ᾱ -ον).

Prepositions

The phrases not in bold are idiomatic expressions well worth noting.

	with the genitive	with the dative	with the accusative
ἀμφί	**concerning, for the sake of** (poetic)	**concerning, for the sake of** (poetic)	**around, about**
			οἱ ἀμφὶ Πλάτωνα followers of (*literally*, those around) Plato
			ἀμφὶ εἴκοσι ἔτη about 20 years
ἀνά			**up, throughout**
ἀντί	**instead of**		
ἀπό	**from, away from** ἀφ' ἵππου on (*literally*, from) horseback		
διά	**through, by means of** δι' ὀλίγου (πολλοῦ) after a short (long) time διὰ δίκης ἰέναι to go to law with		**on account of** see note **1** below
εἰς			**into** (in poetry, often ἐς) εἰς ἑσπέρᾱν towards evening εἰς τριᾱκοσίους up to 300 εἰς καιρόν at the right time
ἐκ, ἐξ	**out of, from** (before a vowel) ἐκ τούτου after this ἐξ ἴσου equally		

	with the genitive	with the dative	with the accusative
ἐν		**in, at**	
		ἐν τούτῳ meanwhile	
		ἐν τῷ παρόντι at present	
		ἐν Πλάτωνος (gen.) at Plato's (house) (see p. 17)	
ἐπί	**on, in the time of** (of time and purpose)	**upon, on**	**to, onto, against, over, for**
	ἐφ' ἵππου on horseback	ἐφ' ἡμῖν ἐστίν it is in our power	ἐπὶ τὸν ἵππον onto a horse
	ἐπὶ τῶν πατέρων in the time of our fathers	ἐπὶ τούτοις on these conditions	ἐπὶ πολὺν χρόνον for a long time
		ἐφ' ᾧ, ἐφ' ᾧτε on condition that (see p. 179)	ἐφ' ὕδωρ for (*i.e.*, to fetch) water
			ἐπὶ μάχην ἐξιέναι to go out for battle
κατά	**down from, down into, against**		**down, on, over, according to, throughout**
	κατ' ἄκρᾶς utterly (from top to bottom)		κατὰ τὸν ποταμόν downstream
	κατὰ τῆς γῆς ἰέναι to go under the earth		κατὰ γῆν καὶ κατὰ θάλατταν by land and sea
	(λόγος) κατὰ Φιλίππου (a speech) against Philip		κατ' ἐκεῖνον τὸν χρόνον about that time
			κατὰ τοὺς νόμους according to the laws
			καθ' Ἑλλάδα throughout Greece
			καθ' ἡμέρᾶν from day to day

	with the genitive	with the dative	with the accusative
μετά	**with, together with**	**among** (poetic)	**after**
			μετὰ ταῦτα after these things see note **2** below
παρά	**from** (a person)	**by the side of, with**	**to the presence of, beside, beyond, contrary to, during**
		παρὰ τῷ βασιλεῖ with the king (in Attic prose only of persons)	παρὰ τὸν βασιλέᾱ ἄγειν to bring before the king
			παρὰ τὸν ποταμόν along the river
			παρ' ὅλον τὸν βίον during my whole life
			παρὰ τοὺς νόμους contrary to the laws
περί	**concerning**	**concerning, around**	**around, about** (of place and time)
	περὶ πολλοῦ (ὀλίγου, οὐδενὸς) ποιεῖσθαι to consider of great (little, no) importance		περὶ ἑβδομήκοντα about 70
			οἱ περὶ Ἡράκλειτον Heraclitus and his school/associates
πρό	**before, in front of** (of place and time), **rather than**		
πρός	**in the name of, by**	**close by, near, in addition to**	**to, towards, against**
	πρὸς τῶν θεῶν by the gods!	πρὸς τούτοις beside these things	πρὸς χάριν with a view to pleasing
			πρὸς βίᾱν forcibly
			πρὸς ταῦτα with reference to these things

	with the genitive	with the dative	with the accusative
σύν[1]		**(in company) with** σὺν θεῷ with god's help common in poetry; rare in Attic prose	
ὑπέρ	**above, on behalf of** ὑπὲρ τῆς Ἑλλάδος for the sake of Greece		**beyond, to beyond** ὑπὲρ δύναμιν beyond one's power
ὑπό	**by** (the agent) ἑάλων ὑπὸ τῶν πολεμίων I was captured by the enemy	**under, subject to** ὑπὸ δένδρῳ under a tree ὑπ' Ἀθηναίοις subject to the Athenians	**to under, under, about** or **at** (of time) ὑπὸ νυκτά at nightfall see note **3** below
ὡς			**to** (of people) ὡς Ἄγιν to Agis

Note

1 In compound verbs, διά adds the meaning of either 'thoroughly' or 'right through' or 'parting'.

2 In compound verbs, μετά tends to add the meaning of either 'after' ('follow after', 'send after' (= for)') or 'sharing' or 'changing'.

3 In compound verbs, ὑπό adds the meaning of either 'under' or 'gradually' or 'in an underhand way'.

---

[1] This word, both as a separate preposition and as part of a compound (e.g. συν-άγω (I bring together)) was spelt ξύν in old Attic, but σύν appeared in the fifth century BC and became usual towards the end of it. Thucydides is the only Attic prose writer who consistently uses the ξ. It is the usual spelling in tragedy.

Verbs

1 Most Greek verbs alter their endings according to a single pattern. We give the verb παύω (I stop), παύομαι (I cease) as our example of this. If you master this verb you will be able to understand and form any part of the vast majority of verbs.

There are a significant number of irregular verbs and we give the most frequently used of these in the tables of grammar and in the lists of principal parts. We divide the principal parts into two sections. The 'top 101' are the commonest and the effort of learning them will prove worthwhile. The second list can be used for reference.

2 In the following tables, the numbers 1, 2 and 3 refer to **persons**. In the singular 1 is 'I', 2 is 'you' and 3 is 'he', 'she' or 'it'. In the plural, 1 is 'we', 2 is 'you' and 3 is 'they'. For agreement of persons, see **7** on p. 219.

3 There are three **voices** in Greek, active, middle and passive. The **middle voice** generally tells us that the subject performs an action upon himself or herself, or for personal benefit, e.g. παύω = I stop (something), παύομαι = I stop myself, i.e. I come to a stop, I cease.

Sometimes, however, verbs have an active meaning but only middle (or middle and passive) forms, e.g. βούλομαι (I wish). We call such verbs **deponent**. If they do make use of passive as well as middle forms, the passive forms will usually be confined to the aorist.

4 The middle and the passive have the same forms as each other <u>except</u> in the future and the aorist. We give only the future and aorist tenses under the middle in the tables, referring readers to the passive table for the other tenses.

5 Almost all of the tenses we use when talking about Greek verbs are used in English grammar. But note the following:

imperfect tense – this tense usually expresses continuous or repeated or incomplete action in the past, e.g. 'I was stopping ...'. It can also have the meaning of 'I tried to ...' (conative, from the Latin 'cōnor' (I try)).

aorist tense – this tense simply tells us that a single event happened in the past, e.g. 'I did this'. It is often used with the force of the English pluperfect.

Outside the aorist indicative and its participles (but see p.137), i.e. in imperatives, infinitives, subjunctives and optatives, the aorist does not tell us the time at which the action happened.[1] It tells us that it was a single <u>event</u>, and the event can take place in the present and the future as well as the past. Thus ἐλθέ (aorist imperative) δεῦρο means 'Come here (and be quick about it)!' The imperfect tense, which usually suggests that the action should be seen as a continuing process, makes a helpful contrast with this use of the aorist to convey a single crisp event. We refer to the distinction between ways of expressing events and actions as **aspect**.

pluperfect tense – this tense is rarely used in subordinate time clauses. The aorist is preferred, e.g. ἐπεὶ εἰσήλθομεν = when we had come in. The pluperfect is in fact rarely used altogether.

future perfect tense – 'I shall have stopped', 'you will have stopped', etc. This tense is very rarely found.

finite verb – a verb in a tense with a personal ending.

indicative – this term tells us that a finite verb is not in the subjunctive, optative (see below) or imperative. It is usually making a statement or asking a question.

the **subjunctive** and **optative** – the various uses of the subjunctive and optative will become increasingly evident as this grammar is studied. However, it is worth remarking that a mood which is certainly not the indicative is used in English. The following citations are taken from 'The Oxford English Grammar' (published in 1996):

Israel insists that it <u>remain</u> in charge on the borders ...

If they decide that it's necessary, then so <u>be</u> it.

... you can teach him if need <u>be</u>.

... more customers are demanding that financial services <u>be tailored</u> to their needs.

He said Sony would not object even if Columbia <u>were to make</u> a movie critical of the late Emperor Hirohito.

Words such as 'may', 'might', 'would', 'should' and 'could' can also be helpful when translating the Greek subjunctive and optative.

[1] However, note the use of the infinitive in indirect statement and the optative in indirect statement and indirect questions, both of them in 'the tense actually used' (see pp. 155 & 164).

| Verbs in ω

Active παύω / *stop*

	indicative	imperative	subjunctive	optative
present				
sg 1	παύ-ω		παύ-ω	παύ-οιμι
2	παύ-εις	παῦ-ε	παύ-ῃς	παύ-οις
3	παύ-ει	παυ-έτω	παύ-ῃ	παύ-οι
pl 1	παύ-ομεν		παύ-ωμεν	παύ-οιμεν
2	παύ-ετε	παύ-ετε	παύ-ητε	παύ-οιτε
3	παύ-ουσι(ν)	παυ-όντων	παύ-ωσι(ν)	παύ-οιεν

Infinitive: παύ-ειν Participle: παύ-ων, -ουσα, -ον (see p. 38)

	indicative	imperative	subjunctive	optative
imperfect				
sg 1	ἔ-παυ-ον			
2	ἔ-παυ-ες			
3	ἔ-παυ-ε(ν)			
pl 1	ἐ-παύ-ομεν			
2	ἐ-παύ-ετε			
3	ἔ-παυ-ον			

	indicative	imperative	subjunctive	optative
future				
sg 1	παύσ-ω			παύσ-οιμι
2	παύσ-εις			παύσ-οις
3	παύσ-ει			παύσ-οι
pl 1	παύσ-ομεν			παύσ-οιμεν
2	παύσ-ετε			παύσ-οιτε
3	παύσ-ουσι(ν)			παύσ-οιεν

Infinitive: παύσ-ειν Participle: παύσ-ων, -ουσα, -ον (see p. 38)

1st aorist (for 2nd aorist, see p. 69)

	indicative	imperative	subjunctive	optative
sg 1	ἔ-παυσ-α		παύσ-ω	παύσ-αιμι
2	ἔ-παυσ-ας	παῦσ-ον	παύσ-ῃς	παύσ-ειας *or* -αις
3	ἔ-παυσ-ε(ν)	παυσ-άτω	παύσ-ῃ	παύσ-ειε(ν) *or* -αι
pl 1	ἐ-παύσ-αμεν		παύσ-ωμεν	παύσ-αιμεν
2	ἐ-παύσ-ατε	παύσ-ατε	παύσ-ητε	παύσ-αιτε
3	ἔ-παυσ-αν	παυσ-άντων	παύσ-ωσι(ν)	παύσ-ειαν *or* -αιεν

Infinitive: παῦσ-αι Participle: παύσ-ᾱς, -ᾱσα, -αν (see p. 39)

	indicative	imperative	subjunctive	optative
perfect				
sg 1	πέ-παυκ-α		πε-παύκ-ω	πε-παύκ-οιμι
2	πέ-παυκ-ας		πε-παύκ-ῃς	πε-παύκ-οις
3	πέ-παυκ-ε(ν)		πε-παύκ-ῃ	πε-παύκ-οι
pl 1	πε-παύκ-αμεν		πε-παύκ-ωμεν	πε-παύκ-οιμεν
2	πε-παύκ-ατε		πε-παύκ-ητε	πε-παύκ-οιτε
3	πε-παύκ-ᾱσι(ν)		πε-παύκ-ωσι(ν)	πε-παύκ-οιεν

Infinitive: πε-παυκ-έναι **Participle:** πε-παυκ-ώς, -υῖα, -ός (see p. 41)

pluperfect

sg 1	ἐ-πε-παύκ-η
2	ἐ-πε-παύκ-ης
3	ἐ-πε-παύκ-ει(ν)
pl 1	ἐ-πε-παύκ-εμεν
2	ἐ-πε-παύκ-ετε
3	ἐ-πε-παύκ-εσαν

Note

1 All past indicatives add ἐ- as a prefix (the **augment**) except for the perfect, which reduplicates. (In fact, the perfect does not count as a past tense at all since it denotes a present state.) For details, see p. 67.

2 Forms of the verb which are not indicative do not have an augment.

3 There is no future subjunctive.

4 The perfect subjunctive and optative are rare.

Passive παύομαι *I am stopped*

	indicative	imperative	subjunctive	optative
present				
sg 1	παύ-ομαι		παύ-ωμαι	παυ-οίμην
2	παύ-ει *or* -ῃ	παύ-ου	παύ-ῃ	παύ-οιο
3	παύ-εται	παυ-έσθω	παύ-ηται	παύ-οιτο
pl 1	παυ-όμεθα		παυ-ώμεθα	παυ-οίμεθα
2	παύ-εσθε	παύ-εσθε	παύ-ησθε	παύ-οισθε
3	παύ-ονται	παυ-έσθων	παύ-ωνται	παύ-οιντο

Infinitive: παύ-εσθαι Participle: παυ-όμεν-ος, -η, -ον

imperfect				
sg 1	ἐ-παυ-όμην			
2	ἐ-παύ-ου			
3	ἐ-παύ-ετο			
pl 1	ἐ-παυ-όμεθα			
2	ἐ-παύ-εσθε			
3	ἐ-παύ-οντο			

future				
sg 1	παυσθήσ-ομαι			παυσθησ-οίμην
2	παυσθήσ-ει *or* -ῃ			παυσθήσ-οιο
3	παυσθήσ-εται			παυσθήσ-οιτο
pl 1	παυσθησ-όμεθα			παυσθησ-οίμεθα
2	παυσθήσ-εσθε			παυσθήσ-οισθε
3	παυσθήσ-ονται			παυσθήσ-οιντο

Infinitive: παυσθήσ-εσθαι Participle: παυσθησ-όμεν-ος, -η, -ον

aorist				
sg 1	ἐ-παύσ-θην		παυσ-θῶ	παυσ-θείην
2	ἐ-παύσ-θης	παύσ-θητι	παυσ-θῇς	παυσ-θείης
3	ἐ-παύσ-θη	παυσ-θήτω	παυσ-θῇ	παυσ-θείη
pl 1	ἐ-παύσ-θημεν		παυσ-θῶμεν	παυσ-θεῖμεν
2	ἐ-παύσ-θητε	παύσ-θητε	παυσ-θῆτε	παυσ-θεῖτε
3	ἐ-παύσ-θησαν	παυσ-θέντων	παυσ-θῶσι(ν)	παυσ-θεῖεν

Infinitive: παυσ-θῆναι Participle: παυσ-θείς, -θεῖσα, -θέν (see p. 40)

	indicative	imperative	subjunctive	optative

perfect (for verbs with consonant stems, see p. 68)

sg 1	πέ-παυ-μαι		πεπαυμένος ὦ	πεπαυμένος εἴην
2	πέ-παυ-σαι		πεπαυμένος ᾖς	πεπαυμένος εἴης
3	πέ-παυ-ται		πεπαυμένος ᾖ	πεπαυμένος εἴη
pl 1	πε-παύ-μεθα		πεπαυμένοι ὦμεν	πεπαυμένοι εἴημεν
2	πέ-παυ-σθε		πεπαυμένοι ἦτε	πεπαυμένοι εἴητε
3	πέ-παυ-νται		πεπαυμένοι ὦσι(ν)	πεπαυμένοι εἶεν

Infinitive: πε-παύ-σθαι **Participle:** πε-παυ-μέν-ος, -η, -ον

pluperfect

sg 1	ἐ-πε-παύ-μην
2	ἐ-πέ-παυ-σο
3	ἐ-πέ-παυ-το
pl 1	ἐ-πε-παύ-μεθα
2	ἐ-πέ-παυ-σθε
3	ἐ-πέ-παυ-ντο

future perfect

sg 1	πε-παύσ-ομαι			πε-παυσ-οίμην
2	πε-παύσ-ει *or* -ῃ			πε-παύσ-οιο
3	πε-παύσ-εται			πε-παύσ-οιτο
pl 1	πε-παυσ-όμεθα			πε-παυσ-οίμεθα
2	πε-παύσ-εσθε			πε-παύσ-οισθε
3	πε-παύσ-ονται			πε-παύσ-οιντο

Infinitive: πε-παύσ-εσθαι **Participle:** πε-παυσ-όμεν-ος, -η, -ον

Note

1 Many verbs do <u>not</u> (like παύω) add -σ- before the -θήσομαι and -θην endings of the future and aorist passive, e.g. λύω (I loose) – λυ-θήσομαι, ἐ-λύ-θην; πιστεύω (I trust) – πιστευ-θήσομαι, ἐ-πιστευ-θήν.

2 The perfect subjunctive and optative, and the future perfect optative are rare.

3 The 1 pl. ending -μεθα often appears as -μεσθα in epic and tragedy for metrical reasons.

4 Note the altenative forms for εἴημεν, εἴητε and εἶεν in the perfect optative: εἶμεν, εἶτε and εἴησαν.

Middle παύομαι *I stop myself*

indicative	imperative	subjunctive	optative

present, imperfect, perfect, pluperfect and **future perfect**
for these tenses, the middle is identical to the passive given on the previous two pages

future

	indicative	imperative	subjunctive	optative
sg 1	παύσ-ομαι			παυσ-οίμην
2	παύσ-ει *or* -ῃ			παύσ-οιο
3	παύσ-εται			παύσ-οιτο
pl 1	παυσ-όμεθα			παυσ-οίμεθα
2	παύσ-εσθε			παύσ-οισθε
3	παύσ-ονται			παύσ-οιντο

Infinitive: παύσ-εσθαι **Participle:** παυσ-όμεν-ος, -η, -ον

1st aorist (for 2nd aorist, see pp. 69–70)

	indicative	imperative	subjunctive	optative
sg 1	ἐ-παυσ-άμην		παύσ-ωμαι	παυσ-αίμην
2	ἐ-παύσ-ω	παῦσ-αι	παύσ-ῃ	παύσ-αιο
3	ἐ-παύσ-ατο	παυσ-άσθω	παύσ-ηται	παύσ-αιτο
pl 1	ἐ-παυσ-άμεθα		παυσ-ώμεθα	παυσ-αίμεθα
2	ἐ-παύσ-ασθε	παύσ-ασθε	παύσ-ησθε	παύσ-αισθε
3	ἐ-παύσ-αντο	παυσ-άσθων	παύσ-ωνται	παύσ-αιντο

Infinitive: παύσ-ασθαι **Participle:** παυσ-άμεν-ος, -η, -ον

Note

Many middle verbs become passive in form (but not in meaning) in the aorist. Note the following:

βούλομαι → ἐβουλήθην	I wish
δέομαι → ἐδεήθην	I beg
ἥδομαι → ἥσθην	I find pleasure in
μιμνήσκομαι → ἐμνήσθην	I remember
διαλέγομαι → διελέχθην	I converse
οἴομαι → ᾠήθην	I think
φοβέομαι → ἐφοβήθην	I fear
ὀργίζομαι → ὠργίσθην	I grow angry

| The augment expressing time, and reduplication

1 You can tell the past tenses of the indicative because, apart from the perfect (a special case since it is not really a past tense – see p. xiv), they all have an 'augment' (= something added at the start) in all three voices:

(a) If the verb begins with a consonant, this is the letter ἐ-, e.g. ἔ-παυον (imperfect), ἔ-παυσα (aorist).

(b) If the verb begins with a vowel, the vowel will lengthen as follows:

original vowel	vowel with augment
α	η
ᾳ, αι, ει	ῃ
αυ, ευ	ηυ
ε	η, rarely ει
ι	ῑ
ο	ω
οι	ῳ
υ	ῡ

2 The augment is added to the uncompounded verb, not its prefix. Thus the aorist of ἀποπαύω (I stop) is ἀπ-έπαυσα (the augment dislodging the ο of ἀπο-). Compare:

καταπέμπω → aor. κατ-έπεμψα	I send down
ἐπιβουλεύω → aor. ἐπ-εβούλευσα	I plot against

But note:

ἐγκρύπτω → aor. ἐν-έκρυψα	I hide in
ἐκπαιδεύω → aor. ἐξ-επαίδευσα	I educate
περιβαίνω → impf. περι-έβαινον	I go around (the ι of περι remains)

προβαίνω → impf. προ-έβαινον or προὔβαινον	I go forward

3 (a) The perfect 'reduplicates' (see p. xv) if the verb begins with a consonant, making use of the vowel ε. Thus:

παύω → pf. πέ-παυκα	I stop
λύω → pf. λέ-λυκα	I release

(b) θ, φ, χ reduplicate with τ, π, κ, e.g.,

θύω → pf. τέ-θυκα	I sacrifice
φεύγω → pf. πέ-φευγα	I flee
χαίρω → pf. κε-χάρηκα	I rejoice

(c) If the verb begins with a vowel, the same lengthening process is followed as with the augment (see 1 (b) above).

4 The pluperfect <u>both</u> has an augment <u>and</u> reduplicates. When the pluperfect is formed from the perfect of a verb beginning with a vowel, no further change is made.

| Forming the perfect passive

The perfect passive of verbs with stems ending in vowels is formed like
that of παύω (see p. 65), but when the stem ends in a consonant, almost all
the regular endings have to be changed for reasons of sound. Study of the
perfect passives of λείπω (I leave) and πράττω (I do) will indicate the
nature of these changes:

	λείπω	πράττω
perfect passive (indicative)		
sg 1	λέλειμμαι	πέπρᾱγμαι
2	λέλειψαι	πέπρᾱξαι
3	λέλειπται	πέπρᾱκται
pl 1	λελείμεθα	πεπράγμεθα
2	λέλειφθε	πέπρᾱχθε
3	λελειμμένοι εἰσί(ν)	πεπρᾱγμένοι εἰσί(ν)

Infinitive: λελεῖφθαι Participle: λελειμμένος Infinitive: πεπρᾶχθαι Participle: πεπρᾱγμένος

☑ Where the forms of the perfect passive are made up of the perfect
passive participle and a part of εἰμί (I am), the participle must agree
in number and gender with the subject of the verb, e.g.
αἱ γυναῖκες λελειμμέναι εἰσίν.
The women have been left behind.

| Verbs with a 2nd aorist

Many very common verbs which form all their other tenses regularly like παύω form those based on the aorist stem in a different way. This is the **2nd aorist** and is often distinguished by having an aorist stem which is shorter than the present stem. In the tables of principal parts, a verb which forms a 2nd aorist will have the ending -ον or -όμην in the aorist column.

While the formation is different, the meaning is the same. Compare English, where the 'regular' past tense is formed with -ed, as 'walked' from 'walk'. The Greek 2nd aorist can be compared with the past tense of verbs like 'sing' and 'run', where we find (with a vowel change) 'sang' and 'ran'. Sometimes in both languages, a different stem is used in different tenses. For example, the aorist of αἱρέω (I take) is εἷλον, from the stem ἑλ-. Cf. English 'go' beside 'went'.

The forms are given in full below, but note that the endings are identical to those of the regular imperfect for the indicative and to those of the present for all the other forms. The aorist <u>passive</u> is formed from its own separate stem.

Active λαμβάνω *I take*

	indicative	imperative	subjunctive	optative
aorist				
sg 1	ἔ-λαβ-ον		λάβ-ω	λάβ-οιμι
2	ἔ-λαβ-ες	λαβ-έ	λάβ-ῃς	λάβ-οις
3	ἔ-λαβ-ε	λαβ-έτω	λάβ-ῃ	λάβ-οι
pl 1	ἐ-λάβ-ομεν		λάβ-ωμεν	λάβ-οιμεν
2	ἐ-λάβ-ετε	λάβ-ετε	λάβ-ητε	λάβ-οιτε
3	ἔ-λαβ-ον	λαβ-όντων	λάβ-ωσι(ν)	λάβ-οιεν

Infinitive: λαβ-εῖν **Participle:** λαβ-ών, -οῦσα, -όν (accentuation like ἑκών, p. 38)

Note

Note also the following common imperatives: εἰπέ (say!), ἐλθέ (come!), εὑρέ (find!), ἰδέ (see!).

Middle λαμβάνομαι *I take for myself*

	indicative	imperative	subjunctive	optative
aorist				
sg 1	ἐ-λαβ-όμην		λάβ-ωμαι	λαβ-οίμην
2	ἐ-λάβ-ου	λαβ-οῦ	λάβ-ῃ	λάβ-οιο
3	ἐ-λάβ-ετο	λαβ-έσθω	λάβ-ηται	λάβ-οιτο
pl 1	ἐ-λαβ-όμεθα		λαβ-ώμεθα	λαβ-οίμεθα
2	ἐ-λάβ-εσθε	λάβ-εσθε	λάβ-ησθε	λάβ-οισθε
3	ἐ-λάβ-οντο	λαβ-έσθων	λάβ-ωνται	λάβοιντο

Infinitive: λαβ-έσθαι **Participle:** λαβ-όμεν-ος, -η, -ον

Note
The accents on 2nd aorist verb forms can be different from those on other verbs. For the details, see **4** on p. 226.

| Root aorists

Some verbs form the aorist by just adding endings onto the root of the verb. For example, the active aorists of βαίνω (root βη-) and γιγνώσκω (root γνω-) are as follows:

βαίνω / go

	indicative	imperative	subjunctive	optative
aorist				
sg 1	ἔβην		βῶ	βαίην
2	ἔβης	βῆθι	βῇς	βαίης
3	ἔβη	βήτω	βῇ	βαίη
pl 1	ἔβημεν		βῶμεν	βαῖμεν
2	ἔβητε	βῆτε	βῆτε	βαῖτε
3	ἔβησαν	βάντων	βῶσι(ν)	βαῖεν

Infinitive: βῆναι **Participle:** βάς, βᾶσα, βάν (stem βάντ-)

γιγνώσκω / get to know

	indicative	imperative	subjunctive	optative
aorist				
sg 1	ἔγνων		γνῶ	γνοίην
2	ἔγνως	γνῶθι	γνῷς	γνοίης
3	ἔγνω	γνώτω	γνῷ	γνοίη
pl 1	ἔγνωμεν		γνῶμεν	γνοῖμεν
2	ἔγνωτε	γνῶτε	γνῶτε	γνοῖτε
3	ἔγνωσαν	γνόντων	γνῶσι(ν)	γνοῖεν

Infinitive: γνῶναι **Participle:** γνούς, γνοῦσα, γνόν (stem γνόντ-)

Note

1 Other verbs which have root aorists are:

Present	Aorist	
ἁλίσκομαι	ἑάλων	be captured (used as passive of αἱρέω)
βιόω	ἐβίων	live
-διδράσκω	-έδρᾱν	run
-δύω	-έδῡν	enter, put on

Note: List continues on p. 72

ἵστημι	ἔστην	aor. = I stood (intr.)
σβέννυμι	ἔσβην	extinguish
φθάνω	ἔφθην	anticipate X (acc.) in doing, act *or* be first
φύω	ἔφυν	aor. = I am by nature (intr.)

2 Some verbs have both regular and root aorists. In these cases the root aorist is always intransitive and the regular aorist is often transitive. For example,

ἔφυν	ἔφυσα
I grew, I was by nature	I grew, produced, made to grow
ἔστην	ἔστησα
I stood, was standing	I did set up, made stand (see p. 84)
κατέδυν	κατέδυσα
I sank	I made sink, caused to sink

But φθάνω (I anticipate X (acc.) in doing, act or be first) is both transitive and intransitive in both its aorist forms (ἔφθην and ἔφθασα). And βιόω is intransitive in both of its aorist forms (ἐβίων and ἐβίωσα).

| Contracted verbs

Contracted verbs are verbs whose present stem ends in a vowel (-α-, -ε-, -ο-), e.g. τιμάω, φιλέω, δηλόω.

In the present and imperfect (including the imperative, subjunctive, optative, infinitive and participle), this vowel coalesces with the vowel of the ending. We give these conjugations in full on the following pages.

The following rules should be learnt:

α verbs

    α followed by ε or η becomes ᾱ.
    α followed by ο or ω becomes ω.
    ι is preserved but becomes subscript; υ disappears.

ε verbs

    ε followed by ε becomes ει.
    ε followed by ο becomes ου.
    ε followed by a long vowel or diphthong disappears.

ο verbs

    ο followed by a long vowel becomes ω.
    ο followed by a short vowel becomes ου.
    Any combination with ι becomes οι.

N.B. The endings of contracted verbs follow those of παύω with the application of the above rules, <u>except</u> in the singular of the present optative active.

    From τῑμάω, this is τῑμ-ῴην, τῑμ-ῴης, τῑμ-ῴη.
    From φιλέω, this is φιλ-οίην, φιλ-οίης, φιλ-οίη.
    From δηλόω, this is δηλ-οίην, δηλ-οίης δηλ-οίη.

| Contracted verbs in α

Active τῑμῶ (άω) *I honour*

	indicative	imperative	subjunctive	optative
present				
sg 1	τῑμ-ῶ		τῑμ-ῶ	τῑμ-ῴην
2	τῑμ-ᾷς	τίμ-ᾱ	τῑμ-ᾷς	τῑμ-ῴης
3	τῑμ-ᾷ	τῑμ-άτω	τῑμ-ᾷ	τῑμ-ῴη
pl 1	τῑμ-ῶμεν		τῑμ-ῶμεν	τῑμ-ῷμεν
2	τῑμ-ᾶτε	τῑμ-ᾶτε	τῑμ-ᾶτε	τῑμ-ῷτε
3	τῑμ-ῶσι(ν)	τῑμ-ώντων	τῑμ-ῶσι(ν)	τῑμ-ῷεν

Infinitive: τῑμ-ᾶν **Participle:** τῑμ-ῶν, -ῶσα, -ῶν

imperfect				
sg 1	ἐ-τίμ-ων			
2	ἐ-τίμ-ᾱς			
3	ἐ-τίμ-ᾱ			
pl 1	ἐ-τῑμ-ῶμεν			
2	ἐ-τῑμ-ᾶτε			
3	ἐ-τίμ-ων			

Note

1 Note that the present infinitive active of these verbs usually ends in -ᾶν. The ι of the regular infinitive ending -ειν (originally -εεν) is not found in contracted verbs.

2 Some α verbs (including ζάω (I live) and χράομαι (I use)) contract to η instead of ᾱ when α is followed by ε or η, e.g. ζῆν (to live), χρῆσθαι (to use).

Middle/Passive τιμῶμαι

	indicative	imperative	subjunctive	optative
present				
sg 1	τῑμ-ῶμαι		τῑμ-ῶμαι	τῑμ-ῴμην
2	τῑμ-ᾷ	τῑμ-ῶ	τῑμ-ᾷ	τῑμ-ῷο
3	τῑμ-ᾶται	τῑμ-άσθω	τῑμ-ᾶται	τῑμ-ῷτο
pl 1	τῑμ-ώμεθα		τῑμ-ώμεθα	τῑμ-ῴμεθα
2	τῑμ-ᾶσθε	τῑμ-ᾶσθε	τῑμ-ᾶσθε	τῑμ-ῷσθε
3	τῑμ-ῶνται	τῑμ-άσθων	τῑμ-ῶνται	τῑμ-ῷντο

Infinitive: τῑμ-ᾶσθαι **Participle:** τῑμ-ώμεν-ος, -η, -ον

imperfect	
sg 1	ἐ-τῑμ-ώμην
2	ἐ-τῑμ-ῶ
3	ἐ-τῑμ-ᾶτο
pl 1	ἐ-τῑμ-ώμεθα
2	ἐ-τῑμ-ᾶσθε
3	ἐ-τῑμ-ῶντο

| Other tenses

For their <u>future</u>, <u>aorist</u> and <u>perfect</u>, contracted verbs lengthen their vowel before the ending, with α becoming η. The forms of the first person singular in these tenses are:

	active	**middle**	**passive**
future	τῑμή-σω	τῑμή-σομαι	τῑμη-θήσομαι
aorist	ἐ-τίμη-σα	ἐ-τῑμη-σάμην	ἐ-τῑμή-θην
perfect	τε-τίμη-κα	τε-τίμη-μαι	τε-τίμη-μαι

| Contracted verbs in ε

Active φιλῶ (έω) / love

	indicative	imperative	subjunctive	optative
present				
sg 1	φιλ-ῶ		φιλ-ῶ	φιλ-οίην
2	φιλ-εῖς	φίλ-ει	φιλ-ῇς	φιλ-οίης
3	φιλ-εῖ	φιλ-είτω	φιλ-ῇ	φιλ-οίη
pl 1	φιλ-οῦμεν		φιλ-ῶμεν	φιλ-οῖμεν
2	φιλ-εῖτε	φιλ-εῖτε	φιλ-ῆτε	φιλ-οῖτε
3	φιλ-οῦσι(ν)	φιλ-ούντων	φιλ-ῶσι(ν)	φιλ-οῖεν

Infinitive: φιλ-εῖν Participle: φιλ-ῶν, -οῦσα, -οῦν

imperfect	
sg 1	ἐ-φίλ-ουν
2	ἐ-φίλ-εις
3	ἐ-φίλ-ει
pl 1	ἐ-φιλ-οῦμεν
2	ἐ-φιλ-εῖτε
3	ἐ-φίλ-ουν

Note

1 When stems in ε are only one syllable long, e.g. πλέ-ω (I sail), δεῖ (it is necessary), they contract <u>only</u> when the ending added to the stem begins with ε. Then they contract to ει. Thus the present tense of πλέω is:

Active πλέω / sail

	indicative	imperative	subjunctive	optative
present				
sg 1	πλέω		πλέω	πλέοιμι (N.B.)
2	πλεῖς (έ-εις)	πλεῖ	πλέῃς	πλέοις
3	πλεῖ (έ-ει)	πλείτω	πλέῃ	πλέοι
pl 1	πλέομεν		πλέωμεν	πλέοιμεν
2	πλεῖτε (έ-ετε)	πλεῖτε	πλέητε	πλέοιτε
3	πλέουσι(ν)	πλεόντων	πλέωσι(ν)	πλέοιεν

Infinitive: πλεῖν Participle: πλέ-ων, -ουσα, -ον

Middle/Passive φιλοῦμαι

	indicative	imperative	subjunctive	optative
present				
sg 1	φιλ-οῦμαι		φιλ-ῶμαι	φιλ-οίμην
2	φιλ-εῖ *or* -ῇ	φιλ-οῦ	φιλ-ῇ	φιλ-οῖο
3	φιλ-εῖται	φιλ-είσθω	φιλ-ῆται	φιλ-οῖτο
pl 1	φιλ-ούμεθα		φιλ-ώμεθα	φιλ-οίμεθα
2	φιλ-εῖσθε	φιλ-εῖσθε	φιλ-ῆσθε	φιλ-οῖσθε
3	φιλ-οῦνται	φιλ-είσθων	φιλ-ῶνται	φιλ-οῖντο

Infinitive: φιλ-εῖσθαι Participle: φιλ-ούμεν-ος, -η, -ον

imperfect		
sg 1	ἐ-φιλ-ούμην	
2	ἐ-φιλ-οῦ	
3	ἐ-φιλ-εῖτο	
pl 1	ἐ-φιλ-ούμεθα	
2	ἐ-φιλ-εῖσθε	
3	ἐ-φιλ-οῦντο	

| Other tenses

For their <u>future</u>, <u>aorist</u> and <u>perfect</u>, contracted verbs lengthen their vowel before the ending, with ε becoming η. The forms of the first person singular in these tenses are:

	active	middle	passive
future	φιλή-σω	φιλή-σομαι	φιλη-θήσομαι
aorist	ἐ-φίλη-σα	ἐ-φιλη-σάμην	ἐ-φιλή-θην
perfect	πε-φίλη-κα	πε-φίλη-μαι	πε-φίλη-μαι

| Contracted verbs in o

Active δηλῶ (όω) *I show*

	indicative	imperative	subjunctive	optative
present
sg 1	δηλ-ῶ		δηλ-ῶ	δηλ-οίην
2	δηλ-οῖς	δήλ-ου	δηλ-οῖς	δηλ-οίης
3	δηλ-οῖ	δηλ-ούτω	δηλ-οῖ	δηλ-οίη
pl 1	δηλ-ούμεν		δηλ-ῶμεν	δηλ-οῖμεν
2	δηλ-οῦτε	δηλ-οῦτε	δηλ-ῶτε	δηλ-οῖτε
3	δηλ-οῦσι(ν)	δηλ-ούντων	δηλ-ῶσι(ν)	δηλ-οῖεν

Infinitive: δηλ-οῦν Participle: δηλ-ῶν, -οῦσα, -οῦν

| **imperfect** |
sg 1	ἐ-δήλ-ουν
2	ἐ-δήλ-ους
3	ἐ-δήλ-ου
pl 1	ἐ-δηλ-οῦμεν
2	ἐ-δηλ-οῦτε
3	ἐ-δήλ-ουν

Note

Note that the present infinitive active of these verbs ends in -οῦν. The ι of the regular infinitive ending -ειν (originally -εεν) is not found in contracted verbs.

Middle/Passive δηλοῦμαι *I am shown*

	indicative	imperative	subjunctive	optative
present				
sg 1	δηλ-οῦμαι		δηλ-ῶμαι	δηλ-οίμην
2	δηλ-οῖ	δηλ-οῦ	δηλ-οῖ	δηλ-οῖο
3	δηλ-οῦται	δηλ-ούσθω	δηλ-ῶται	δηλ-οῖτο
pl 1	δηλ-ούμεθα		δηλ-ώμεθα	δηλ-οίμεθα
2	δηλ-οῦσθε	δηλ-οῦσθε	δηλ-ῶσθε	δηλ-οῖσθε
3	δηλ-οῦνται	δηλ-ούσθων	δηλ-ῶνται	δηλ-οῖντο

Infinitive: δηλ-οῦσθαι **Participle:** δηλ-ούμεν-ος, -η, -ον

imperfect

sg 1	ἐ-δηλ-ούμην
2	ἐ-δηλ-οῦ
3	ἐ-δηλ-οῦτο
pl 1	ἐ-δηλ-ούμεθα
2	ἐ-δηλ-οῦσθε
3	ἐ-δηλ-οῦντο

| Other tenses

For their <u>future</u>, <u>aorist</u> and <u>perfect</u>, contracted verbs lengthen their vowel before the ending, with o becoming ω. The forms of the first person singular in these tenses are:

	active	**middle**	**passive**
future	δηλώ-σω	δηλώ-σομαι	δηλω-θήσομαι
aorist	ἐ-δήλω-σα	ἐ-δηλω-σάμην	ἐ-δηλώ-θην
perfect	δε-δήλω-κα	δε-δήλω-μαι	δε-δήλω-μαι

| Verbs in μι – τίθημι

Active τίθημι *I put, place*

	indicative	imperative	subjunctive	optative
present				
sg 1	τίθημι		τιθῶ	τιθείην
2	τίθης	τίθει	τιθῇς	τιθείης
3	τίθησι(ν)	τιθέτω	τιθῇ	τιθείη
pl 1	τίθεμεν		τιθῶμεν	τιθ-εῖμεν *or* -είημεν
2	τίθετε	τίθετε	τιθῆτε	τιθ-εῖτε *or* -είητε
3	τιθέᾱσι(ν)	τιθέντων	τιθῶσι(ν)	τιθ-εῖεν *or* -είησαν

Infinitive: τιθέναι **Participle:** τιθείς, τιθεῖσα, τιθέν (stem τιθέντ-)

	indicative	imperative	subjunctive	optative
imperfect				
sg 1	ἐτίθην			
2	ἐτίθεις			
3	ἐτίθει			
pl 1	ἐτίθεμεν			
2	ἐτίθετε			
3	ἐτίθεσαν			

	indicative	imperative	subjunctive	optative
aorist				
sg 1	ἔθηκα		θῶ	θείην
2	ἔθηκας	θές	θῇς	θείης
3	ἔθηκε(ν)	θέτω	θῇ	θείη
pl 1	ἔθεμεν		θῶμεν	θεῖμεν *or* θείημεν
2	ἔθετε	θέτε	θῆτε	θεῖτε *or* θείητε
3	ἔθηκαν, ἔθεσαν	θέντων	θῶσι(ν)	θεῖεν *or* θείησαν

Infinitive: θεῖναι **Participle:** θείς, θεῖσα, θέν (stem θέντ-)

Note

1 In the active, the future, perfect and pluperfect tenses are formed regularly from a stem θη-: θήσω, τέθηκα, ἐτεθήκη.

Passive τίθεμαι *I am put, placed*

	indicative	imperative	subjunctive	optative
present				
sg 1	τίθεμαι		τιθῶμαι	τιθείμην
2	τίθεσαι	τίθεσο	τιθῇ	τιθεῖο
3	τίθεται	τιθέσθω	τιθῆται	τιθεῖτο
pl 1	τιθέμεθα		τιθώμεθα	τιθείμεθα
2	τίθεσθε	τίθεσθε	τιθῆσθε	τιθεῖσθε
3	τίθενται	τιθέσθων	τιθῶνται	τιθεῖντο

Infinitive: τίθεσθαι **Participle:** τιθέμεν-ος, -η, -ον

imperfect

sg 1	ἐτιθέμην
2	ἐτίθεσο
3	ἐτίθετο
pl 1	ἐτιθέμεθα
2	ἐτίθεσθε
3	ἐτίθεντο

Note

The passive of the future and aorist are as follows: τεθήσομαι, ἐτέθην. For the perfect passive, κεῖμαι is used: see p. 92.

Middle τίθεμαι *I put, place*

	indicative	imperative	subjunctive	optative
aorist				
sg 1	ἐθέμην		θῶμαι	θείμην
2	ἔθου	θοῦ	θῇ	θεῖο
3	ἔθετο	θέσθω	θῆται	θεῖτο
pl 1	ἐθέμεθα		θώμεθα	θείμεθα
2	ἔθεσθε	θέσθε	θῆσθε	θεῖσθε
3	ἔθεντο	θέσθων	θῶνται	θεῖντο

Infinitive: θέσθαι **Participle:** θέμεν-ος, -η, -ον

Note

As with all verbs, the middle is only distinct from the passive in the future and aorist tenses. The future middle is formed regularly from a stem θη-: θήσομαι.

ἵημι

Active ἵημι *I send*

	indicative	imperative	subjunctive	optative
present				
sg 1	ἵημι		ἱῶ	ἱείην
2	ἵης	ἵει	ἱῇς	ἱείης
3	ἵησι(ν)	ἱέτω	ἱῇ	ἱείη
pl 1	ἵεμεν		ἱῶμεν	ἱεῖμεν or ἱείημεν
2	ἵετε	ἵετε	ἱῆτε	ἱεῖτε or ἱειήτε
3	ἱᾶσι(ν)	ἱέντων	ἱῶσι(ν)	ἱεῖεν or ἱείησαν

Infinitive: ἱέναι Participle: ἱείς, ἱεῖσα, ἱέν (stem ἱέντ-)

imperfect				
sg 1	ἵην			
2	ἵεις			
3	ἵει			
pl 1	ἵεμεν			
2	ἵετε			
3	ἵεσαν			

aorist				
sg 1	-ἧκα		ὦ	εἵην
2	-ἧκας	ἕς	ᾗς	εἵης
3	-ἧκε(ν)	ἕτω	ᾗ	εἵη
pl 1	εἷμεν		ὦμεν	εἷμεν or εἵημεν
2	εἷτε	ἕτε	ἧτε	εἷτε or εἵητε
3	εἷσαν	ἕντων	ὦσι(ν)	εἷεν or εἵησαν

Infinitive: εἷναι Participle: εἵς, εἷσα, ἕν (stem ἕντ-)

Note

1 A hyphen before a word indicates that it is usually or always found only in compound forms.

2 In the active, the future and perfect tenses are formed as follows: -ἥσω, -εἷκα.

Passive ἵεμαι *I am sent*

	indicative	imperative	subjunctive	optative
present				
sg 1	ἵεμαι		ἱῶμαι	ἱείμην
2	ἵεσαι	ἵεσο	ἱῇ	ἱεῖο
3	ἵεται	ἱέσθω	ἱῆται	ἱεῖτο
pl 1	ἱέμεθα		ἱώμεθα	ἱείμεθα
2	ἵεσθε	ἵεσθε	ἱῆσθε	ἱεῖσθε
3	ἵενται	ἱέσθων	ἱῶνται	ἱεῖντο

Infinitive: ἵεσθαι **Participle:** ἱέμεν-ος, -η, -ον

imperfect	
sg 1	ἱέμην
2	ἵεσο
3	ἵετο
pl 1	ἱέμεθα
2	ἵεσθε
3	ἵεντο

Note

In the passive, the future, aorist, perfect and pluperfect are formed as follows:
-ἐθήσομαι, -εἵθην, -εἷμαι, -εἵμην.

Middle ἵεμαι *I send*

	indicative	imperative	subjunctive	optative
aorist				
sg 1	εἵμην		ὧμαι	εἵμην
2	εἷσο	οὗ	ἧ	εἷο
3	εἷτο	ἕσθω	ἧται	εἷτο
pl 1	εἵμεθα		ὥμεθα	εἵμεθα
2	εἷσθε	ἕσθε	ἧσθε	εἷσθε
3	εἷντο	ἕσθων	ὧνται	εἷντο

Infinitive: ἕσθαι **Participle:** ἕμεν-ος, -η, -ον

Note

As with all verbs, the middle is distinct from the passive only in the future and aorist tenses; the future middle is ἥσομαι.

ἵστημι

Active ἵστημι / make stand, set up (tr.)

	indicative	imperative	subjunctive	optative
present / make stand, set up (tr.)				
sg 1	ἵστημι		ἱστῶ	ἱσταίην
2	ἵστης	ἵστη	ἱστῇς	ἱσταίης
3	ἵστησι(ν)	ἱστάτω	ἱστῇ	ἱσταίη
pl 1	ἵσταμεν		ἱστῶμεν	ἱστ-αῖμεν or -αίημεν
2	ἵστατε	ἵστατε	ἱστῆτε	ἱστ-αῖτε or -αίητε
3	ἱστᾶσι(ν)	ἱστάντων	ἱστῶσι(ν)	ἱστ-αῖεν or -αίησαν

Infinitive: ἱστάναι Participle: ἱστάς, ἱστᾶσα, ἱστάν

imperfect / was setting up (tr.)				
sg 1	ἵστην			
2	ἵστης			
3	ἵστη			
pl 1	ἵσταμεν			
2	ἵστατε			
3	ἵστασαν			

aorist / did set up (tr.)				
sg 1	ἔστησα		στήσω	στήσαιμι
2	ἔστησας	στῆσον	στήσῃς	στήσ-ειας or -αις
3	ἔστησε(ν)	στησάτω	στήσῃ	στήσ-ειε(ν) or -αι
pl 1	ἐστήσαμεν		στήσωμεν	στήσαιμεν
2	ἐστήσατε	στήσατε	στήσητε	στήσαιτε
3	ἔστησαν	στησάντων	στήσωσι(ν)	στήσ-ειαν or -αιεν

Infinitive: στῆσαι Participle: στήσᾱς, στήσᾱσα, στῆσαν

Note

This (transitive) 1st aorist active is formed regularly like ἔπαυσα, but we give it in full to contrast with ἔστην, the intransitive 2nd aorist, given on p. 86. The future is formed regularly: στήσω (I shall set up (tr.)).

Passive ἵσταμαι *I am made to stand, am set up*

	indicative	imperative	subjunctive	optative
present *I am set up*				
sg 1	ἵσταμαι		ἱστῶμαι	ἱσταίμην
2	ἵστασαι	ἵστασο	ἱστῇ	ἱσταῖο
3	ἵσταται	ἱστάσθω	ἱστῆται	ἱσταῖτο
pl 1	ἱστάμεθα		ἱστώμεθα	ἱσταίμεθα
2	ἵστασθε	ἵστασθε	ἱστῆσθε	ἱσταῖσθε
3	ἵστανται	ἱστάσθων	ἱστῶνται	ἱσταῖντο

Infinitive: ἵστασθαι Participle: ἱστάμεν-ος, -η, -ον

imperfect *I was being set up*

sg 1	ἱστάμην
2	ἵστασο
3	ἵστατο
pl 1	ἱστάμεθα
2	ἵστασθε
3	ἵσταντο

future *I shall be set up*

sg 1   σταθήσομαι etc. regularly as παυσθήσομαι

aorist *I was set up*

sg 1   ἐστάθην etc. regularly as ἐπαύσθην

Middle ἵσταμαι *I set up for myself* (tr.)

	indicative	imperative	subjunctive	optative
aorist *I did set up for myself (tr.)*				
sg 1	ἐστησάμην		στήσωμαι	στησαίμην
2	ἐστήσω	στῆσαι	στήσῃ	στήσαιο
3	ἐστήσατο	στησάσθω	στήσηται	στήσαιτο
pl 1	ἐστησάμεθα		στησώμεθα	στησαίμεθα
2	ἐστήσασθε	στήσασθε	στήσησθε	στήσαισθε
3	ἐστήσαντο	στησάσθων	στήσωνται	στήσαιντο

Infinitive: στήσασθαι Participle: στησάμεν-ος, -η, -ον

The middle of the transitive present and imperfect is identical to the passive forms.

Active ἕστηκα / *stand* (intr.)

	indicative	imperative	subjunctive	optative
perfect	/ *have stood up, i.e.* / *am standing,* / *stand*			
sg 1	ἕστηκα		ἑστῶ	ἑσταίην
2	ἕστηκας	ἕσταθι	ἑστῇς	ἑσταίης
3	ἕστηκε	ἑστάτω	ἑστῇ	ἑσταίη
pl 1	ἕσταμεν		ἑστῶμεν	ἑστ-αῖμεν *or* -αίημεν
2	ἕστατε	ἕστατε	ἑστῆτε	ἑστ-αῖτε *or* -αίητε
3	ἑστᾶσι(ν)	ἑστάντων	ἑστῶσι(ν)	ἑστ-αῖεν *or* -αίησαν

Infinitive: ἑστάναι **Participle:** ἑστ-ώς, -ῶσα, -ός (stem ἑστωτ-)

pluperfect	/ *had stood up, i.e.* / *was standing*			
sg 1	εἱστήκη			
2	εἱστήκης			
3	εἱστήκει			
pl 1	ἕσταμεν			
2	ἕστατε			
3	ἕστασαν			

aorist	/ *stood* (2nd aorist)			
sg 1	ἕστην		στῶ	σταίην
2	ἕστης	στῆθι	στῇς	σταίης
3	ἕστη	στήτω	στῇ	σταίη
pl 1	ἕστημεν		στῶμεν	σταῖμεν *or* σταίημεν
2	ἕστητε	στῆτε	στῆτε	σταῖτε *or* σταίητε
3	ἕστησαν	στάντων	στῶσι(ν)	σταῖεν *or* σταίησαν

Infinitive: στῆναι **Participle:** στάς, στᾶσα, στάν

Note

These three tenses indicate a <u>state</u> of standing. ἑστήξω = I shall stand.

Middle ἵσταμαι *I am (in the process of) standing up*

	indicative	imperative	subjunctive	optative
present *I am (in the process of) standing up*				
sg 1	ἵσταμαι		ἱστῶμαι	ἱσταίμην
2	ἵστασαι	ἵστασο	ἱστῇ	ἱσταῖο
3	ἵσταται	ἱστάσθω	ἱστῆται	ἱσταῖτο
pl 1	ἱστάμεθα		ἱστώμεθα	ἱσταίμεθα
2	ἵστασθε	ἵστασθε	ἱστῆσθε	ἱσταῖσθε
3	ἵστανται	ἱστάσθων	ἱστῶνται	ἱσταῖντο

Infinitive: ἵστασθαι Participle: ἱστάμεν-ος, -η, -ον

imperfect *I was (in the process of) standing up*				
sg 1	ἱστάμην			
2	ἵστασο			
3	ἵστατο			
pl 1	ἱστάμεθα			
2	ἵστασθε			
3	ἵσταντο			

future *I shall stand up*				
sg 1	στήσομαι			στησοίμην
2	στήσει *or* στήσῃ			στήσοιο
3	στήσεται			στήσοιτο
pl 1	στησόμεθα			στησοίμεθα
2	στήσεσθε			στήσοισθε
3	στήσονται			στήσοιντο

Infinitive: στήσεσθαι Participle: στησόμεν-ος, -η, -ον

Note

These three tenses indicate the process of standing up.

δίδωμι

Active δίδωμι / give

	indicative	imperative	subjunctive	optative
present				
sg 1	δίδωμι		διδῶ	διδοίην
2	δίδως	δίδου	διδῷς	διδοίης
3	δίδωσι(ν)	διδότω	διδῷ	διδοίη
pl 1	δίδομεν		διδῶμεν	διδ-οῖμεν *or* -οίημεν
2	δίδοτε	δίδοτε	διδῶτε	διδ-οῖτε *or* -οίητε
3	διδόᾱσι(ν)	διδόντων	διδῶσι(ν)	διδ-οῖεν *or* -οίησαν

Infinitive: διδόναι Participle: διδούς, διδοῦσα, διδόν (stem διδόντ-)

imperfect				
sg 1	ἐδίδουν			
2	ἐδίδους			
3	ἐδίδου			
pl 1	ἐδίδομεν			
2	ἐδίδοτε			
3	ἐδίδοσαν			

	indicative	imperative	subjunctive	optative
aorist				
sg 1	ἔδωκα		δῶ	δοίην
2	ἔδωκας	δός	δῷς	δοίης
3	ἔδωκε(ν)	δότω	δῷ	δοίη
pl 1	ἔδομεν		δῶμεν	δοῖμεν *or* δοίημεν
2	ἔδοτε	δότε	δῶτε	δοῖτε *or* δοίητε
3	ἔδωκαν, ἔδοσαν	δόντων	δῶσι(ν)	δοῖεν *or* δοίησαν

Infinitive: δοῦναι Participle: δούς, δοῦσα, δόν (stem δόντ-)

Note

In the active, the future, perfect and pluperfect tenses are formed regularly from a stem δω-: δώσω, δέδωκα, ἐδεδώκη.

Passive δίδομαι *I am given*

	indicative	imperative	subjunctive	optative
present				
sg 1	δίδομαι		διδῶμαι	διδοίμην
2	δίδοσαι	δίδοσο	διδῷ	διδοῖο
3	δίδοται	διδόσθω	διδῶται	διδοῖτο
pl 1	διδόμεθα		διδώμεθα	διδοίμεθα
2	δίδοσθε	δίδοσθε	διδῶσθε	διδοῖσθε
3	δίδονται	διδόσθων	διδῶνται	διδοῖντο

Infinitive: δίδοσθαι **Participle:** διδόμεν-ος, -η, -ον

imperfect				
sg 1	ἐδιδόμην			
2	ἐδίδοσο			
3	ἐδίδοτο			
pl 1	ἐδιδόμεθα			
2	ἐδίδοσθε			
3	ἐδίδοντο			

Note

In the passive, the future, aorist, perfect and pluperfect are as follows: δοθήσομαι, ἐδόθην, δέδομαι, ἐδεδόμην.

Middle δίδομαι *I give, offer*

	indicative	imperative	subjunctive	optative
aorist				
sg 1	ἐδόμην		δῶμαι	δοίμην
2	ἔδου	δοῦ	δῷ	δοῖο
3	ἔδοτο	δόσθω	δῶται	δοῖτο
pl 1	ἐδόμεθα		δώμεθα	δοίμεθα
2	ἔδοσθε	δόσθε	δῶσθε	δοῖσθε
3	ἔδοντο	δόσθων	δῶνται	δοῖντο

Infinitive: δόσθαι **Participle:** δόμεν-ος, -η, -ον

Note

As with all verbs, the middle is only different in form from the passive in the future and aorist tenses; the future middle is formed regularly from a stem δω-: δώσομαι.

δείκνῡμι

Active δείκνῡμι / *show*

	indicative	imperative	subjunctive	optative
present				
sg 1	δείκνῡμι		δεικνύω	δεικνύοιμι
2	δείκνῡς	δείκνῡ	δεικνύῃς	δεικνύοις
3	δείκνῡσι(ν)	δεικνύτω	δεικνύῃ	δεικνύοι
pl 1	δείκνυμεν		δεικνύωμεν	δεικνύοιμεν
2	δείκνυτε	δείκνυτε	δεικνύητε	δεικνύοιτε
3	δεικνύᾱσι(ν)	δεικνύντων	δεικνύωσι(ν)	δεικνύοιεν

Infinitive: δεικνύναι **Participle:** δεικνύς, δεικνῦσα, δεικνύν (stem δεικνύντ-)

imperfect

sg 1	ἐδείκνῡν
2	ἐδείκνῡς
3	ἐδείκνῡ
pl 1	ἐδείκνυμεν
2	ἐδείκνυτε
3	ἐδείκνυσαν

Note

In the active, the aorist, future, perfect and pluperfect tenses are formed as follows:
ἔδειξα, δείξω, δέδειχα, ἐδεδείχη.

Passive δείκνυμαι *I am shown*

	indicative	imperative	subjunctive	optative
present				
sg 1	δείκνυμαι		δεικνύωμαι	δεικνυοίμην
2	δείκνυσαι	δείκνυσο	δεικνύῃ	δεικνύοιο
3	δείκνυται	δεικνύσθω	δεικνύηται	δεικνύοιτο
pl 1	δεικνύμεθα		δεικνυώμεθα	δεικνυοίμεθα
2	δείκνυσθε	δείκνυσθε	δεικνύησθε	δεικνύοισθε
3	δείκνυνται	δεικνύσθων	δεικνύωνται	δεικνύοιντο

Infinitive: δείκνυσθαι Participle: δεικνύμεν-ος, -η, -ον

imperfect	
sg 1	ἐδεικνύμην
2	ἐδείκνυσο
3	ἐδείκνυτο
pl 1	ἐδεικνύμεθα
2	ἐδείκνυσθε
3	ἐδείκνυντο

Note

In the passive, the future, aorist, perfect and pluperfect are formed regularly: δειχθήσομαι, ἐδείχθην, δέδειγμαι, ἐδεδείγμην.

Middle δείκνυμαι *I show*

	indicative	imperative	subjunctive	optative
aorist				
sg 1	ἐδειξάμην etc. regularly as ἐπαυσάμην			

Note

As with all verbs, the middle is different in form from the passive only in the future and aorist tenses; the future middle is δείξομαι.

δύναμαι

Middle δύναμαι *I am able, I can*

	indicative	imperative	subjunctive	optative
present				
sg 1	δύναμαι		δύνωμαι	δυναίμην
2	δύνασαι	δύνασο	δύνῃ	δύναιο
3	δύναται	δυνάσθω	δύνηται	δύναιτο
pl 1	δυνάμεθα		δυνώμεθα	δυναίμεθα
2	δύνασθε	δύνασθε	δύνησθε	δύναισθε
3	δύνανται	δυνάσθων	δύνωνται	δύναιντο

Infinitive: δύνασθαι **Participle:** δυνάμεν-ος, -η, -ον

imperfect	
sg 1	ἐδυνάμην
2	ἐδύνασο
3	ἐδύνατο
pl 1	ἐδυνάμεθα
2	ἐδύνασθε
3	ἐδύναντο

Note

1 Note also the verb κεῖμαι (I lie, am placed) which is used for the passive of τίθημι (I place): κεῖμαι, κεῖσαι, κεῖται, κείμεθα, κεῖσθε, κεῖνται; infinitive κεῖσθαι; participle κείμενος -η -ον; imperfect ἐκείμην, ἔκεισο, ἔκειτο, etc.; future κείσομαι.

| Irregular verbs

εἰμί *I am*

	indicative	imperative	subjunctive	optative
present				
sg 1	εἰμί		ὦ	εἴην
2	εἶ	ἴσθι	ᾖς	εἴης
3	ἐστί(ν)	ἔστω	ᾖ	εἴη
pl 1	ἐσμέν		ὦμεν	εἶμεν *or* εἴημεν
2	ἐστέ	ἔστε	ἦτε	εἶτε *or* εἴητε
3	εἰσί(ν)	ὄντων	ὦσι(ν)	εἶεν *or* εἴησαν

Infinitive: εἶναι **Participle:** ὤν, οὖσα, ὄν

imperfect *I was*	
sg 1	ἦν *or* ἦ
2	ἦσθα
3	ἦν
pl 1	ἦμεν
2	ἦτε
3	ἦσαν

Note

1 The future tense of εἰμί is ἔσομαι and is formed regularly except for the 3 sg., which is ἔσται.

2 The present indicative (except the 2 sg.) is enclitic. However, ἐστί is written ἔστι when it starts a sentence; possibly when it means 'he, she, it <u>exists</u>'; and when it follows οὐκ, μή, εἰ, ὡς, καί, ἀλλά, τοῦτο.

3 Distinguish carefully the indicative forms from those of εἶμι (I shall go); see p. 94.

4 The alternative optative forms are only used in prose. Plato uses εἶμεν; εἶτε occurs only in poetry; εἶεν is used in prose and verse, and is more common than εἴησαν.

εἶμι *I shall go, am going*

	indicative	imperative	subjunctive	optative
present				
sg 1	εἶμι (= *I shall go*)		ἴω	ἴοιμι *or* ἰοίην
2	εἶ	ἴθι	ἴῃς	ἴοις
3	εἶσι(ν)	ἴτω	ἴῃ	ἴοι
pl 1	ἴμεν		ἴωμεν	ἴοιμεν
2	ἴτε	ἴτε	ἴητε	ἴοιτε
3	ἴᾱσι(ν)	ἰόντων	ἴωσι(ν)	ἴοιεν

Infinitive: ἰέναι **Participle:** ἰών, ἰοῦσα, ἰόν

imperfect *I was going, went*				
sg 1	ᾖα *or* ᾔειν			
2	ᾔεισθα *or* ᾔεις			
3	ᾔειν *or* ᾔει			
pl 1	ᾖμεν			
2	ᾖτε			
3	ᾔεσαν *or* ᾖσαν			

Note

1 The 'present' indicative of this verb is future in meaning: for a true present tense, use ἔρχομαι (I go). In the subjunctive, the meaning is always future. In the optative, infinitive and participle, it may be either future or present. The aorist is ἦλθον (I went), the perfect is ἐλήλυθα (I have come) and the pluperfect is ἐληλύθη, all of which are formed regularly. However, ἥκω (I have come) and ἧκον (I came) are frequently used for the perfect and pluperfect respectively.

2 Whether such verbs in a given instance signify coming or going (arrival or departure) must be decided by the context.

οἶδα *I know*

	indicative	imperative	subjunctive	optative
perfect (with present meaning)				
sg 1	οἶδα		εἰδῶ	εἰδείην
2	οἶσθα	ἴσθι	εἰδῇς	εἰδείης
3	οἶδε(ν)	ἴστω	εἰδῇ	εἰδείη
pl 1	ἴσμεν		εἰδῶμεν	εἰδ-εῖμεν *or* -είημεν
2	ἴστε	ἴστε	εἰδῆτε	εἰδ-εῖτε *or* -είητε
3	ἴσᾱσι(ν)	ἴστων	εἰδῶσι(ν)	εἰδ-εῖεν *or* -είησαν

Infinitive: εἰδέναι **Participle:** εἰδώς, -υῖα, -ός (stem εἰδότ-)

pluperfect *I knew*	
sg 1	ἤδη *or* ἤδειν
2	ἤδησθα *or* ἤδεις *or* ἤδεισθα
3	ἤδει(ν)
pl 1	ᾖσμεν
2	ᾖστε
3	ᾖσαν *or* ἤδεσαν

Note

1 This verb is perfect in form but present in meaning. Etymologically it is related to Latin *video* 'I see'. The perfect in Greek thus came to mean 'I know (that) …' from 'I have seen that …'.

2 The aorist of this root became the aorist for ὁράω (*I see*): εἶδον.

φημί *I say*

	indicative	imperative	subjunctive	optative
present				
sg 1	φημί		φῶ	φαίην
2	φής *or* φής	φάθι	φῇς	φαίης
3	φησί(ν)	φάτω	φῇ	φαίη
pl 1	φαμέν		φῶμεν	φαῖμεν
2	φατέ	φάτε	φῆτε	φαίητε
3	φᾶσί(ν)	φάντων	φῶσι(ν)	φαῖεν

Infinitive: φάναι Participle: φάς, φᾶσα, φάν

imperfect

sg 1	ἔφην
2	ἔφησθα *or* ἔφης
3	ἔφη
pl 1	ἔφαμεν
2	ἔφατε
3	ἔφασαν

Note

1 The present participle of φάσκω (I say) is used instead of φάς in Attic prose: φάσκων, -ουσα, -ον.
2 The imperfect of φάσκω is used for repeated assertion: ἔφασκον.
3 The present indicative (except the 2 sg.) is enclitic.
4 οὐ φημί means 'I say no, refuse, say … not'. See p. 156.

Tables of principal parts

The list of verbs is divided into two groups. The first table contains the 101 most common verbs, and is well worth learning. The second table is provided for reference.

Note:

- compound verbs are generally given without their prefix. The most common prefix is given in brackets. Note that, in general, prose prefers the compounded forms, whereas verse uses both compound forms and forms without a prefix.

- a form beginning with a hyphen indicates that the verb is not found (or is rarely found) without a prefix in this tense or voice but that compounds of it are.

- italics indicate forms which are rarely or never found in Attic prose.

- where the word in the first column is deponent (i.e. middle in form but active in meaning) the forms given for the perfect middle/passive and aorist passive are also generally active in meaning.

Top 101 irregular verbs

Present	Meaning	Future	Aorist
ἀγγέλλω	I announce	ἀγγελῶ (έω)	ἤγγειλα
ἄγω	I lead	ἄξω	ἤγαγον
αἰνέω (ἐπ-)	I praise	-αινέσω	-ήνεσα
αἱρέω	I take (act.) I choose (mid.)	αἱρήσω	εἷλον
αἴρω	I lift, remove	ἀρῶ (έω)	ἦρα
αἰσθάνομαι	I perceive	αἰσθήσομαι	ἠσθόμην
αἰσχΰνω	I disgrace (act.) I am ashamed (pass.)	αἰσχυνῶ (έω)	ἤσχῡνα
ἀκούω	I hear	ἀκούσομαι	ἤκουσα
ἁλίσκομαι	I am captured	ἁλώσομαι	ἑάλων
ἁμαρτάνω	I make a mistake, miss	ἁμαρτήσομαι	ἥμαρτον
ἀνᾱλίσκω	I spend	ἀνᾱλώσω	ἀνήλωσα
ἄρχω	I begin, rule	ἄρξω	ἦρξα
ἀφικνέομαι	I arrive	ἀφίξομαι	ἀφῑκόμην
βαίνω	I walk, go	-βήσομαι	-ἔβην
βάλλω	I throw	βαλῶ (έω)	ἔβαλον
βιόω [ζάω]	I live	βιώσομαι ζήσω, ζήσομαι	ἐβίων (ἔζων, ἔζην impf.)
βούλομαι	I want, wish	βουλήσομαι	—

Perfect	Perfect Middle/Passive	Aorist Passive	Future Passive
ἤγγελκα	ἤγγελμαι	ἠγγέλθην	ἀγγελθήσομαι
-ἦχα	ἦγμαι	ἤχθην	ἀχθήσομαι
-ἤνεκα	-ἤνημαι	-ηνέθην	-αινεθήσομαι
ᾕρηκα	ᾕρημαι	ᾑρέθην	αἱρεθήσομαι
ἦρκα	ἦρμαι	ἤρθην	ἀρθήσομαι
—	ᾔσθημαι (tr.)	—	—
—	—	ᾐσχύνθην	αἰσχυνοῦμαι (έο) αἰσχυνθήσομαι
ἀκήκοα	—	ἠκούσθην	ἀκουσθήσομαι
ἑάλωκα	—	—	—
ἡμάρτηκα	ἡμάρτημαι	ἡμαρτήθην	—
ἀνήλωκα	ἀνήλωμαι	ἀνηλώθην	ἀνᾱλωθήσομαι
ἦρχα	ἦργμαι	ἤρχθην	*ἀρχθήσομαι*
—	ἀφῖγμαι	—	—
βέβηκα	—	—	—
βέβληκα	βέβλημαι	ἐβλήθην	βληθήσομαι
βεβίωκα	—	—	—
—	βεβούλημαι	ἐβουλήθην	*βουληθήσομαι*

Present	Meaning	Future	Aorist
γαμέω	*I take as my wife* (act.) *I take as my husband* (mid.)	γαμῶ (έω)	ἔγημα
γελάω	*I laugh*	γελάσομαι	ἐγέλασα
γίγνομαι	*I become*	γενήσομαι	ἐγενόμην
γιγνώσκω	*I recognise*	γνώσομαι	ἔγνων
δάκνω	*I bite*	δήξομαι	ἔδακον
δεῖ	*it is necessary*	δεήσει	ἐδέησε
δείκνῡμι	*I show*	δείξω	ἔδειξα
διδάσκω	*I teach*	διδάξω	ἐδίδαξα
δίδωμι	*I give*	δώσω	ἔδωκα
δοκέω	*I seem*	δόξω	ἔδοξα
δύναμαι	*I can, am able*	δυνήσομαι	—
ἐάω	*I allow*	ἐάσω	εἴᾱσα (εἴων (αο) impf.)
ἐγείρω	*I arouse*	ἐγερῶ (έω)	ἤγειρα
ἐθέλω	*I wish*	ἐθελήσω	ἠθέλησα
εἰμί	*I am*	ἔσομαι	ἦν (impf.)
ἐλαύνω	*I drive*	ἐλῶ (άω)	ἤλασα
ἕλκω	*I drag*	-ἕλξω	εἵλκυσα
ἕπομαι	*I follow*	ἕψομαι	ἑσπόμην (εἱπόμην impf.)

Perfect	Perfect Middle/Passive	Aorist Passive	Future Passive
γεγάμηκα	γεγάμημαι	—	—
—	—	ἐγελάσθην	—
γέγονα	γεγένημαι	—	—
ἔγνωκα	ἔγνωσμαι	ἐγνώσθην	γνωσθήσομαι
—	δέδηγμαι	ἐδήχθην	δηχθήσομαι
δέδειχα	δέδειγμαι	ἐδείχθην	δειχθήσομαι
δεδίδαχα	δεδίδαγμαι	ἐδιδάχθην	διδάξομαι
δέδωκα	δέδομαι	ἐδόθην	δοθήσομαι
—	δέδογμαι	—	—
—	δεδύνημαι	ἐδυνήθην	—
εἴακα	εἴαμαι	εἰάθην	ἐάσομαι
ἐγρήγορα (intr.)	—	ἠγέρθην	ἐγερθήσομαι
ἠθέληκα	—	—	—
—	—	—	—
-ελήλακα	ἐλήλαμαι	ἠλάθην	—
-εἵλκυκα	-εἵλκυσμαι	-εἱλκύσθην	-ελκυσθήσομαι
—	—	—	—

Present	Meaning	Future	Aorist
ἔρχομαι	I go	εἶμι ἥξω, ἐλεύσομαι	ἦλθον
ἐρωτάω	I ask	ἐρωτήσω ἐρήσομαι	ἠρόμην ἠρώτησα
ἐσθίω	I eat	ἔδομαι	ἔφαγον
εὑρίσκω	I find	εὑρήσω	ηὗρον εὗρον
ἔχω	I have	ἕξω σχήσω	ἔσχον (εἶχον impf.)
ἥδομαι	I am pleased, enjoy	—	—
θάπτω	I bury	θάψω	ἔθαψα
θνήσκω (ἀπο-)	I die	θανοῦμαι (έο)	ἔθανον
ἵημι	I send, shoot	ἥσω	ἧκα
ἵστημι	I make stand (tr.) I stand (intr.)	στήσω	ἔστησα (tr.) ἔστην (intr.)
καίω	I burn	καύσω	ἔκαυσα
καλέω	I call	καλῶ (έω)	ἐκάλεσα
κλαίω κλάω (in prose)	I weep	κλαύσομαι κλᾱήσω	ἔκλαυσα
κλέπτω	I steal	κλέψω	ἔκλεψα
κρίνω	I judge	κρινῶ (έω)	ἔκρῑνα
κτάομαι	I obtain, gain	κτήσομαι	ἐκτησάμην
κτείνω (ἀπο-)	I kill	κτενῶ (έω)	ἔκτεινα ἔκτανον

Perfect	Perfect Middle/Passive	Aorist Passive	Future Passive
ἐλήλυθα ἥκω	—	—	—
ἠρώτηκα	ἠρώτημαι	ἠρωτήθην	—
ἐδήδοκα	-εδήδεσμαι	ἠδέσθην	
ηὕρηκα εὕρηκα	ηὕρημαι εὕρημαι	ηὑρέθην εὑρέθην	εὑρεθήσομαι
ἔσχηκα	-ἔσχημαι	—	—
—	—	ἥσθην	ἡσθήσομαι
—	τέθαμμαι	ἐτάφην	ταφήσομαι
τέθνηκα	—	—	—
εἷκα	εἷμαι	εἷθην	ἑθήσομαι
ἕστηκα (intr.)	*ἕσταμαι*	ἐστάθην	σταθήσομαι
-κέκαυκα	κέκαυμαι	ἐκαύθην	-καυθήσομαι
κέκληκα	κέκλημαι	ἐκλήθην	κληθήσομαι
—	κέκλαυμαι κέκλαυσμαι	*ἐκλαύσθην*	*κλαυσθήσομαι*
κέκλοφα	κέκλεμμαι	ἐκλάπην	—
κέκρικα	κέκριμαι	ἐκρίθην	κριθήσομαι
—	κέκτημαι	ἐκτήθην	—
-ἔκτονα	—	—	—

Present	Meaning	Future	Aorist
λαμβάνω	I take	λήψομαι	ἔλαβον
λανθάνω	I escape the notice of	λήσω	ἔλαθον
λέγω	I say	ἐρῶ (έω) λέξω	εἶπον ἔλεξα
λείπω	I leave	λείψω	ἔλιπον
μανθάνω	I learn	μαθήσομαι	ἔμαθον
μάχομαι	I fight	μαχοῦμαι (έο)	ἐμαχεσάμην
μέλει	it concerns	μελήσει	ἐμέλησε
μέλλω	I intend, am about (to)	μελλήσω	ἐμέλλησα
μένω	I stay, remain	μενῶ (έω)	ἔμεινα
μιμνήσκω (ἀνα-)	I remind (act.) I remember (mid.)	-μνήσω	-έμνησα
νομίζω	I think, consider	νομιῶ (έω)	ἐνόμισα
οἴγνῡμι (ἀν-)	I open	-οίξω	-έῳξα
οἶδα	I know	εἴσομαι	ᾔδη (impf.)
ὄλλῡμι (ἀπ-)	I destroy (act.) I perish (mid.)	-ολῶ (έω)	-ώλεσα -ωλόμην (intr. mid.)
ὄμνῡμι	I swear	ὀμοῦμαι (έο)	ὤμοσα
ὁράω	I see	ὄψομαι	εἶδον (ἑώρων (αο) impf.)
ὀφείλω	I owe	ὀφειλήσω	ὠφείλησα ὤφελον

Perfect	Perfect Middle/Passive	Aorist Passive	Future Passive
εἴληφα	εἴλημμαι	ἐλήφθην	ληφθήσομαι
λέληθα	-λέλησμαι	—	—
εἴρηκα	εἴρημαι λέλεγμαι	ἐρρήθην ἐλέχθην	εἰρήσομαι ῥηθήσομαι λεχθήσομαι
λέλοιπα	λέλειμμαι	ἐλείφθην	λειφθήσομαι
μεμάθηκα	—	—	—
—	μεμάχημαι	—	—
μεμέληκε	—	—	—
—	—	—	—
μεμένηκα	—	—	—
—	μέμνημαι	ἐμνήσθην	μνησθήσομαι
νενόμικα	νενόμισμαι	ἐνομίσθην	νομισθήσομαι
-έῳχα	-έῳγμαι	-εῴχθην	—
—	—	—	—
-ολώλεκα (tr.) -όλωλα (intr.)	—	—	—
ὀμώμοκα	—	ὠμόθην ὠμόσθην	ὀμοσθήσομαι
ἑόρᾱκα, ἑώρᾱκα ὄπωπα	ἑώρᾱμαι ὦμμαι	ὤφθην	ὀφθήσομαι
ὠφείληκα	—	—	—

Present	Meaning	Future	Aorist
πάσχω	I suffer	πείσομαι	ἔπαθον
πείθω	I persuade (act.) I obey (mid.)	πείσω πείσομαι (mid.)	ἔπεισα (act.) ἐπιθόμην (mid.)
πέμπω	I send	πέμψω	ἔπεμψα
πίμπλημι (ἐμ-/ἐν-)	I fill	-πλήσω	-έπλησα
πίνω	I drink	πίομαι	ἔπιον
πίπτω	I fall	πεσοῦμαι (έο)	ἔπεσον
πλέω	I sail	πλεύσομαι πλευσοῦμαι (έο)	ἔπλευσα
πρᾱ́ττω	I act, do	πρᾱ́ξω	ἔπρᾱξα
πυνθάνομαι	I enquire, find out	πεύσομαι	ἐπυθόμην
πωλέω ἀποδίδομαι	I sell	πωλήσω ἀποδώσομαι	ἐπώλησα ἀπεδόμην
ῥήγνῡμι	I break	-ρήξω	ἔρρηξα
στέλλω (ἀπο-, ἐπι-)	I send	-στελῶ (έω)	ἔστειλα
σῴζω	I save	σώσω	ἔσωσα
τέμνω	I cut	τεμῶ (έω)	ἔτεμον
τίθημι	I place, put	θήσω	ἔθηκα
τίκτω	I give birth to, beget	τέξομαι	ἔτεκον
τιτρώσκω	I wound	τρώσω	ἔτρωσα

Perfect	Perfect Middle/Passive	Aorist Passive	Future Passive
πέπονθα	—	—	—
πέπεικα (tr.) πέποιθα (intr. (= *trust*))	πέπεισμαι	ἐπείσθην	πεισθήσομαι
πέπομφα	πέπεμμαι	ἐπέμφθην	πεμφθήσομαι
-πέπληκα	-πέπλησμαι	-επλήσθην	-πλησθήσομαι
πέπωκα	-πέπομαι	-επόθην	-ποθήσομαι
πέπτωκα	—	—	—
πέπλευκα	—	—	—
πέπρᾱχα (tr.) πέπρᾱγα (tr. & intr. (= *have fared*))	πέπρᾱγμαι	ἐπρᾱ́χθην	πρᾱχθήσομαι
—	πέπυσμαι	—	—
πέπρᾱκα	πέπρᾱμαι	ἐπρᾱ́θην	πεπρᾱ́σομαι
-ἔρρωγα (intr.)	-*ἔρρηγμαι*	ἐρράγην	-ραγήσομαι
-ἔσταλκα	ἔσταλμαι	ἐστάλην	-σταλήσομαι
σέσωκα	σέσωσμαι	ἐσώθην	σωθήσομαι
-τέτμηκα	τέτμημαι	ἐτμήθην	*τμηθήσομαι*
τέθηκα	κεῖμαι (see p. 92)	ἐτέθην	τεθήσομαι
τέτοκα	—	—	—
—	τέτρωμαι	ἐτρώθην	τρωθήσομαι

Present	Meaning	Future	Aorist
τρέπω	I turn (tr.)	τρέψω	ἔτρεψα ἐτραπόμην (I fled)
τρέφω	I nourish, support	θρέψω	ἔθρεψα
τρέχω	I run	δραμοῦμαι (εο) -θεύσομαι	ἔδραμον
τυγχάνω	I happen	τεύξομαι	ἔτυχον
ὑπισχνέομαι	I promise	ὑποσχήσομαι	ὑπεσχόμην
φαίνω	I reveal (act.) I appear, seem (mid.)	φανῶ (έω)	ἔφηνα
φέρω	I carry, bear	οἴσω	ἤνεγκα ἤνεγκον
φεύγω	I flee	φεύξομαι	ἔφυγον
φημί	I say	φήσω	ἔφησα (ἔφην impf.)
φθάνω	I anticipate	φθήσομαι	ἔφθασα ἔφθην (like ἔστην)
φθείρω (δια-)	I destroy, corrupt	φθερῶ (έω)	ἔφθειρα
φοβέομαι	I fear	φοβήσομαι	—
φύω	I produce (tr.) I am by nature (intr.)	φύσω (tr.)	ἔφῦσα (tr.) ἔφῦν (intr.)
χρή	it is necessary	—	(ἐ)χρῆν (impf.)
ὠνέομαι	I buy	ὠνήσομαι	ἐπριάμην

Perfect	Perfect Middle/Passive	Aorist Passive	Future Passive
τέτροφα	τέτραμμαι	ἐτρέφθην ἐτράπην (intr.)	τραπήσομαι
τέτροφα	τέθραμμαι	ἐτράφην	τραφήσομαι
-δεδράμηκα	—	—	—
τετύχηκα	—	—	—
—	ὑπέσχημαι	—	—
πέφαγκα (tr.) πέφηνα (intr.)	πέφασμαι	ἐφάνθην ἐφάνην (intr.)	φανήσομαι
ἐνήνοχα	ἐνήνεγμαι	ἠνέχθην	-ενεχθήσομαι οἰσθήσομαι
πέφευγα	—	—	—
—	—	—	—
ἔφθακα	—	—	—
ἔφθαρκα -έφθορα (tr. & intr. (= *am ruined*))	ἔφθαρμαι	ἐφθάρην	-φθαρήσομαι
—	πεφόβημαι	ἐφοβήθην	—
—	—	—	—
πέφῡκα (intr.)			
—	—	—	—
—	ἐώνημαι (= *have bought* or *have been bought*)	ἐωνήθην	—

More principal parts

Present	Meaning	Future	Aorist
ἄγνῡμι	I break	-άξω	-έᾱξα
ᾄδω	I sing	ᾄσομαι	ᾖσα
αἰδέομαι	I respect, feel shame	αἰδέσομαι	—
ἀλείφω	I anoint	ἀλείψω	ἤλειψα
ἀλλάσσω ἀλλάττω	I change	ἀλλάξω	ἤλλαξα
ἅλλομαι	I leap	ἁλοῦμαι (έο)	ἡλάμην
ἅπτω	I fasten, kindle	ἅψω	ἧψα
ἀρέσκω	I please	ἀρέσω	ἤρεσα
ἁρμόττω ἁρμόζω	I fit	ἁρμόσω	ἥρμοσα
αὐξάνω αὔξω	I increase	αὐξήσω	ηὔξησα
βλάπτω	I hurt	βλάψω	ἔβλαψα
βλώσκω	I go	μολοῦμαι (έο)	ἔμολον
γράφω	I write	γράψω	ἔγραψα
δαρθάνω (κατα)	I sleep	—	-έδαρθον
δέχομαι	I receive	δέξομαι	ἐδεξάμην
δέω	I bind	δήσω	ἔδησα

Perfect	Perfect Middle/Passive	Aorist Passive	Future Passive
-έᾱγα	—	-εάγην	—
—	ᾖσμαι	ᾔσθην	—
—	ᾔδεσμαι	ᾐδέσθην	αἰδεσθήσομαι
-αλήλιφα	ἀλήλιμμαι	ἠλείφθην	ἀλειφθήσομαι
-ἤλλαχα	ἤλλαγμαι	ἠλλάγην ἠλλάχθην (poetic)	-αλλαγήσομαι -αλλαχθήσομαι (poetic)
—	—	—	—
—	ἧμμαι	ἥφθην	—
—	—	*ἠρέσθην*	—
—	ἥρμοσμαι	ἡρμόσθην	*ἁρμοσθήσομαι*
ηὔξηκα	ηὔξημαι	ηὐξήθην	αὐξηθήσομαι
βέβλαφα	βέβλαμμαι	ἐβλάφθην ἐβλάβην	βλαβήσομαι
μέμβλωκα	—	—	—
γέγραφα	γέγραμμαι	ἐγράφην	γραφήσομαι
-δεδάρθηκα	—	—	—
—	δέδεγμαι	-εδέχθην	—
δέδεκα	δέδεμαι	ἐδέθην	δεθήσομαι

Present	Meaning	Future	Aorist
διώκω	I pursue	διώξομαι	ἐδίωξα
δράω	I do	δράσω	ἔδρᾱσα
ἐλέγχω	I cross-examine, refute	ἐλέγξω	ἤλεγξα
ἐξετάζω	I investigate	ἐξετάσω	ἐξήτασα
ἐπίσταμαι	I know, understand	ἐπιστήσομαι	ἠπιστάμην (impf.)
εὕδω (καθ-)	I sleep	-εὑδήσω	-ηὗδον (impf.) ἐκάθευδον (N.B., impf.)
εὔχομαι	I pray, boast	εὔξομαι	ηὐξάμην
ζεύγνῡμι	I yoke	ζεύξω	ἔζευξα
ζέω	I boil (intr.)	-ζέσω	ἔζεσα
θύω	I sacrifice	θύσω	ἔθῡσα
καθαίρω	I purify	καθαρῶ (έω)	ἐκάθηρα
καλύπτω	I cover	καλύψω	ἐκάλυψα
κάμνω	I toil, am tired	καμοῦμαι (έο)	ἔκαμον
κείρω	I shear	κερῶ (έω)	ἔκειρα
κεράννῡμι	I mix	—	ἐκέρασα
κερδαίνω	I gain	κερδανῶ (έω)	ἐκέρδᾱνα
κηρῡ́ττω	I proclaim	κηρύξω	ἐκήρῡξα
κομίζω	I care for, carry	κομιῶ (έω)	ἐκόμισα

Perfect	Perfect Middle/Passive	Aorist Passive	Future Passive
δεδίωχα	—	ἐδιώχθην	διωχθήσομαι
δέδρᾱκα	δέδρᾱμαι	ἐδράσθην	—
—	ἐλήλεγμαι	ἠλέγχθην	ἐλεγχθήσομαι
ἐξήτακα	ἐξήτασμαι	ἐξητάσθην	ἐξετασθήσομαι
—	—	ἠπιστήθην	—
—	—	—	—
—	ηὖγμαι	—	—
—	ἔζευγμαι	*ἐζύγην* *ἐζεύχθην*	—
—	*-έζεσμαι*	*-εζέσθην*	—
τέθυκα	τέθυμαι	ἐτύθην	*τυθήσομαι*
—	κεκάθαρμαι	ἐκαθάρθην	—
—	κεκάλυμμαι	ἐκαλύφθην	*καλυφθήσομαι*
κέκμηκα	—	—	—
—	κέκαρμαι	—	—
—	κέκρᾱμαι	ἐκράθην ἐκεράσθην	*κρᾱθήσομαι*
-κεκέρδηκα	—	—	—
-κεκήρῡχα	κεκήρῡγμαι	ἐκηρύχθην	κηρῡχθήσομαι
κεκόμικα	κεκόμισμαι (usually mid.)	ἐκομίσθην	κομισθήσομαι

Present	Meaning	Future	Aorist
κρεμάννῡμι	*I hang* (tr.)	κρεμῶ (άω)	ἐκρέμασα
λαγχάνω	*I obtain by lot*	λήξομαι	ἔλαχον
μαίνω	*I madden*	—	ἔμηνα
μείγνῡμι μῑγνῡμι	*I mix*	μείξω	ἔμειξα
νέμω	*I distribute, pasture*	νεμῶ (έω)	ἔνειμα
νέω	*I swim*	νευσοῦμαι (έο)	-ένευσα
ὄζω	*I smell* (intr.)	ὀζήσω	ὤζησα
οἶμαι οἴομαι	*I think*	οἰήσομαι	ᾠμην (impf.)
ὀνίνημι	*I benefit*	ὀνήσω	ὤνησα
ὀργίζω	*I enrage*	-οργιῶ (έω)	ὤργισα
ὀρύττω	*I dig*	-ορύξω	ὤρυξα
ὀσφραίνομαι	*I smell* (tr.)	ὀσφρήσομαι	ὠσφρόμην
ὀφλισκάνω	*I owe, incur a penalty*	ὀφλήσω	ὦφλον
παίω	*I strike*	παίσω	ἔπαισα
περαίνω	*I accomplish*	περανῶ (έω)	ἐπέρᾱνα
πέρδομαι	*I fart*	-παρδήσομαι	-έπαρδον
πετάννῡμι (ἀνα-)	*I spread out*	-πετῶ (άω)	-επέτασα
πέτομαι	*I fly*	-πτήσομαι	-επτόμην

Perfect	Perfect Middle/Passive	Aorist Passive	Future Passive
—	—	ἐκρεμάσθην	—
εἴληχα	εἴληγμαι	ἐλήχθην	—
μέμηνα (= am mad)	—	ἐμάνην	—
—	μέμειγμαι	ἐμίγην ἐμείχθην	μειχθήσομαι
-νενέμηκα	νενέμημαι	ἐνεμήθην	νεμηθήσομαι
-νένευκα	—	—	—
—	—	—	—
—	—	ᾠήθην	—
—	—	ὠνήθην	—
—	ὤργισμαι	ὠργίσθην	ὀργισθήσομαι
-ορώρυχα	ὀρώρυγμαι	ὠρύχθην	-ορυχθήσομαι
—	—	ὠσφράνθην	—
ὤφληκα	ὤφλημαι	—	—
-πέπαικα	—	ἐπαίσθην	—
—	πεπέρασμαι	ἐπεράνθην	—
πέπορδα	—	—	—
—	-πέπταμαι	—	—
—	—	—	—

Present	Meaning	Future	Aorist
πήγνῡμι	*I fix*	πήξω	ἔπηξα
πίμπρημι (ἐμ-/ἐν-)	*I burn*	-πρήσω	-έπρησα
πλήττω	*I strike*	-πλήξω	-έπληξα
πνέω	*I breathe, blow*	πνευσοῦμαι (έο) πνεύσομαι	ἔπνευσα
ῥέω	*I flow*	ῥυήσομαι	—
ῥίπτω	*I throw*	ῥίψω	ἔρρῑψα
σβέννῡμι	*I extinguish*	σβέσω	ἔσβεσα ἔσβην (intr. (= *went out*))
σημαίνω	*I show*	σημανῶ (έω)	ἐσήμηνα
σκάπτω	*I dig*	σκάψω	-έσκαψα
σπάω	*I draw, drag*	-σπάσω	ἔσπασα
σπείρω	*I sow*	σπερῶ (έω)	ἔσπειρα
σπένδω	*I pour a libation*	-σπείσω	ἔσπεισα
στρέφω	*I turn*	-στρέψω	ἔστρεψα
σφάλλω	*I trip up, deceive*	σφαλῶ (έω)	ἔσφηλα
τάττω	*I arrange, draw up*	τάξω	ἔταξα
τείνω	*I stretch*	τενῶ (έω)	-έτεινα
τελέω	*I finish, accomplish*	τελῶ (έω)	ἐτέλεσα

Perfect	Perfect Middle/Passive	Aorist Passive	Future Passive
πέπηγα (intr. (= *am fixed*))	—	ἐπάγην	παγήσομαι
—	-πέπρημαι	-επρήσθην	—
πέπληγα	-πέπληγμαι	ἐπλήγην -επλάγην	πληγήσομαι -πλαγήσομαι
-πέπνευκα	—	—	—
ἐρρύηκα	—	ἐρρύην (intr.)	—
ἔρρῑφα	ἔρρῑμμαι	ἐρρίφθην	*-ρρῑφθήσομαι*
-έσβηκα (intr. (= *have gone out*))	*ἔσβεσμαι*	ἐσβέσθην	—
—	σεσήμασμαι	ἐσημάνθην	-σημανθήσομαι
-έσκαφα	ἔσκαμμαι	-εσκάφην	—
-έσπακα	ἔσπασμαι	-εσπάσθην	-σπασθήσομαι
—	ἔσπαρμαι	ἐσπάρην	σπαρήσομαι
—	ἔσπεισμαι	—	—
—	ἔστραμμαι	ἐστράφην (usu. intr.) ἐστρέφθην	-στραφήσομαι
—	ἔσφαλμαι	ἐσφάλην	σφαλήσομαι
τέταχα	τέταγμαι	ἐτάχθην	ταχθήσομαι
-τέτακα	τέταμαι	-ετάθην	-ταθήσομαι
τετέλεκα	τετέλεσμαι	ἐτελέσθην	τελεσθήσομαι

Present	Meaning	Future	Aorist
τήκω	*I melt*	τήξω	ἔτηξα
τίνω	*I pay, expiate*	τείσω	ἔτεισα
τρίβω	*I rub*	τρίψω	ἔτρῑψα
ὑφαίνω	*I weave*	ὑφανῶ (έω)	ὕφηνα
φείδομαι	*I spare*	φείσομαι	ἐφεισάμην
φράζω	*I tell, declare*	φράσω	ἔφρασα
φυλάττω	*I guard*	φυλάξω	ἐφύλαξα
χαίρω	*I rejoice*	χαιρήσω	—
χέω	*I pour*	χέω	ἔχεα
χρῑω	*I anoint*	χρῑσω	ἔχρῑσα
ψεύδω	*I deceive*	ψεύσω	ἔψευσα
ὠθέω	*I push*	ὤσω	ἔωσα ἐώθουν (εο) (impf.)

Perfect	Perfect Middle/Passive	Aorist Passive	Future Passive
τέτηκα (intr. (= I am molten))	—	ἐτάκην (intr. (= I became molten))	—
τέτεικα	-τέτεισμαι	-ἐτείσθην	—
τέτριφα	τέτρῑμμαι	ἐτρίβην ἐτρίφθην	-τριβήσομαι
—	ὕφασμαι	ὑφάνθην	—
—	—	—	—
πέφρακα	πέφρασμαι	ἐφράσθην (tr. (= I told))	—
πεφύλαχα	πεφύλαγμαι (intr. (= I am on my guard))	ἐφυλάχθην	—
κεχάρηκα	κεχάρημαι κέχαρμαι	ἐχάρην	—
κέχυκα	κέχυμαι	ἐχύθην	χυθήσομαι
—	κέχρῑμαι	ἐχρίσθην	—
—	ἔψευσμαι (tr. or pass. in meaning)	ἐψεύσθην	ψευσθήσομαι
—	ἔωσμαι	ἐώσθην	ὠσθήσομαι

Constructions

The definite article

The hero was saved by a woman.

In this sentence 'the' is the **definite article** and 'a' (written 'an' before a vowel) the **indefinite article**. Greek has no word for the indefinite article, though it often uses the indefinite pronoun τις (some, a certain) after the noun to perform the same function (see p. 149). It does, however, have a definite article: ὁ, ἡ, τό (for the full declension, see p. 24).

Greek uses the definite article much as English does, but note the following points. They include a number of instances where the word 'the' must be omitted in translation into English:

1 In English, the names of *people* and *places* almost never have the article, but in Greek, they very often do. It may well not be used the first time a name occurs. For example, Herodotus begins his history by declaring that it is the work Ἡροδότου Ἁλικαρνησσέος (of Herodotus from Halicarnassus) and Thucydides says that Θουκῡδίδης Ἀθηναῖος ξυνέγραψε τὸν πόλεμον (Thucydides the Athenian wrote the history of the war).[1] But after a name has been mentioned once, subsequent uses generally need the article.

   With famous names, however, the article can be used on their first occurrence, e.g. ὁ τῶν ἑπτὰ σοφώτατος Σόλων (Solon, the wisest of the Seven (Sages), Plato, *Timaeus* 20d).

2 Where English uses possessive adjectives (my, your, her, etc.) Greek employs the definite article unless there is doubt about the identity of the possessor:

   Κῦρός τε καταπηδήσᾱς ἀπὸ τοῦ ἅρματος τὸν θώρᾱκα ἐνεδύετο.
   (Xenophon, *Anabasis* 1.8.3)
   And after leaping down from his chariot, Cyrus put on his breastplate.

3 Abstract nouns are generally found with the article. Note therefore that ἡ ἀνδρείᾱ must be translated as 'courage' and not 'the courage'.

---

[1] The supremely important king of Persia is referred to simply as βασιλεύς, without the article.

4 The article can be used with adjectives functioning as nouns, e.g.:

| οἱ ἀνδρεῖοι | brave men |
| τὸ δίκαιον | justice (*literally,* the just thing) |

5 The article can be used with participles, e.g.:

ὁ βουλόμενος	anyone who wishes, the first to volunteer
ὁ ἐπιτυχών ὁ ἐντυχών	} { *literally,* the man who meets, i.e. the first man one meets, the man in the street
τὰ γεγενημένα	the things that have occurred, events
οἱ ἀληθῆ λέγοντες	those speaking the truth, those who speak the truth

The article with the participle is frequently found with the meaning of a relative clause. See p. 138.

6 The article is used with nouns or adjectives which describe whole classes. We call this usage **generic**:

ὁ ἄνθρωπος οἱ ἄνθρωποι	} { a man, men, mankind (as opposed to other living creatures)
αἱ γυναῖκες	women
οἱ γέροντες	old people
οἱ σοφοί	the wise

7 The article can be used with adverbs or adverbial phrases and without nouns in such expressions as:

οἱ ἐκεῖ	the people there
οἱ ἐνθάδε	the people here
οἱ νῦν	people nowadays
οἱ πάλαι	people in the old days
οἱ τότε	people then
οἱ ἐν ἡλικίᾳ	those in the prime of life
οἱ ἐν τελεῖ	the people in authority

8 ὁ δέ, ἡ δέ, τὸ δέ and/but he, and/but she, and/but it

Here the article refers back to a noun in a previous clause which was <u>not</u> the subject of that clause:

Ἰνάρως ... Ἀθηναίους ἐπηγάγετο. οἱ δὲ ... ἦλθον. (Thucydides 1.104.1–2)
Inaros invited the Athenians; and they came.

9 ὁ μέν ... ὁ δέ   this one ... and (or but) that one ...
οἱ μέν ... οἱ δέ   some ... others

... οὐ πάσᾱς χρὴ τὰς δόξᾱς τῶν ἀνθρώπων τῑμᾶν, ἀλλὰ τὰς μέν, τὰς δ' οὔ; (Plato, *Crito* 47a)
... so one shouldn't respect all the opinions of men, but (only) some and not others?

Note also:
τὸ μέν ... τὸ δέ   on the one hand ... and on the other hand ...

10 The neuter singular of the definite article (τό) with the infinitive creates a verbal noun (also called a **gerund**). In English, the verbal noun ends in '-ing', or the infinitive can be used. Examples are:

<u>Communicating</u> (or to communicate) is difficult.
I like <u>walking</u> (or to walk).

τὸ πράττειν   accomplishing, to accomplish
τὸ τοῦτο πράττειν   accomplishing this

The subject of the infinitive, if expressed at all, is in the accusative:

τὸ ἐμὲ τοῦτο πράττειν   my accomplishing this

This verbal noun declines:

nom.   τὸ πράττειν
gen.   τοῦ πράττειν
dat.   τῷ πράττειν
acc.   τὸ πράττειν

Negative μή.
τῷ μὴ τοῦτο πράττειν   by not accomplishing this, by
                      failing to accomplish this, through
                      failure to accomplish this

11 The original use of the definite article as a deictic pronoun (see p. ix) is frequently met in Homer and Herodotus:

τὴν δ' ἐγὼ οὐ λύσω. (Homer, *Iliad* 1.29)
But <u>her</u> I will not release.

12 In Homer, forms identical with the article are used as the relative pronoun (see p. 227):

πυρὰ πολλὰ τὰ καίετο (Homer, *Iliad* 10.12)
many fires which were burning ...

This is found in Herodotus and tragedy too:

κτείνουσα τοὺς οὐ χρὴ κτανεῖν (Euripides, *Andromache* 810)
killing those whom it is not right to kill

We never find this relative form in Attic prose or comedy.

The definite article and word order

1 Adjectives or adjectival phrases normally come between the article and the noun or (less commonly) after the noun with the article repeated. We call these positions **attributive**:

ἡ σοφὴ γυνή *or* ἡ γυνὴ ἡ σοφή
the wise woman

οἱ ἐν ἄστει κεραμεῖς *or* οἱ κεραμεῖς οἱ ἐν ἄστει
the potters in the city

ὁ δεινὸς λεγόμενος γεωργός (Xenophon, *Oeconomicus* 19.14)
the man who is called a skilful farmer

Cf. ἡ τῆς μητρὸς οἰκίᾱ (the mother's house): ἡ οἰκίᾱ τῆς μητρός is less common.

The genitive of deictic and reflexive pronouns (e.g. ταύτης, ἐκείνου, τοῦδε, σεαυτοῦ, ἑαυτοῦ) takes the attributive position:

ἀπέκτεινεν ἑαυτὸν τῷ ἑαυτοῦ ξίφει.
He killed himself with his own sword.

See also **3** on p. 147.

2 If the adjective is not in this position, i.e. stands outside the article and noun, the verb 'to be' will be understood in some way, e.g.

ἡ γυνὴ σοφή
The woman (is) clever.

ἀθάνατον τὴν περὶ αὐτῶν μνήμην καταλείψουσιν. (Isocrates 1.9.3)
They will leave behind a memory of themselves (that will be) immortal.

We call this the **predicative position**.

A noun without the article can be used in this way, e.g.

στρατηγὸς ὁ Ἴων
Ion (is) a general.

☑ The following words will be found in the predicative position, i.e. either before the article or after the noun:

οὗτος	this — e.g. οὗτος ὁ παῖς
	or ὁ παῖς οὗτος = this child
ὅδε	this
ἐκεῖνος	that
ἕκαστος	each
ἑκάτερος	each of two
ἄμφω/ἀμφότεροι	both
πᾶς, ἅπᾶς, σύμπᾶς	all, each and every (used attributively, it means 'as a whole', e.g. οἱ πάντες πολῖται = the whole body of citizens)

| Practice sentences

Translate into English or Greek as appropriate:

1 τοὺς μὲν ἀπέκτεινε, τοὺς δὲ ἐξήλασεν. (Thucydides 5.82.2)
2 [δεῖ] τὸν στρατιώτην φοβεῖσθαι μᾶλλον τὸν ἄρχοντα ἢ τοὺς πολεμίους. (Xenophon, *Anabasis* 2.6.10)
3 τὰς ἡδονὰς θήρευε τὰς μετὰ δόξης (= good repute). (Isocrates 1.16)
4 οὐκ ἀπορήσετε τῶν ἐθελησόντων ὑπὲρ ὑμῶν κινδυνεύειν. (Demosthenes 20.166)
5 ὁ δὲ παῖς πάντων θηρίων ἐστὶ δυσμεταχειριστότατον. (Plato, *Laws* 808d)
6 τὰς τριήρεις ἀφείλκυσαν κενάς. (Thucydides 2.93.4)
7 The Persian king loved his friends and hated his enemies.
8 Courage is (a) better (thing) than cowardice.
9 My wife admires the brave men of old more than (she does) people nowadays.
10 I told the first person I met what had happened.
11 I hate Pericles. But he does not respect a man who wrongs him.
12 By hurrying, the desperate man reached his own house.

Relative clauses

This is the man <u>who</u> betrayed me.
I am the man <u>whom</u> she betrayed.
There is the woman <u>for whom</u> he left me.
That is the relationship <u>that</u> she preferred.

The relative pronoun (who, which, whom, whose, that) is one of the few English words which can change according to its function in the sentence. Note, however, that in English the word 'whom' is now used very little. The second of the above sentences could be rewritten:

I am the woman (who/that) he betrayed.

As you can see, the word 'who', 'whom' or 'that' may be omitted.

The relative pronoun refers back to a noun or pronoun, in the above sentences 'man', 'woman', 'woman' and 'relationship' respectively. We call this word the **antecedent**.

In Greek, the most common word for 'who' is ὅς, ἥ, ὅ (see p. 50 — after the nominative singular and plural, this is the same as the definite article without the τ).[1] It agrees in gender and number with its antecedent, but its case depends on its function in the relative clause which it introduces.

εἶδον τοὺς ἄνδρας οἳ ἀφίκοντο.
I saw the men who arrived.

ἀπέκτεινα τοὺς ἄνδρας οὓς εἶδες.
I killed the men (whom) you saw.

In the first sentence, οἳ is masculine and plural because it agrees with its antecedent τοὺς ἄνδρας in gender and number. It is nominative because it is the subject of the verb ἀφίκοντο.

In the second sentence, οὓς is masculine and plural because it agrees with its antecedent τοὺς ἄνδρας in gender and number. It is accusative

---

[1] ἥ, οἱ and αἱ do not have accents when they are the definite articles, but <u>do</u> have them (ἥ, οἳ and αἵ) when they are relative pronouns.

<u>not</u> because τοὺς ἄνδρας is accusative, but because it is the object of the verb εἶδες.

If you are translating from English into Greek, you can discover the case that the relative pronoun should be in by phrasing the English relative clause as a full sentence. In the second sentence above, you can change 'whom you saw' to 'You saw them (the men)'. In this sentence, 'the men' would be accusative in Greek, and so they will also be accusative in the corresponding relative clause. The Greek for 'the men' is masculine and plural. Hence οὕς.

αὕτη ἐστὶν ἡ γυνὴ ἣν ἐζητοῦμεν.
This is the woman whom we were looking for.

ὃν γὰρ θεοὶ φιλοῦσιν ἀποθνῄσκει νέος. (Menander, *Sententiae* 425)
For he whom the gods love dies young.

Notice how the antecedent has to be understood in this example (i.e. it is not given in the Greek).

Four more relative pronouns

- ὅσπερ, ἥπερ, ὅπερ is especially definite:

 ταὐτόν μοι ἔδοξαν ἔχειν ἁμάρτημα ὅπερ καὶ οἱ ποιηταί. (Plato, *Apology* 22d)
 They seemed to me to be making exactly the same mistake as the poets.

- ὅστις, ἥτις, ὅτι when used as a relative is generalized, i.e. it does not refer to a specific person:

 ἀνελεύθερος πᾶς ὅστις εἰς δόξαν βλέπει. (Cleanthes, a Stoic philosopher)
 Every man who looks to fame is unfree.

- οἷος, -ᾱ, -ον (of the kind that) and ὅσος, -η, -ον (sg. as much as, pl. as many as) are commonly used. See p. 51.

| Attraction of the relative

A relative pronoun which would be in the accusative is frequently attracted into the case of the antecedent if that antecedent is in the genitive or dative.

Μήδων μέντοι ὅσων (for ὅσους) ἑώρᾱκα ... πολὺ οὗτος ὁ ἐμὸς πάππος κάλλιστος. (Xenophon, *Education of Cyrus* 1.3.2)
However, of all the Medes that I have seen ... this man, my grandfather, is by far the most handsome.

ἐπαινῶ σε ἐφ᾽ οἷς (for ἐπὶ τούτοις ἃ) λέγεις. (Xenophon, *Anabasis* 1.3.45)
I praise you for what you say.

Note how the antecedent is omitted in the above sentence. This is usual when the relative is attracted into the case of a deictic pronoun (see p. ix). Cf. Milton, *Paradise Lost* 6.808: 'Vengeance is his, or whose he sole appoints.' Here 'whose' stands for 'that of the individual whom'.

Attraction of the relative is by no means inevitable. It happens with ὅς, οἷος and ὅσος, but <u>not</u> ὅστις.

☑ In translating ὅσος in the plural, it is likely that you will find yourself including the word 'all', as in the first example above.

N.B. The article with the participle is frequently found with the meaning of a relative clause. See **5** on p. 123.

ἀλλ᾽, οἶμαι, οἱ τιθέμενοι τοὺς νόμους οἱ ἀσθενεῖς ἄνθρωποί εἰσιν καὶ οἱ πολλοί. (Plato, *Gorgias* 483b)
But, I think, those who enact the laws are the weak men and the mass of the people.

Here οἱ τιθέμενοι τοὺς νόμους is a participial phrase which could also have been expressed by a relative clause, i.e. ἐκεῖνοι οἳ τίθενται τοὺς νόμους.

| Practice sentences

Translate into English or Greek as appropriate:
1 ἦν δέ τις ἐν τῇ στρατιᾷ Ξενοφῶν Ἀθηναῖος, ὃς οὔτε στρατηγὸς οὔτε λοχᾱγὸς οὔτε στρατιώτης ὢν συνηκολουθεῖ. (Xenophon, *Anabasis* 3.1.4)
2 μακάριος ὅστις οὐσίᾱν καὶ νοῦν ἔχει. (Menander, *Sententiae* 340)

3 ἴσως γὰρ ἀναλίσκουσιν οὐκ εἰς ἃ δεῖ μόνον, ἀλλὰ καὶ εἰς ἃ βλάβην φέρει αὐτῷ (the master of the house) καὶ τῷ οἴκῳ. (Xenophon, *Oeconomicus* 3.5)

4 ὦ πρέσβυ, Ταφίων ὅς ποτ᾽ ἐξεῖλες πόλιν ... [This is not a complete sentence.] (Euripides, *Heracles* 60)

5 ἐγὼ δέ, ὦ Κῦρε, καὶ ὧν ἐγὼ κρατῶ μενοῦμεν. (Xenophon, *Education of Cyrus* 5.1.26)

6 I am the famous Heracles whom the gods love, the hero whose father is Zeus.

7 This is the girl I gave the book to.

8 The girl will give me all (use ὅσος) the apples she has.

9 She read none of the books that I gave her. (Attract the relative.)

10 Is it Athens that you are travelling to? (Use πρός + acc.)

Time, place and space

Time

- In Greek, the <u>accusative</u> expresses *time how long*:

  αἱ δὲ σπονδαὶ ἐνιαυτὸν ἔσονται. (Thucydides 4.118.10)
  And the truce will be for a year.

  ἔτη γεγονὼς ἑβδομήκοντα (Plato, *Apology* 17d)
  born for seventy years, *i.e.* seventy years old [The life is seventy years <u>long</u>.]

  With an ordinal number, the accusative expresses *how long since*:

  ἑβδόμην ... ἡμέραν τῆς θυγατρὸς αὐτῷ τετελευτηκυίας. (Aeschines 3.77)
  After his daughter had died six days before (this being the seventh (ἑβδόμην) day of the duration of her death).

- The <u>genitive</u> expresses *time within which*:
  | νυκτός | in the course of the night |
  | χειμῶνος | in the course of the winter |

- The <u>dative</u> expresses *time when*:
  | τῇ ὑστεραίᾳ | on the next day |
  | τραγῳδοῖς καινοῖς | at the presentation of the new tragedies (from an inscription) |

  ἐν is often found before the dative, especially in prose, e.g.

  ἐν οὕτως ὀλίγῳ χρόνῳ
  in so brief a time

Some expressions of time:
ἅμ' ἡμέρᾳ	at daybreak
ἅμα (τῇ) ἕῳ	at dawn
ἐν μεσημβρίᾳ	at midday
δείλης	in the afternoon
πρὸς ἑσπέραν	towards evening

ἑσπέρᾱς	in the evening
ὑπὸ νύκτα	at nightfall
πρῴ	early (in the day)
ὀψέ	late
τῇ προτεραίᾳ	on the day before
τῇ ὑστεραίᾳ	on the next day
χθές	yesterday
τήμερον	today
αὔριον	tomorrow
θέρους	in summer
χειμῶνος	in winter
ἦρος	in spring
τοῦ λοιποῦ	in the future
ἐκ τοῦ	from that time
ἐν τῷ παρόντι	at present
ἐν τούτῳ	in the meantime
ἐκ τούτου μετὰ ταῦτα	} after this
ἐπὶ Κρόνου, etc.	in the time of Cronus, etc.
ἐφ' ἡμῶν	in our lifetime
δι' ὀλίγου	after a short interval
εἰς καιρόν	at the right time

| Place

In Greek, prepositions are generally used to indicate place:

- *motion towards* involves prepositions followed by the <u>accusative</u>:
πρὸς τὸ ἄστυ	towards/to the city
εἰς τὸ ἄστυ	into the city
ὡς Φαρνάβαζον	to Pharnabazus (the preposition ὡς is used with *people* only, not *places*)

- *motion away from* involves prepositions followed by the <u>genitive</u>:
ἀπὸ τοῦ ἄστεως	away from the city
ἐκ τοῦ ἄστεως	out of the city
παρὰ βασιλέως	from the Persian king (παρά is commonly used with *people*)

- *place where* commonly involves prepositions followed by the <u>dative</u>:
  ἐν τῇ πόλει   in the city
  πρὸς τῷ ἄστει   near *or* at the city

  But in poetry the dative is used without ἐν, and in prose place names can be found both with and without ἐν. Plato has an example of both alongside each other:

  τῶν τε Μαραθῶνι μαχεσαμένων καὶ τῶν ἐν Σαλαμῖνι ναυμαχησάντων
  (Plato, *Menexenus* 241b)
  both those who fought at Marathon and were in the sea battle at Salamis

---

☑ While the dative, with or without ἐν, generally expresses *place where*, an older dative plural ending survives for the first declension which is also used with this meaning. This ends in -ᾱσι or -ησι (compare Πλαταιᾶσι (at Plataea) with the later dative Πλαταιαῖς). In addition a small number of fossilized examples of the old locative (the case which expresses *place where*) survive, e.g. οἴκοι and χαμαί (see below). For the sake of convenience, we classify all of these as locatives.

Note the following:
- the <u>locative</u>:
  οἴκοι   at home (but beware of ποῖ (= to where))
  χαμαί   on the ground
  Ἀθήνησι   at Athens
  Πλαταιᾶσι   at Plataea
- the suffix -θεν indicates *place from where*:
  πανταχόθεν   from every side
  Ἀθήνηθεν   from Athens
  οἴκοθεν   from home
- the suffix -δε or -σε indicates *place to where*:
  πανταχόσε   in every direction
  Ἀθήναζε   to Athens
  οἴκαδε   to home, homewards

  Why the ζ in Ἀθήναζε? Because the suffix -δε is being added to the accusative Ἀθήνᾱς and the combination σδ is naturally written with a zeta (see p. 1).

Some place words:

Ἀθήνησι	Ἀθήνηθεν	Ἀθήναζε
at Athens	from Athens	to Athens
ἄλλοθι	ἄλλοθεν	ἄλλοσε
elsewhere	from elsewhere	to somewhere else
ἀμφοτέρωθι	ἀμφοτέρωθεν	
in both ways	from both sides	
αὐτοῦ	αὐτόθεν	αὐτόσε
in the very place, exactly there, exactly here	from the very place	to the very place
ἐκεῖ	ἐκεῖθεν	ἐκεῖσε
there	from there	to there
ἐνθάδε	ἐνθένδε	ἐνθάδε
here, there	from here	to here, to there
ἐνταῦθα	ἐντεῦθεν	ἐνταῦθα
here, there	from here, from there	to here, to there
οὐδαμοῦ	οὐδαμόθεν	οὐδαμόσε
nowhere, in no place	from no place	to no place
οἴκοι	οἴκοθεν	οἴκαδε
at home	from home	to home
ὁμοῦ	ὁμόθεν	ὁμόσε
at the same place	from the same place	to the same place
πανταχοῦ	πανταχόθεν	πανταχόσε
everywhere	from every direction	in all directions
Ὀλυμπίασι	Ὀλυμπίαθεν	Ὀλυμπίαζε
at Olympia	from Olympia	to Olympia

| Space

• the <u>accusative</u> expresses *extent of space*:

ἀπέχει τὸ ἄστυ τρία στάδια.
The town is three stades away.

ἐξελαύνει διὰ τῆς Λυδίας σταθμοὺς τρεῖς, παρασάγγας εἴκοσι καὶ δύο.
(Xenophon, *Anabasis* 1.2.5)
He advances the length of three days' marches, twenty-two parasangs,
through Lydia.

• τὸ μῆκος in length   τὸ εὖρος in breadth   τὸ ὕψος in height

Greek generally uses a <u>genitive</u> of the measurement with an <u>accusative</u>
of respect (e.g. in length, breadth, etc.). The article is included with the
accusative of respect:

τεῖχος ὀκτὼ σταδίων τὸ μῆκος
a wall eight stades long (*literally*, in length)

Some space words:

σταθμός m.	a day's march
στάδιον n.	a stade, 606 ³/₄ English feet (in the plural it can be either οἱ στάδιοι or τὰ στάδια)
παρασάγγης m.	a parasang, 30 stades

| Practice sentences

Translate into English or Greek as appropriate:

1 ἀπέχει δὲ ἡ Πλάταια τῶν Θηβῶν σταδίους ἑβδομήκοντα.
(Thucydides 2.5.2)

2 οὐκοῦν ἡδὺ μέν (ἐστι) θέρους (τὴν οἰκίαν) ψύχεινὴν (= cool) ἔχειν,
ἡδὺ δὲ χειμῶνος ἀλεεινήν (= warm); (Xenophon, *Memorabilia*
3.8.9)

3 ἀφίκετο ὡς Περδίκκᾱν καὶ ἐς τὴν Χαλκιδικήν. (Thucydides 4.79.1)

4 καὶ ταύτην μὲν τὴν ἡμέρᾱν καὶ τὴν ἐπιοῦσαν νύκτα ἐν φυλακῇ εἶχον
αὐτοὺς οἱ Ἀθηναῖοι· τῇ δ' ὑστεραίᾳ ... τἆλλα διεσκευάζοντο ὡς ἐς
πλοῦν. (Thucydides 4.38.4)

5 I shall stay in Athens for five days.

6 My sister died during the night and was buried the next day.

7 He sailed to Athens and went to Pericles.

8 The queen built a road a hundred stades long.

Participles

I ran away from the <u>collapsing</u> house.

Newly <u>rebuilt</u>, the house will last a hundred years.

<u>Hanging</u> in the art gallery, I saw the picture.

Participles are verbal adjectives, i.e. they are formed from verbs and so describe an action, but they are adjectives and so in Greek almost always agree with a noun or pronoun. If you think about the ambiguity in the third sentence above, you will see that English indicates agreement through the order of the words. In Greek agreement is indicated through the case, gender and number of the agreeing words.

- The **present participle** describes an action going on at the same time as the main verb:

  ταῦτα ἔπρᾱττε στρατηγῶν.
  He did this while he was general.

- The **future participle** unsurprisingly looks forward in time. It is likely to express purpose, often in conjunction with ὡς:

  συλλαμβάνει Κῦρον ὡς ἀποκτενῶν. (Xenophon, *Anabasis* 1.1.3)
  He arrests Cyrus in order to put him to death.

  After verbs of motion ὡς is frequently omitted:

  ὁ δ' ἀνὴρ αὐτῆς λαγὼς ᾤχετο θηρᾱσων. (Xenophon, *Anabasis* 4.5.24)
  But her husband had gone to hunt hares.

- The **aorist participle** usually communicates an action which has occurred before the action of the main verb:

  δειπνήσᾱς ἐχώρει. (Thucydides 3.112.2)
  After having his dinner, he went off.

But note:

ἐπομόσᾱς ἔφη ...   he said on oath ...
γελάσᾱς ἔφη ...   he said with a laugh ...

In these two cases he will have respectively sworn and laughed <u>before</u> he started speaking, but the actions of the participles presumably continued <u>while</u> he spoke. In the first example, his words were the expression of his oath; in the second, they were accompanied by laughter.

* The **perfect participle** communicates a present state which has resulted from a past event, e.g.

οἱ τεθνηκότες
those who have died, *i.e.* the dead

| More uses of the participle

Note the following uses of the participle:

<u>causal</u> – (a) with ἅτε, οἷα or οἷον (inasmuch as, seeing that)

ἅτε, οἷα and οἷον are used when the writer advances the cause as a fact:

ἥκομεν τῇ προτεραίᾳ ἑσπέρᾱς ἐκ Ποτιδαίᾱς ἀπὸ τοῦ στρατοπέδου, οἷον δὲ διὰ χρόνου ἀφῑγμένος ἀσμένως ᾖα ἐπὶ τὰς συνήθεις διατριβάς. (Plato, *Charmides* 153a)

We had come in the evening of the day before from the camp in Potideia and, inasmuch as I had arrived after a long absence, I went with pleasure to my usual haunts.

– (b) with ὡς (on the grounds that)

ὡς implies that the cause is the thought or statement of the main verb <u>without</u> suggesting that it is also the idea of the writer:

τὸν ... Περικλέᾱ ἐν αἰτίᾳ εἶχον ὡς πείσαντα σφᾶς πολεμεῖν καὶ δι᾽ ἐκεῖνον ταῖς συμφοραῖς περιπεπτωκότες. (Thucydides 2.59.2)

They kept blaming Pericles on the grounds that he had persuaded them to make war and that it was through him that they had fallen into disaster.

The negative in both these causal uses is οὐ.

'although' = καίπερ

> ἐποικτίρω δέ νιν … καίπερ ὄντα δυσμενῆ. (Sophocles, *Ajax* 121–2)
> But I pity him, although he is my enemy.

Negative οὐ.

comparison – with ὥσπερ (as, as if)

> ὠρχοῦντο … ὥσπερ ἄλλοις ἐπιδεικνύμενοι. (Xenophon, *Anabasis* 5.4.34)
> They danced as if they were showing off to others.

Negative οὐ.

conditional

> σὺ δὲ κλύων εἴσει τάχα. (Aristophanes, *Birds* 1390)
> If you listen, you will find soon out.

Here κλύων could be expanded to ἐὰν κλύῃς (see pp. 184–5).

Negative μή. If μή is used with the participle, it is likely to have this conditional force:

> οὐκ ἂν δύναιο μὴ καμὼν εὐδαιμονεῖν. (Euripides, fragment 461.1)
> You couldn't be happy unless you were to work.

Here μὴ καμών could be expanded to εἰ μὴ κάμοις.

'with' – note the following participles which are frequent equivalents to the English word 'with':

ἔχων	having
ἄγων	leading, bringing
φέρων	carrying, bringing
	(mainly with *inanimate objects*)
λαβών	having taken
χρώμενος (+ dat.)	using

> ἔχων στρατιὰν ἀφικνεῖται. (Thucydides 4.30.2)
> He arrives with (*literally,* having) an army.

> βοῇ τε χρώμενοι (Thucydides 2.84.3)
> and with (*literally,* using) a shout

with the article – note pp. 123 & 129.

Study the following sentence:

> οἱ Ἀθηναῖοι οἱ ἐν τῇ πόλει ὄντες καταφρονοῦσι τῶν τοὺς ἀγροὺς οἰκούντων.
> The Athenians who are in the city despise those who live in the country.

with certain verbs

The following verbs are used with participles:

τυγχάνω	I happen, am just now ...	παρὼν ἐτύγχανε.[1] He happened to be there.
λανθάνω	I escape (the) notice (of)	τοὺς φύλακας ἔλαθεν εἰσέλθων. He entered unnoticed by the guards.
		φονέᾱ τοῦ παιδὸς ἐλάνθανε βόσκων. (Herodotus 1.44) He didn't realize he was entertaining his son's murderer.
φθάνω	I anticipate, get in first	αὐτοὶ φθήσονται αὐτὸ δράσαντες. (Plato, *Republic* 375c) They will do this themselves first.
		ἔφθασε τὸν φίλον τρέχων. He beat his friend in running.
διατελέω	I continue, keep on	διατελεῖ μῖσῶν. He continues to hate (*or* hating).
		ἑπτὰ γὰρ ἡμέρᾱς ... μαχόμενοι διετέλεσαν. (Xenophon, *Anabasis* 4.3.2) For they continued fighting for seven days.
ἄρχομαι[2]	I begin	ἄρξομαι δὲ ἀπὸ τῆς ἰᾱτρικῆς λέγων. (Plato, *Symposium* 186b) But I shall begin by talking about medicine.
λήγω, παύομαι	I stop, cease	παῦσαι λέγουσα. (Euripides, *Hippolytus* 706) Stop talking!
ἀνέχομαι	I hold out, endure	οὐκ ἀνέξομαι ζῶσα. (Euripides, *Hippolytus* 354) I shall not hold out and live on (*literally*, endure living).

---

[1] This can also mean: 'He was actually there.'

[2] ἄρχομαι λέγειν means simply 'I begin to speak'.

φαίνομαι	I am obviously	φαίνεται τἀληθῆ λέγων. He is evidently speaking the truth.

☑ With φαίνομαι + the participle, appearance and reality coincide. As in English, the use of the infinitive suggests that the appearance may be false:

φαίνεται τἀληθῆ λέγειν.
He appears <u>to be speaking</u> the truth (but may not be).

δῆλός εἰμι φανερός εἰμι	} I am obviously	
χαίρω ἥδομαι τέρπομαι	} I am pleased, enjoy	χαίρω γε διαλεγόμενος τοῖς σφόδρα πρεσβύταις. (Plato, *Republic* 328d) I enjoy talking to very old men.
ἀγανακτέω ἄχθομαι χαλεπῶς φέρω	{ I am displeased, annoyed	
ὀργίζομαι	I am angry	
μεταμέλομαι	I am sorry, regret	μετεμέλοντο τὰς σπονδὰς οὐ δεξάμενοι. (Thucydides 4.27.3) They were sorry they had not accepted the truce.

| Genitive absolute

In all the examples above, the participles have agreed with the subject or object of a verb. They could also have agreed with a noun or pronoun which forms some other part of the clause it belongs to, as in this sentence:

Ἀθήναζε εἶμι μετά σου, φιλτάτης οὔσης.
I shall go to Athens with you, (being) my dearest friend.

Often, however, the participial phrase (i.e. the noun + the participle) is independent of the structure of the rest of the sentence:

καὶ ταῦτ' ἐπράχθη Κόνωνος ... στρατηγοῦντος. (Isocrates 9.56)
And these things were done while Conon was general.
  (*literally,* These things were done, Conon being the general.)

Here, στρατηγοῦντος agrees with Κόνωνος, who is neither the subject nor the object of the main verb. His name is <u>independent</u> of the clause in which it sits. Compare:

τούτων λεχθέντων ἀνέστησαν. (Xenophon, *Anabasis* 3.3.1)
After these things had been said (*literally,* these things having been said), they got up.

The technical term for this is **absolute** (from the Latin word for 'loosed from' or 'set free from', i.e. 'independent'). In phrases such as this, both noun and participle are in the <u>genitive</u> case.

Κῦρος ... ἀνέβη ἐπὶ τὰ ὄρη οὐδενὸς κωλύοντος. (Xenophon, *Anabasis* 1.2.22)
Cyrus went up to the mountains without opposition (*literally,* no one hindering).

| Accusative absolute

Where the participle has no subject, i.e. with impersonal verbs (see pp. 190–1), the **accusative absolute** is used in place of the genitive absolute:

δέον	it being necessary
ἐξόν	} it being possible
παρόν	
προσῆκον	it being fitting
μετόν	there being a share
μεταμέλον	it being a matter of regret
παρέχον	it being in one's power
παρασχόν	an opportunity having presented itself
δόξαν	since it was resolved
εἰρημένον	since it has been stated *or* told
ἄδηλον ὄν	it being unclear

δυνατὸν ὄν	it being possible
ἀδύνατον ὄν	it being impossible
αἰσχρὸν ὄν	it being shameful
καλὸν ὄν	it being fine or honourable

For more information on the impersonal verbs, see pp. 190–1.

τί δή, ὑμᾶς ἐξὸν ἀπολέσαι, οὐκ ἐπὶ τοῦτο ἤλθομεν; (Xenophon, *Anabasis* 2.5.22)

Why indeed, when it was possible for us to destroy you, did we not proceed to do it?

μετεμέλοντό τε ὅτι μετὰ τὰ ἐν Πύλῳ, καλῶς παρασχόν, οὐ ξυνέβησαν. (Thucydides 5.14.2)

And they regretted that after what had occurred at Pylos, when a favourable opportunity had presented itself, they had not come to terms.

Note that words such as ἅτε, ὡς and καίπερ (see pp. 137–8) can be used in conjunction with the accusative absolute.

| Practice sentences

Translate into English or Greek as appropriate:

1 ἡμεῖς οὔτε συνήλθομεν ὡς βασιλεῖ πολεμήσοντες οὔτε ἐπορευόμεθα ἐπὶ (= against) βασιλέᾱ. (Xenophon, *Anabasis* 2.31.21)

2 οὐδεὶς τὸ μεῖζον (κακὸν) αἱρήσεται ἐξὸν τὸ ἔλαττον (αἱρεῖσθαι). (Plato, *Protagoras* 358d)

3 καὶ νῦν μὲν, ἔφη, δειπνεῖτε παρ' ἡμῖν. δειπνήσαντες δὲ ἀπελαύνετε ὅποι ὑμῖν θυμός. (Xenophon, *Education of Cyrus* 3.1.37)

4 ὁ δὲ Κῦρος, ἅτε παῖς ὤν καὶ φιλόκαλος καὶ φιλότῑμος, ἥδετο τῇ στολῇ. (Xenophon, *Education of Cyrus* 1.3.3)

5 πῶς δῆτα, Δίκης οὔσης, ὁ Ζεὺς οὐκ ἀπόλωλεν, τὸν πατέρ' αὑτοῦ δήσᾱς; (Aristophanes, *Clouds* 904–5)

6 συμβουλεύω δέ σοι καίπερ νεώτερος ὤν. (Xenophon, *Education of Cyrus* 4.5.32)

7 ἀνὴρ γὰρ ὅστις ἥδεται λέγων ἀεί,
λέληθεν αὑτὸν τοῖς ξυνοῦσιν ὢν βαρύς. (Sophocles, fragment 103 (Pearson))

8 The Athenians killed Socrates on the grounds that he had corrupted the young men.

9 Inasmuch as it was still winter, the young men did not go to the gymnasium.

10 Since it is impossible for me to marry you, I advise you to go home.

11 After setting out at dawn the queen of the Amazons reached the city with a thousand women.

12 The girl is obviously highly intelligent. The boy, on the other hand, appears to be stupid.

13 Since the night was dark, he escaped unnoticed by the soldiers.

14 If you do not know anything (use participle), how can you continue teaching? (not ... anything = μηδέν)

Pronouns

1 | Deictic pronouns

οὗτος, αὕτη, τοῦτο this ἐκεῖνος, ἐκείνη, ἐκεῖνο that (there)
(see p. 49) (see p. 49)

ὅδε, ἥδε, τόδε this (here)
(see p. 49) [ὅδε is often used in tragedy to refer to the speaker]

In prose, these pronouns are regularly used <u>with</u> the definite article, and are placed outside the article and the noun, i.e in the predicative position (see pp. 125–6):

αὕτη ἡ γυνή ὁ ἀνὴρ ἐκεῖνος
this woman that man

Since these pronouns point to what they describe, they are called **deictic** (from δείκνῡμι (I show)).

ὅδε and its adverb ὧδε (thus) usually point forward to what follows:

τάδε εἶπεν.
He spoke as follows.

οὗτος points to something near or something just mentioned, ἐκεῖνος to something further away. Thus ἐκεῖνος can mean 'the former' and οὗτος can mean 'the latter', e.g.

ἀλλ᾽ ἐκεῖνος μὲν σκληφρός, οὗτος δὲ προφερὴς καὶ καλὸς καὶ ἀγαθὸς τὴν ὄψιν. (Plato, *Euthydemus* 271b)
But the former is without grace while the latter is well-developed, handsome and good-looking.

'-ί' can be added to οὗτος in all its forms for emphasis, e.g. οὑτοσί (this man here).

Other deictic pronouns are:

| τοιόσδε, τοιάδε, τοιόνδε | of such a kind | } pointing forward |
| τοσόσδε, τοσήδε, τοσόνδε | { so much, so many, so great | } to what follows |

| τοιοῦτος, τοιαύτη, τοιοῦτο | of such a kind | } pointing backward |
| τοσοῦτος, τοσαύτη, τοσοῦτο | { so much, so many, so great | } to what came before |

καὶ ὁ Κῦρος, ἀκούσᾱς τοῦ Γωβρύᾱ τοιαῦτα, τοιάδε πρὸς αὐτὸν ἔλεξε.
(Xenophon, *Education of Cyrus* 5.2.31)
And after hearing such words from Gobryas, Cyrus addressed him as follows.

Study the declension of αὐτός on p. 46. It is important to distinguish it from οὗτος (p. 49), especially in the feminine nominative singular and plural:

	f. nom. sg.	f. nom. pl.
αὐτός →	αὐτή	αὐταί
οὗτος →	αὕτη	αὗται

- οὗτος and sometimes ἐκεῖνος can be used to mean 'well-known':

  Γοργίᾱς οὗτος   ἐκεῖνος Θουκῡδίδης
  the celebrated Gorgias   that famous Thucydides

  τούτους τοὺς σῡκοφάντᾱς (Plato, *Crito* 45a)
  these infamous informers (they are not actually present, though the article is used)

- Note the exclamatory use of οὗτος:

  οὗτος, τί ποιεῖς; (Aristophanes, *Frogs* 198)
  You there, what are you doing?

Cf. τοῦτ' ἐκεῖνο. (Aristophanes, *Acharnians* 41)
That's it! (*literally*, That's what this (is)!)

2 | αὐτός αὐτή αὐτό

αὐτός (see p. 46) has three different meanings, depending on how it is used:

1 In the accusative, genitive and dative, αὐτός means 'him', 'her', 'it' or 'them':

ἐρῶ αὐτῆς   ἀπέκτεινα αὐτόν
I love her   I killed him

N.B. With this meaning, it is a pronoun and <u>never</u> appears in the nominative. Unless emphatic, it does not stand at the beginning of a sentence.

2 Standing by itself or outside the article and the noun, αὐτός means 'self':

ταῦτα ἐποιεῖτε αὐτοί   you were doing these things yourselves

αὐτὸς ὁ στρατηγός   the general himself

ἡ γυνὴ αὐτή   the woman herself[1]

For this meaning, the article is not necessary, as with names, e.g.

Θουκῡδίδης αὐτός
Thucydides himself

Note the use of αὐτός with ordinal numbers, e.g.

τρίτος αὐτός   himself the third (*i.e.*, with two others)

πέμπτος αὐτός   himself the fifth (*i.e.*, with four others)

αὐτός is always the chief person.

3 When it is preceded by the definite article, αὐτός means 'the same':

ἡ αὐτὴ γυνή   ταὐτά (= τὰ αὐτά)
the same woman   the same things[1]

For this meaning, the article <u>is</u> necessary.

---

[1] Note how in these usages the word order is the same in Greek and English.

☑ αὐτοῖς X = 'X and all'

A common Greek idiom using αὐτός in the dative plural (usually without the article) suggests inclusive accompaniment (see p. 20):

μίαν τούτων [τῶν νεῶν] αὐτοῖς ἀνδράσιν (Thucydides 4.14.1)
one of these ships with all its crew (with its men and all)

εἶπεν ... ἥκειν εἰς τὰς τάξεις αὐτοῖς στεφάνοις. (Xenophon, *Education of Cyrus* 3.3.40)

He told them to come to their posts, crowns and all.

3 | Personal pronouns and their adjectives

These are given on p. 46.

The adjectives generally come after the article, the pronouns generally after the article + noun group, e.g.

ἡ σὴ μήτηρ
ἡ μήτηρ ἡ σή   } your mother
ἡ μήτηρ σοῦ

ἡ πατρὶς ἡμῶν   our country

αὐτοῦ, αὐτῆς, αὐτοῦ (pl. αὐτῶν) his, her, its (pl. their) (*literally,* of him, etc.) come outside the article and noun:

ὁρῶ τὸν φίλον αὐτοῦ (αὐτῆς).
I see his (her) friend.

γιγνώσκων αὐτοῦ τὴν ἀνδρείᾱν (Plato, *Protagoras* 310d)
knowing his courage

4 | Reflexive pronouns

These are given on p. 47.[2] They refer back to the subject of their sentence or clause.

γνῶθι σεαυτόν.
Know thyself.

δίδωμί σοι ἐμαυτὸν δοῦλον. (Xenophon, *Education of Cyrus* 4.6.2)
I give myself to you as a slave.

Ὀρέστης ... ἔπεισεν Ἀθηναίους ἑαυτὸν κατάγειν. (Thucydides 1.111.1)
Orestes persuaded the Athenians to restore him.

In the last example the reflexive pronoun refers back to the subject not of its own clause (ἑαυτὸν κατάγειν) but to that of the main clause. We call reflexive pronouns used in this way **indirect reflexives**. Cf.

> <u>Philip</u> gave Olympias the crown which the Macedonians had given <u>to him</u>.

- Note the following reflexive forms:

singular

dat.   οἷ   to himself, herself, itself

plural

gen.	σφῶν	of themselves
dat.	σφίσι(ν)	to themselves
acc.	σφᾶς	themselves

often joined with αὐτῶν, etc.

ἠρώτα ... αὐτὴν εἰ ἐθελήσοι διακονῆσαί οἷ. (Antiphon 1.16)
He asked her if she would be willing to do him a service.

ἔλεξαν ὅτι πέμψειε σφᾶς ὁ Ἰνδῶν βασιλεύς. (Xenophon, *Education of Cyrus* 2.4.7)
They said that the king of the Indians had sent them.

κελεύουσι γὰρ ἡμᾶς κοινῇ μετὰ σφῶν καὶ μετὰ Κορινθίων πολεμεῖν. (Andocides 3.27)
For they urge us to make war in common with them and the Corinthians.

---

[2] See also the description of the middle voice on pp. xii & 60.

In Attic prose these reflexive forms are generally used as indirect reflexives. In Homer, Herodotus and the Attic poets, they are generally simply personal pronouns, though they may be reflexives:

αὐτίκα δέ οἱ εὕδοντι ἐπέστη ὄνειρος. (Herodotus 1.34)
and very soon a dream came to him in his sleep (*literally,* to him sleeping).

☑ The genitive of reflexive pronouns as well as of deictic pronouns takes the attributive position (see p. 125) when it is possessive:

ἀπέκτεινεν ἑαυτὸν τῷ ἑαυτοῦ ξίφει.
He killed himself with his own sword.

5 | The indefinite pronoun (τις, τι)

τις, τι (some one; any, some; a certain, a, an) is an enclitic, i.e. it will, if possible, put its accent on the last syllable of the word in front of it. Therefore it cannot stand first word in its word-group.

τοῦτο λέγει τις	some one says this
ἄνθρωπός τις	some/a certain man
δεινός τις ἄνθρωπος ἄνθρωπός τις δεινός }	an alarming man

As you can see, τις can perform the function of the indefinite article. See p. xi.

With adjectives, adverbs and numbers, τις may suggest that the word to which it is joined should not be taken completely literally:

δεινός τις ἔρως (Xenophon, *Education of Cyrus* 5.1.24)
a strange longing

τριάκοντα μέν τινας ἀπέκτειναν. (Thucydides 8.73.6)
They killed some thirty (about thirty).

6 | Other pronouns

- **ἀλλήλων one another, each other** (plural, not nominative — see p. 47)

  ὡς δ᾽ εἰδέτην (dual, see pp. 232–3) ἀλλήλους ἡ γυνὴ καὶ ὁ
  Ἀβραδάτας, ἠσπάζοντο ἀλλήλους. (Xenophon, *Education of Cyrus*
  6.1.47)
  When Abradatas and his wife saw one another, they embraced each
  other.

- **ἄλλος, -η, -ο other**

ἄλλαι γυναῖκες	other women
αἱ ἄλλαι γυναῖκες	(all) the other women, the rest of the women

  ὁ δὲ Βρασίδας τῷ μὲν ἄλλῳ στρατῷ ἡσύχαζεν …, ἑκατὸν δὲ
  πελταστὰς προπέμπει. (Thucydides 4.111.1)
  Brasidas did nothing with the rest of the army but sent forward a
  hundred peltasts.

- ἄλλος followed by another form of the same word can make a two-fold
  statement, as follows (cf. English 'different' – 'different people do
  different things'):

  ἄλλος ἄλλα λέγει. (Xenophon, *Anabasis* 2.1.15)
  one says one thing, another says another (*literally*, other things).

  ἄλλοι ἄλλοθεν
  some from one place, others from another

- Note also:

ὁ ἕτερος, -ᾱ, -ον	one *or* the other of two
οἱ ἕτεροι	one of two groups
ἕκαστος, -η, -ον	each
ἑκάτερος, -ᾱ, -ον	each (one) of two
ἑκάτεροι	each (one) of two groups
ἀμφότεροι	both, either
οὐδέτερος, -ᾱ, -ον μηδέτερος, -ᾱ, -ον }	neither of the two

  When used with nouns, all of the above, apart from the first two, are
  placed outside the article and the noun.

| Practice sentences

Translate into English or Greek as appropriate:

1 τοὺς παῖδας τοὺς ἐμοὺς ᾔσχῡνε καὶ ἐμὲ αὐτὸν ὕβρισεν εἰς τὴν οἰκίαν τὴν ἐμὴν εἰσιών. (Lysias 1.4)

2 οἱ τοὺς αὐτοὺς αἰεὶ περὶ τῶν αὐτῶν λόγους λέγοντες πιστότεροί εἰσι τῶν διαφερομένων σφίσιν αὐτοῖς. (Antiphon 5.50)

3 οἱ δὲ ἡττώμενοι ἅμα ἑαυτούς τε καὶ τὰ ἑαυτῶν πάντα ἀποβάλλουσιν. (Xenophon, *Education of Cyrus* 3.3.45)

4 ἐνταῦθα λέγεται Ἀπόλλων ἐκδεῖραι Μαρσύᾱν νῑκήσᾱς ἐρίζοντά οἱ περὶ σοφίᾱς. (Xenophon, *Anabasis* 1.2.8)

5 μετεπέμψατο τὴν ἑαυτοῦ θυγατέρα καὶ τὸν παῖδα αὐτῆς. (Xenophon, *Education of Cyrus* 1.3.1)

6 I admire both Agathon and Socrates. The former is very friendly, the latter very wise.

7 The celebrated Socrates remembered these words: 'Know thyself.'

8 I (my)self do not always do the same things.

9 My father gave you a book which you must give back to him.

10 Opinions differ.

Sequence of tenses and moods

In Greek, the tense of the main verb can determine whether a subjunctive or optative is used in a subordinate clause where one of those moods is needed. A similar process can operate in English too:

> I am wooing the rich widow so that I <u>can/may</u> enjoy her money.

> I was wooing her so that I <u>could/might</u> enjoy her money.

We call this pattern of agreement **sequence of tenses and moods** and it falls into two divisions, which we call **primary** (the main verb is usually in a present or future tense) and **historic** or **secondary** (the main verb is in a past tense).

| Primary sequence

Tense of verb in main clause	Mood of verb in subordinate clause
present	
future	
perfect (describes a present state)	subjunctive
future perfect	

Main verbs in the subjunctive and the imperative also fall into this category.

| Historic sequence

Tense of verb in main clause	Mood of verb in subordinate clause
imperfect	
aorist	} optative
pluperfect	

Main verbs in the optative also fall into this category.

In the indicative, the historic tenses all begin with an augment (ἐ-).

☑ You will discover that a subjunctive can be used in purpose clauses and clauses of fearing in historic sequence. See pp. 174–5 and p. 180.

Indirect statement

Direct speech	Indirect speech
I am going to Athens.	I said <u>I was going to Athens</u>.
I have gone to Athens.	I told her <u>that I had gone to Athens</u>.
I shall go to Athens.	I promised <u>that I would go to Athens</u>.

An **indirect statement** comes after a verb in which the *voice, mind* or *one of the senses* is used (e.g. say, hear, discover, see, observe, know, think) followed by 'that' or with 'that' understood, e.g.

I think that I am intelligent. I think he is a fool.

It can be seen from the examples above that in English the words of direct speech are liable to be changed when they are converted into indirect speech. The Greek words usually change too, but this will depend on which of three different Greek constructions they follow. Here are the English equivalents of these three Greek constructions:

1 I think that she is a fool.

2 I believe her to be a fool.

3 I regard her as being foolish.

1 | ὅτι and ὡς

After verbs of *saying* (though not φημί), the clause of the indirect statement is usually introduced by ὅτι or ὡς. ὅπως is also used, most often in poetry and Xenophon. Negative οὐ.

The verb in the indirect statement remains in the tense of the direct speech (the tense actually used by the speaker), e.g.

εἶπον ὅτι Ἀθήναζε προσέρχομαι.
I said that I was on my way to Athens.

αὐτῷ ἤγγειλα ὡς Ἀθήναζε προσεῖμι.
I told him that I would (*literally*, shall) come to Athens.

Note

1 In historic sequence (i.e. after a main verb in a past tense — see pp. 152–3), the *optative* can be used. It will still be in the same tense as the indicative would have been (i.e. the tense actually used):

εἶπον ὅτι ὁ Φίλιππος μῶρος εἴη.
I said that Philip was stupid.

The optative is less 'vivid' than the indicative when used in sentences like this. In the example above, if ἐστί had been used instead of εἴη, it would have lent emphasis to the assertion of Philip's stupidity.

2 ὅτι and ὡς are chiefly found after λέγω (I say) and εἶπον (I said), and sometimes after ἀγγέλλω (I announce).

2 | The infinitive construction

After verbs of *saying, thinking, believing, hoping, promising* and *swearing*, the verb in the indirect statement goes into the infinitive in the tense of the direct speech (the tense actually used by the speaker).

If the subject of the infinitive is the same as that of the main verb, it is usually omitted in Greek. If it is included, which happens rarely, it will be in the nominative. If the subject of the infinitive is different from that of the main verb, it will be in the accusative. Negative οὐ — as it would have been in the direct speech which is being reproduced.

αὕτη φησὶν Ἀθήναζε προσχωρήσειν.
This women says that she will come to Athens.

[Κλέων] οὐκ ἔφη αὐτός, ἀλλ᾽ ἐκεῖνον [Νῑκίᾱν] στρατηγεῖν.
   (Thucydides 4.28.2)
[Cleon] said that it was not himself who was the general, but that man [Nicias].

αὗται ἔφασαν τὴν ἀδελφὴν ἄρτι ἀπελθεῖν.
These women said that their sister had just gone away.

The imperfect indicative becomes the present infinitive.

τότε ἐβασίλευεν ὁ Δαρεῖος.
Darius was king at the time.

ἔφη τότε βασιλεύειν τὸν Δαρεῖον.
He said that Darius was king at the time.

The pluperfect indicative becomes the perfect infinitive.

ἔφη ... χρήμαθ' ἑαυτῷ τοὺς Θηβαίους ἐπικεκηρῦχέναι. (Demosthenes 19.21)
He said that the Thebans had proclaimed a reward for him.

Note

1 The Greek for 'I say ... not' is οὔ φημι:

οὔ φησι δώσειν μοι τὴν βίβλον.
He says that he will not give me the book.

2 The verbs ἐλπίζω (I hope), ὑπισχνέομαι (I promise) and ὄμνῡμι (I swear) are generally followed by a <u>future infinitive</u> because their meaning usually causes them to refer to the future. Negative μή.

ὑπέσχοντο μὴ κλέψεσθαι τὸ ἀργύριον.
They promised not to steal the money, *i.e.* that they would not steal it.

There is nothing irregular about this, but English speakers need to be on their guard since English tends to use what appears to be a present infinitive in this context, and this can prove misleading when translating English into Greek.

The following verbs are among those which are followed by the infinitive construction:

φημί	I say
ἡγέομαι	
οἶμαι, οἴομαι	I think, consider
δοκέω	
νομίζω	
ὑπολαμβάνω	I suppose
ὑποπτεύω	I suspect
εἰκάζω	I guess
πιστεύω	I believe, feel sure that, trust
ἀπιστέω	I do not believe, disbelieve
ὁμολογέω	I agree

3 | The participle construction

After verbs of *knowing* and *perceiving*, the verb in the indirect statement is found in the participle. The participle is in the tense of the direct speech (the tense actually used by the speaker). If the subject of the participle is the same as that of the main verb, it is either omitted or is in the nominative. If it is different, it is in the accusative. The participle agrees in case, number and gender with its subject. Negative οὐ.

ἐπιλελήσμεσθ' ἡδέως γέροντες ὄντες. (Euripides, *Bacchae* 189)
We have gladly forgotten that we are old.

οἶδα αὐτὸν μῶρον ὄντα.
I know that he is stupid.

ἔγνω τὴν ἐσβολὴν ἐσομένην. (Thucydides 2.13)
He knew that the invasion would take place.

μέμνημαι Κριτίᾳ τῷδε ξυνόντα σε. (Plato, *Charmides* 156a)
I remember that you were together with Critias here.

In the third example, the present participle is used to replace the imperfect 'actually used'. This is regular. In the same way, the perfect participle replaces the pluperfect 'actually used'.

Note

1 When ἀκούω (I hear) is used in the context of hearing something actually happening, it is followed by the genitive and the participle:

ἤκουσαν τῆς Κίρκης ᾀδούσης.
They heard Circe singing.

Compare:

ἀκούω αὐτὸν παρόντα.
I hear that he is present.

ἀκούω is regularly followed by the genitive of the *person heard from* and the accusative of the *thing heard*.

2 When οἶδα (I know) and γιγνώσκω (I get to know) are used in the context of knowledge *of a fact*, they are often followed by the ὅτι or ὡς construction (**1** above):

ᾖσαν ὅτι εἰσπλέουσιν οἱ πολέμιοι εἰς τὸν λιμένα.
They knew that the enemy were sailing into the harbour.

The idea is that they did not simply know but had been *told* of the fact; it had been *spoken* to them. Hence the same construction as that with λέγω is used.

These verbs are among those which are usually followed by the participle construction. The asterisked verbs can be followed by the infinitive construction as well:

οἶδα	I know
ἐπίσταμαι	
ἐννοέω	
μανθάνω	
πυνθάνομαι*	I learn, get to know
γιγνώσκω	
ἔγνων	
αἰσθάνομαι*	I perceive, realize
ἀγνοέω	I don't know
ἀκούω*	I hear
μέμνημαι	I remember (*literally*, I have been reminded)
ἐπιλανθάνομαι	I forget
δηλόω	
(ἐπι)δείκνῡμι	I show
(ἀπο)φαίνω	
ἀγγέλλω*	I announce (usually with ὅτι or ὡς)

Herodotus uses both the infinitive and the participle constructions after πυνθάνομαι in the same sentence:

οἱ ... Πέρσαι πυθόμενοι *συνᾱλίσθαι* τοὺς Παίονας καὶ τὴν πρὸς θαλάσσης ἐσβολὴν *φυλάσσοντας*, ... τράπονται. (Herodotus 5.15)
The Persians, discovering that the Paionians had assembled and were guarding the approach by sea, ... turned away.

| Subordinate clauses in indirect statement

> She said that she hated the king <u>because his breath smelt</u>.

In one interpretation of this sentence, the subordinate clause 'because his breath smelt' is part of what she said. In that case, it is part of the indirect statement. Subordinate clauses in indirect statement, regardless of the construction used, follow these rules:

1 If the main verb is primary (i.e. present, future or perfect – see p. 152), the mood and tense of the verb in the subordinate clause do not change.

> ... *φησὶ* ... ποιήσειν ὃ μήτ' αἰσχύνην μήτ' ἀδοξίαν αὐτῷ *φέρει*.
> (Demosthenes 19.41)

He says he will do whatever does not bring shame or dishonour to him.

2 If the main verb is historic (i.e. in a past tense – see p. 153), the mood and tense of the verb in the subordinate clause may be retained.

> ... *ἔφασαν* ... τοὺς ἄνδρας ἀποκτενεῖν οὓς *ἔχουσι* ζῶντας. (Thucydides
> 2.5.5)

They said that they would kill the men whom they had alive.

It may also be put into the optative (keeping the same tense), i.e. in this example ἔχοιεν. However, past tenses of the indicative may not be put into the optative. They remain unchanged.

> *ἤλπιζον* τοὺς Σικελοὺς ταύτῃ, οὓς *μετεπέμψαντο*, ἀπαντήσεσθαι.
> (Thucydides 7.80.6)

They hoped that the Sikels whom they had sent for would meet them there.

The following is included here for the sake of completeness. It can only be understood once the indefinite construction (see pp. 195–6) has been mastered.

If a subjunctive with ἄν becomes optative, ἄν is dropped, ἐάν, ὅταν, etc. becoming εἰ, ὅτε, etc.

ἐξελθὼν δέ τις αὐτόμολος εἶπεν ὅτι ἐπιτίθεσθαι μέλλοιεν αὐτῷ, ὁπότε ἀπάγοι τὸ στράτευμα. (Xenophon, *Education of Cyrus* 7.5.2)
A deserter came out and said that they intended to attack him when he led his forces away. (The 'when' clause in the direct speech would have been ὁπόταν ἀπάγῃς τὸ στράτευμα).

ἀπεκρίνατο ὅτι μανθάνοιεν ἃ οὐκ ἐπίσταιντο. (Plato, *Euthydemus* 276e)
He answered that they were learning what they did not understand.

☑ The same rules apply to subordinate clauses within indirect questions (see pp. 164–6) and indirect commands (see pp. 170–1).

| Practice sentences

Translate into English or Greek as appropriate:

1 ἧκε δ' ἀγγέλλων … τις ὡς Ἐλάτεια κατείληπται. (Demosthenes 18.169)
2 κἄπειτα ἐπειρώμην αὐτῷ δεικνύναι ὅτι οἴοιτο μὲν εἶναι σοφός, εἴη δ' οὔ. (Plato, *Apology* 21c)
3 λέγει πρὸς αὐτὸν ἡ παῖς· 'ὦ βασιλεῦ, διαβεβλημένος ὑπὸ Ἀμάσιος οὐ μανθάνεις;' (Herodotus 3.1)
4 ὀμόσας ἀπάξειν οἴκαδ', ἐς Τροίαν μ' ἄγει. (Sophocles, *Philoctetes* 941)
5 οὐ γὰρ ᾔδεσαν αὐτὸν τεθνηκότα. (Xenophon, *Anabasis* 1.10.16)
6 λέγουσι δὴ αὐτοῖσι ταῦτα, Ξέρξης ὑπὸ μεγαλοφροσύνης οὐκ ἔφη ὅμοιος ἔσεσθαι Λακεδαιμονίοισι. (Herodotus 7.136)
7, 8 Translate in <u>two</u> different ways:
I said that I was not willing to give my brother the book.
9 I promise not to betray the city to the enemy.
10 I thought that you knew that I was stupid.
11 I realize that he is a coward, but I believe that he will help us.
12 He said that he was not a philosopher himself but Plato (was). (use φημί)

Direct and indirect questions

| Direct questions

What are you thinking?
Where are you going?
You aren't going to say that to her, are you?

Greek has two ways of asking single direct questions. In both of them the verb is regularly in the indicative.

Open or 'wh-' questions

If the question is introduced by a word that asks a question (e.g. who? when? why? etc.), the word is likely to be one of those in column **1** below:

1. Direct (and indirect)	2. Indirect
τίς, τί who, what?	ὅστις, ἥτις, ὅτι who, what
πότερος, -ᾱ, -ον which of two?	ὁπότερος, -ᾱ, -ον which of two
ποῖος, -η, -ον of what sort?	ὁποῖος, -η, -ον of what sort
πόσος, -η, -ον how great? how much?	ὁπόσος, -η, -ον how great, how much
πόσοι, -αι, -α how many?	ὁπόσοι, -αι, -α how many
ποῦ where?	ὅπου where
πόθεν from where? where … from?	ὁπόθεν from where, where … from
ποῖ to where? where … to?	ὅποι to where, where … to

πότε	ὁπότε
when?	when
πῶς	ὅπως
how?	how
τί, διὰ τί	τί, διὰ τί
why?	why

Some examples:

τί πράττει;
What's he doing?

πότε ἦλθεν;
When did he come?

πόσους παῖδας ἔχει ὁ βασιλεύς;
How many children does the king have?

διὰ τί ταύτην τὴν γυναῖκα ἔγημας;
Why did you marry this woman?

☑ Greek π-, English wh- (and Latin qu-) are etymologically related.

Other questions

If the question is not introduced by one of the interrogative pronouns, adjectives or adverbs in column **1** above, see which of the following applies in the Greek:

1 A question beginning with ἆρα or ἦ (the latter is chiefly poetic) implies nothing as to the answer expected, which can be either <u>yes</u> or <u>no</u>.

ἆρ' εἰμὶ μάντις; (Sophocles, *Antigone* 1212)
Am I a prophet?

ἦ τέθνηκεν Οἰδίπου πατήρ; (Sophocles, *Oedipus Tyrannus* 943)
Do you mean that Oedipus' father is dead?

However, just as in English, a question can be indicated by the sense or context, without the reinforcement of ἆρα or ἦ. Look out for (and don't forget to use) the question mark (;).

2 If the question begins with ἆρα οὐ (ἆρ' οὐ), οὐκοῦν or οὐ, it will expect the answer <u>yes</u>.

ἆρ' οὐ βούλεσθε χορεύειν; *or* οὐ βούλεσθε χορεύειν;
You do want to dance, don't you? Surely you want to dance?

οὐκοῦν σοι δοκεῖ ... σύμφορον εἶναι; (Xenophon, *Education of Cyrus* 2.4.15)
So doesn't it seem to you to be advantageous?

3 If the question begins with ἆρα μή, μή or μῶν, it will expect the answer <u>no</u>.

ἆρα μὴ βούλεσθε χορεύειν; *or* μὴ βούλεσθε χορεύειν;
You don't want to dance, do you? Surely you don't want to dance?

μή τι νεώτερον ἀγγελεῖς; (Plato, *Protagoras* 310b)
No bad news, I hope?

Note that μῶν does not always have this negative force:

μῶν Πιτθέως τι γῆρας εἴργασται νέον; (Euripides, *Hippolytus* 794)
Nothing has happened to old Pittheus, has it? (The speaker fears that it has, but hopes that it has not.)

4 If a question begins with πότερον (πότερα) followed, though not immediately, by ἤ (whether ... or), it is a double question:

πότερον ἐᾷς [αὐτὸν] ἄρχειν ἢ ἄλλον καθίστης ἀντ' αὐτοῦ; (Xenophon, *Education of Cyrus* 3.1.12)
Do you allow him to rule or do you appoint someone else instead of him?

πότερα δ' ἡγῇ, ὦ Κῦρε, ἄμεινον εἶναι σὺν τῷ σῷ ἀγαθῷ τὰς τιμωρίας ποιεῖσθαι ἢ σὺν τῇ σῇ ζημίᾳ; (Xenophon, *Education of Cyrus* 3.1.15)
Do you think, Cyrus, that it is better to inflict the punishments for your own good or to your own detriment?

You need not find a translation for πότερον (πότερα) in direct questions. It simply informs you that a second half to the question is coming up.

☑ πότερον (πότερα) is often omitted:

ἢν χρήματα πολλὰ ἔχῃ, ἐᾷς πλουτεῖν ἢ πένητα ποιεῖς; (Xenophon, *Education of Cyrus* 3.1.12)
If he has a lot of money, do you let him (go on) be(ing) rich or make him poor?

Deliberative questions

In questions where the speaker asks what he <u>is to</u> do or say, the present or aorist subjunctive is used. Negative μή.

εἴπωμεν ἢ σῑγῶμεν; (Euripides, *Ion* 758)
Are we to speak or keep silent?

ποῖ τράπωμαι; ποῖ πορευθῶ; (Euripides, *Hecuba* 1099)
Where can I turn? Where can I go to?

Deliberative questions can be introduced by βούλει or βούλεσθε (θέλεις, θέλετε in poetry):

βούλει εἴπω ταῦτα;
Do you want me to say these things? (*literally,* Am I to say these things? Do you want me to?)

| Indirect questions

Socrates asked his wife <u>why she nagged him so much</u>.

A verb in which the *voice, ears, mind* or *one of the senses* is used (e.g. ask, know, deliberate, discover) followed by a word which asks a question (who? when? why?, etc.) is followed in Greek by an interrogative pronoun plus a verb in the indicative, though in historic sequence (see pp. 152–3) the optative may be used — with a less 'vivid' force than the indicative. (Cf. Indirect statement with ὅτι and ὡς (pp. 154–5).)

The interrogatives used in direct questions (column **1** above, pp. 161–2) can be used, but the indirect interrogative pronouns, adjectives and adverbs (column **2** above) are more commonly found.

Note that εἰ (less frequently ἆρα) = whether, if.

If the indicative is used, the verb in the indirect question is in the tense of the direct question (the tense actually used). If the optative is used, it too will be in the tense actually used by the questioner.

ἐρωτῶντες εἰ λῃσταί εἰσιν (Thucydides 1.5.2)
asking if they were pirates

ἠρώτησα εἰ βούλοιτο (βούλεται) χορεύειν.
I asked if he wanted to dance.

ἐρωτᾷ ὅτι βούλεσθε.
He is asking what you want.

ἤρετο αὐτὸν εἰ βληθείη (ἐβλήθη). (Xenophon, *Education of Cyrus* 8.3.30)
He asked him if he had been hit.

ἴδωμεν ἆρ᾽ οὑτωσὶ γίγνεται πάντα. (Plato, *Phaedo* 70d)
Let us see whether everything is produced exactly like this.

Double indirect questions:

πότερον (πότερα) ... ἤ ...
εἰ ... ἤ ...   } whether ... or ...
εἴτε ... εἴτε ...

διηρώτα τὸν Κῦρον πότερον βούλοιτο (βούλεται) μένειν ἢ ἀπιέναι.
(Xenophon, *Education of Cyrus* 1.3.15)
She asked Cyrus whether he wanted to stay or go away.

Note that a deliberative subjunctive (see p. 164) in an indirect question in historic sequence can either remain in the subjunctive or be replaced by an optative, e.g.

ὁρῶντες δὲ αὐτοὺς οἱ Πλαταιῆς ἀπειλημμένους ἐβουλεύοντο εἴτε κατακαύσωσιν ὥσπερ ἔχουσιν, ἐμπρήσαντες τὸ οἴκημα, εἴτε τι ἄλλο χρήσωνται. (Thucydides 2.4.6)
Seeing that they were cut off, the Plataeans deliberated whether they should burn them as they were, by setting fire to the house, or dispose of them in some other way.

The verbs in the indirect question could have been κατακαύσειαν and χρήσαιντο.

The negative in indirect questions is generally οὐ, but after εἰ both οὐ and μή are found:

ἤρετο τὸν δῆμον εἰ οὐκ αἰσχύνοιντο γελῶντες. (Aeschines 1.84)
He asked the people whether they were not ashamed of laughing.

ἤρετό με … εἰ μὴ μέμνημαι. (Aeschines 2.36)
He asked me whether I did not remember.

☑ After verbs of *saying*, *knowing* and *perceiving* (but <u>not</u> after verbs of *asking* and rarely after negatives), the relative pronoun is often used:

οἶδά σε ὃς εἶ.
I know (you) who you are. ['I know thee who thou art.']

Note how the subject of the subordinate clause has been extracted from it and made the object of the main verb. This happens in a number of constructions.

| Practice sentences

Translate into English or Greek as appropriate:

1 οἴμοι, τίς ἀνήρ; ἆρ' Ὀδυσσέως κλύω; (Sophocles, *Philoctetes* 976)
2 μῶν τί σε ἀδικεῖ Πρωταγόρᾶς; (Plato, *Protagoras* 310d)
3 ἆρ' οὐχ ὕβρις τάδ[ε]; (Sophocles, *Oedipus at Colonus* 883)
4 τί οὖν ποιήσαντος, ὦ ἄνδρες Ἀθηναῖοι, κατεχειροτονήσατε τοῦ Εὐάνδρου; (Demosthenes 21.176)
5 οἴμοι, τί δράσω; ποῖ φύγω μητρὸς χέρας; (Euripides, *Medea* 1271)
6 ἀλλὰ ποῦ δὴ βούλει καθιζόμενοι ἀναγνῶμεν; (Plato, *Phaedrus* 228e)
7 ἐπειδάν τίς τινα φιλῇ, πότερος ποτέρου φίλος γίγνεται, ὁ φιλῶν τοῦ φιλουμένου ἢ ὁ φιλούμενος τοῦ φιλοῦντος; (Plato, *Lysis* 212a-b)
8 ἠρώτᾱ αὐτὸν πόσον χρῡσίον ἔχοι. (Xenophon, *Anabasis* 7.8.1)
9 θαυμάζω πότερα ὡς κρατῶν βασιλεὺς αἰτεῖ τὰ ὅπλα ἢ ὡς διὰ φιλίᾱν δῶρα. (Xenophon, *Anabasis* 2.1.10)
10 ἀπορῶν ποῖ τράποιτο ἐπὶ λόφον τινὰ καταφεύγει (historic present, see p. 218). (Xenophon, *Education of Cyrus* 3.1.4)
11 κατάλεξον· τίς πόθεν εἰς [this would be εἶ in Attic] ἀνδρῶν; (Homer, *Odyssey* 1.169)

12 I asked him how many soldiers he was bringing and what sort of hopes he had.

13 I asked him who the handsome man was.

14 Where are you now? Where did you set out from, and where are you going to?

15 Are you stupid? You are stupid, aren't you? Surely you aren't stupid?

16 Are you stupid or intelligent, (my) husband?

17 What am I to do?

18 I do not know who she is.

19 My wife asked me if I knew how (ὡς) weak she was.

20 I am at a loss (about) whether she is stupid or intelligent.

21 I am aware of your intelligence (=I know you, how intelligent you are).

22 My wife will tell you whether she is coming to Athens or not.

Commands, exhortations and wishes

Do this. Don't do that.
Let's do this.
If only we were doing this.
I told her not to do that.

| Commands

Commands are expressed by the **imperative**:

λέγε.   εἰπέ.
Speak!   Speak!

ποίει τοῦτο.   ἐλθέτω δεῦρο.
Do this!   Let him come here!

χαιρόντων.
Let them rejoice!

For the use of the aorist imperative as opposed to the present imperative, see the note on aspect on p. 61.

| Prohibitions

Prohibitions are expressed <u>either</u> by μή with the present imperative <u>or</u> by μή with the aorist subjunctive.

μὴ ποίει τοῦτο.
Do not do this! (*i.e.,* Don't keep doing this!)

μὴ ποιήσῃς τοῦτο.
Do not do this!

For the distinction between the present and the aorist, see p. 61.

The third person of the aorist imperative can occur in prohibitions.

Note that ὅπως and ὅπως μή are used with the future indicative to express commands and prohibitions (often colloquially):

νῦν οὖν ὅπως σώσεις μ[ε]. (Aristophanes, *Clouds* 1177)
So now save me!

ὅπως μοι … μὴ ἐρεῖς ὅτι ἔστι τὰ δώδεκα δὶς ἕξ. (Plato, *Republic* 337b)
See to it that you do not tell me that twelve is twice six.

It seems as if a word such as σκόπει or σκοπεῖτε (=see to it!) has dropped out in front of ὅπως.

| Exhortations

Exhortations are expressed by the first person of the subjunctive. Negative μή.

ἴωμεν.   μὴ τοῦτο ποιῶμεν.
Let's go!   Let's not do this

μαχώμεθα ἀνδρείως.
Let's fight bravely!

☑ Imperatives and subjunctives can be preceded by ἄγε (ἄγετε), φέρε or ἴθι (come!). The singular form can still be used when the verb that follows is in the plural:

ἀλλ' ἄγε μίμνετε πάντες. (Homer, *Iliad* 2.331)
But come on, all of you, wait!

| Wishes

Wishes for the future are expressed by the optative, either with or without an introductory εἴθε or εἰ γάρ (if only!). Negative μή.

εἴθ', ὦ λῷστε σύ, φίλος ἡμῖν γένοιο. (Xenophon, *Hellenica* 4.1.38)
If only, you excellent fellow, you would become our friend!

μηκέτι ζῴην ἐγώ. (Aristophanes, *Clouds* 1255)
May I no longer live!

Wishes for the present or past, if they are unattained, are expressed by the imperfect or the aorist indicative, introduced by εἴθε or εἰ γάρ, <u>which cannot be omitted</u>. The imperfect expresses present time or continuous past time; the aorist expresses past momentary time. Negative μή.

εἴθε τοῦτο ἐποίει.
If only he was doing this!

εἰ γὰρ μὴ ἐγένετο τοῦτο.
If only this had not happened!

Wishes for the present and the past can also be expressed, chiefly in poetry, by ὤφελον (=ought — aorist of ὀφείλω (I owe)) in the appropriate person, followed by the present or aorist infinitive. ὤφελον can be preceded by εἴθε, εἰ γάρ or ὡς. Negative μή.

εἰ γὰρ ὤφελον, ὦ Κρίτων, οἷοί τ᾽ εἶναι οἱ πολλοὶ τὰ μέγιστα κακὰ
ἐργάζεσθαι. (Plato, *Crito* 44d)
If only, Crito, the majority were able to do the greatest evils! (present infinitive — referring to now)

ὤφελε τοῦτο ποιῆσαι.
If only he had done this! (aorist infinitive — referring to the past)

εἰ γὰρ ὤφελον can stand on its own, meaning 'If only!'

| Indirect commands

Indirect commands are expressed by the infinitive, as in English. Negative μή (just as μή would have been used in the direct command).

κελεύω αὐτοὺς ἀπιέναι.
I order them to go away.

ἔλεγον αὐτοῖς μὴ ἀδικεῖν. (Thucydides 2.5.5)
They told them not to act unjustly.

Some useful verbs of commanding:

κελεύω	I order
παρακαλέω	I encourage
ἀπαγορεύω	I forbid (always with μή)

The following take the dative with the infinitive:

διακελεύομαι	I encourage, direct
παραινέω	I encourage, advise
ἀγγέλλω	I bring a message to, command
παραγγέλλω	I give orders
(προ)εῖπον	I commanded

| Practice sentences

Translate into English or Greek as appropriate:

1 ἄγε δὴ ἀκούσατε καὶ ἄλλα. (Xenophon, *Apology of Socrates* 14)
2 μὴ κατὰ τοὺς νόμους δικάσητε, ἄνδρες δικασταί· μὴ βοηθήσητε τῷ πεπονθότι δεινά· μὴ εὐορκεῖτε. (Demosthenes 21.211 — the context is ironical.)
3 μή μ᾽ ἐκδίδασκε τοῖς φίλοις εἶναι κακήν. (Sophocles, *Electra* 395)
4 ὅπως οὖν ἔσεσθε ἄξιοι τῆς ἐλευθερίας ἧς κέκτησθε. (Xenophon, *Anabasis* 1.7.3)
5 ἐβόων ... ἀλλήλοις μὴ θεῖν δρόμῳ ἀλλ᾽ ἐν τάξει ἕπεσθαι. (Xenophon, *Anabasis* 1.8.19)
6 μήποτ᾽ ὤφελον λιπεῖν τὴν Σκῦρον. (Sophocles, *Philoctetes* 969)
7 Let's not dispute but converse.
8 Come on, go away (pl.) and-don't (μηδέ) stay here.
9 If only I were not in Athens! If only I could go to Cyprus!
10 I advise you to leave the city as quickly as possible.
11 I told my wife not to desire older men.

Because

The cause of an action is often expressed in Greek by the participle with ἅτε, ὡς, etc. (see p. 137). The words below, followed by a finite verb, are also used:

ὅτι[1]
διότι
διόπερ
οὕνεκα (poetic)
} because (i.e. the causal clause explains what has preceded it, e.g. 'I am looking after you because you are sick')

ἐπεί
ἐπειδή
ὅτε
ὁπότε
} since (i.e. the causal clause comes first, e.g. 'Since you are sick, I am looking after you')

ὡς as, because, since (i.e. the causal clause comes first or second)

The verb in the causal clause is regularly in the indicative. However, if the reason is *alleged* or *reported*, the optative is used after a verb in a historic tense (see pp. 152–3). This is because indirect statement is clearly implied (see p. 155).

> κήδετο γὰρ Δαναῶν, ὅτι ῥα θνῄσκοντας ὁρᾶτο. (Homer, *Iliad* 1.56)
> For she pitied the Danaans because she saw them dying.

> [οἱ Ἀθηναῖοι] τὸν Περικλέᾱ ... ἐκάκιζον ὅτι στρατηγὸς ὢν οὐκ ἐπεξάγοι. (Thucydides 2.21.3)
> The Athenians abused Pericles on the grounds that, though he was a general, he did not lead them out.

Cause can also be expressed by a relative clause:

> θαυμαστὸν ποιεῖς ὃς ἡμῖν ... οὐδὲν δίδως. (Xenophon, *Memorabilia* 2.7.13)
> You are doing something astonishing in giving us nothing.

---

[1] The 'ι' of ὅτι does not elide.

| Practice sentences

Translate into English or Greek as appropriate:

1 ὅτε τοίνυν τοῦθ' οὕτως ἔχει, προσήκει προθύμως ἐθέλειν ἀκούειν τῶν βουλομένων συμβουλεύειν. (Demosthenes 1.1)

2 ἐτύγχανε γὰρ ἐφ' ἁμάξης πορευόμενος διότι ἐτέτρωτο. (Xenophon, *Anabasis* 2.2.14)

3 I admire her because she happens to be so virtuous.

4 The Athenians condemned Socrates to death (see pp. 15–16) on the grounds that he corrupted the young men.

Purpose clauses

	to see	
I went to Athens	in order to see	the poet.
	so as to see	

To express purpose, Greek most frequently uses ἵνα, ὅπως, ὡς[1] (in order that). Negative μή.[2]

The sequence of tenses (pp. 152–3) means that if the verb in the main clause is in a <u>primary</u> tense, the verb in the purpose clause will be in the <u>subjunctive</u>. If the verb in the main clause is in a <u>historic</u> tense, the verb in the purpose clause <u>may</u> be in the <u>optative</u>:

> παρακαλεῖς ἰατροὺς ὅπως μὴ ἀποθάνῃ; (Xenophon, *Memorabilia* 2.10.2)
> Are you calling in doctors so that he may not die?

> φίλων ᾤετο δεῖσθαι, ὡς συνέργους ἔχοι. (Xenophon, *Anabasis* 1.9.21)
> He thought he needed friends in order that he might have helpers.

However, after a historic main verb, the subjunctive is often found in place of the optative:

> (τὰ πλοῖα) Ἀβροκόμας … κατέκαυσεν ἵνα μὴ Κῦρος διαβῇ.
> (Xenophon, *Anabasis* 1.4.18)
> Abrocomas burnt the boats so that Cyrus might (may) not cross.

In this vivid usage, we enter Abrocomas' mind and find him thinking 'I will burn the boats so that Cyrus <u>may</u> not cross'. In fact, Xenophon, together with Plato and the poets, prefers the optative. Herodotus and Thucydides prefer the vivid subjunctive:

> ξυνεβούλευε … τοῖς ἄλλοις ἐκπλεῦσαι ὅπως ἐπὶ πλέον ὁ σῖτος ἀντίσχῃ. (Thucydides 1.65.1)
> He advised the others to sail out so that the food might last longer.

---

[1] ἵνα is preferred by Aristophanes, Herodotus, Plato and the orators, ὅπως by Thucydides and Xenophon. ὡς is rare in prose, except in Xenophon, but common in tragedy.

[2] ἵνα (etc.) μηδείς *or* μή τις (in order that … no one); ἵνα (etc.) μήποτε (in order that … never); etc.

☑ μή can be used in place of ἵνα μή, etc. to mean 'in order that not':

μὴ σπεῦδε πλουτεῖν μὴ ταχὺς πένης γένῃ. (Menander, *Sententiae* 358)
Do not hasten to be rich, lest you swiftly become poor.

This use of μή is common in poetry and in Xenophon and Plato.

Note two other ways of expressing purpose:
1 with the future participle (see p. 136).
2 with the relatives, especially ὅς, ἥ, ὅ or (less commonly) ὅστις, ἥτις,
ὅτι, with the future indicative (even after historic tenses). Negative μή.

φημὶ δὴ δεῖν ἡμᾶς ... πρεσβείαν πέμπειν, ἣ τοὺς μὲν διδάξει ταῦτα,
τοὺς δὲ παροξυνεῖ. (Demosthenes 2.11)
I say that we must send an embassy to tell (*literally,* which will tell)
some people these things and provoke others.

κρύψω τόδ᾽ ἔγχος τοὐμόν ... ἔνθα μή τις ὄψεται. (Sophocles, *Ajax*
659)
I shall hide this sword of mine where no one will see it.

☑ When translating English into classical Greek, be very careful to obey
the above rules and do NOT use the infinitive, which is probably the
most common way of expressing purpose in English. In order to
discover in what person to put the verb in a purpose clause introduced
by the English infinitive, it can be helpful to change the 'to' of the
infinitive to 'in order that' and adjust the English accordingly, e.g.:

I went to Athens to see the comedy.
I went to Athens in order that I might see the comedy.

N.B. Purpose clauses are often referred to as **final clauses**.

| Practice sentences

Translate into English or Greek as appropriate:

1 ἀφῖκόμην ὅπως σοῦ πρὸς δόμους ἐλθόντος εὖ πράξαιμί τι.
   (Sophocles, *Oedipus Tyrannus* 1005)

2 κατάμενε ἵνα καὶ περὶ σοῦ βουλευσώμεθα. (Xenophon, *Anabasis* 6.6.28)

3 ὁ βάρβαρος τῷ μεγάλῳ στόλῳ ἐπὶ τὴν Ἑλλάδα δουλωσόμενος ἦλθεν. (Thucydides 1.18.2)

4 [δεῖ ἡμᾶς] πρεσβείαν ... πέμπειν ἥτις ταῦτ' ἐρεῖ καὶ παρέσται τοῖς πράγμασιν. (Demosthenes 1.2)

5 [οὐ] χρημάτων ἕνεκα ἔπρᾱξα ταῦτα, ἵνα πλούσιος ἐκ πένητος γένωμαι. (Lysias 1.4)

6, 7, Translate in <u>three</u> different ways:
& 8 I sent my sister to find the girls and bring them here.

9 Medea will deceive her husband in order to punish him.

10 I was working carefully to avoid making a mistake.

Result clauses

Arachne wove <u>so</u> skilfully that she even challenged Athene.
Atalanta ran <u>too</u> fast for anyone to catch her.

In these sentences you can see how the words 'so' and 'too' <u>signpost</u> the result clause. A result clause in Greek is often signposted by one of the following words:

οὕτως (οὕτω before consonants)	in such a way, so (with adjectives and adverbs)
τοιοῦτος, τοιαύτη, τοιοῦτο	such
τοσοῦτος, τοσαύτη, τοσοῦτο(ν)	so great, so much
ἐς τοσοῦτο(ν)	so far, to such an extent, to such a pitch (of)

The result is then expressed by ὥστε or sometimes ὡς (as, that, so that)

(a) followed by the infinitive (negative μή) when the result arises naturally or as a likelihood from the action of the main verb, i.e. when the action of the main verb is as important to the meaning as the action of the verb in the result clause.

κραυγὴν πολλὴν ἐποίουν καλοῦντες ἀλλήλους ὥστε καὶ τοὺς πολεμίους ἀκούειν. (Xenophon, *Anabasis* 2.2.17)
They were making a loud noise as they called each other so that (with the result that) even the enemy could hear.

The subject of the infinitive is in the accusative if it is <u>different</u> from that of the main verb. If it is the same, it is either omitted or in the nominative.

The infinitive will almost always be used in a result clause when the main verb is negative:

οὐδεὶς πώποτ' εἰς τοσοῦτ' ἀναιδείας ἀφῖκεθ' ὥστε τοιοῦτόν τι τολμῆσαι ποιεῖν. (Demosthenes 21.62)
No one has ever reached such a pitch of shamelessness as to dare to do anything of that kind.

(b) followed by the indicative (negative οὐ) when the actual occurrence of the result is stressed, i.e. when the action of the verb in the subordinate clause is more important than that of the verb in the main clause.

οὕτω διάκειμαι ὑφ' ὑμῶν ὡς οὐδὲ δεῖπνον ἔχω ἐν τῇ ἐμαυτοῦ χώρᾳ. (Xenophon, *Hellenica* 4.1.33)
I have been treated by you in such a way that I can't even have a meal in my own land.

At times it is difficult to distinguish between these two usages in Greek.

Note

1 The comparative adjective or adverb with ἤ ὥστε can represent the English word 'too':

τοὺς ... παῖδας αὐτῶν ζηλῶ ὅτι νεώτεροί εἰσιν ἤ ὥστε εἰδέναι οἵων πατέρων ἐστέρηνται. (Lysias, *Epitaphius* 72)
I envy their children because they are too young to know (*literally,* more young than so as to know) what sort of father they have been deprived of.

When used in this way, ὥστε must be followed by the infinitive. However, it is not a common usage.

2 The infinitive with ὥστε can express purpose:

πᾶν ποιοῦσιν ὥστε δίκην μὴ διδόναι. (Plato, *Gorgias* 479c)
They do everything so as not to be punished.

Here they are doing everything to achieve the <u>result</u> of not being punished.

3 ὥστε can simply introduce a sentence as a connecting word meaning 'the result was that ...', 'so', 'therefore'. Used in this way, it has no effect on the verb that follows. The sentence in **(a)** on the previous page concludes as follows:

... ὥστε καὶ τοὺς πολεμίους ἀκούειν· ὥστε οἱ μὲν ἐγγύτατα τῶν πολεμίων καὶ ἔφυγον. (Xenophon, *Anabasis* 2.2.17)
... so that even the enemy could hear; as a result, those of the enemy who were nearest actually fled.

4 Result clauses are often called **consecutive clauses**.

| ἐφ' ᾧ and ἐφ' ᾧτε *on condition that*

ἐφ' ᾧ and ἐφ' ᾧτε (on condition that) are followed usually by the infinitive, or occasionally by the future indicative. The negative is almost always μή.

ἀφίεμέν σε, ἐπὶ τούτῳ μέντοι, ἐφ' ᾧτε μηκέτι ... φιλοσοφεῖν. (Plato, *Apology* 29c)
We release you, but on this condition, that you will no longer be a philosopher.

ξυνέβησαν ... ἐφ' ᾧ ἐξίασιν ἐκ Πελοποννήσου ὑπόσπονδοι καὶ μηδέποτε ἐπιβήσονται αὐτῆς. (Thucydides 1.103)
They made an agreement on condition that they should leave the Peloponnese under a truce and never set foot on it again.

| Practice sentences

Translate into English or Greek as appropriate:

1 ἐπιπίπτει (historic present – see p. 218) χιὼν ἄπλετος (immense, *i.e.*, an immense fall of) ὥστε ἀπέκρυψε καὶ τὰ ὅπλα καὶ τοὺς ἀνθρώπους. (Xenophon, *Anabasis* 4.4.11)

2 καὶ εἰς (= on) μὲν τὴν ὑστεραίαν οὐχ ἧκεν· ὥσθ' οἱ Ἕλληνες ἐφρόντιζον. (Xenophon, *Anabasis* 2.3.25)

3 οὐκ ἔχομεν ἀργύριον ὥστε ἀγοράζειν τὰ ἐπιτήδεια. (Xenophon, *Anabasis* 7.3.5)

4 ᾔσθοντο αὐτὸν ἐλάττω ἔχοντα δύναμιν ἢ ὥστε τοὺς φίλους ὠφελεῖν. (Xenophon, *Hellenica* 4.8.23)

5 οἱ δὲ ἔφασαν ἀποδώσειν (τοὺς νεκροὺς) ἐφ' ᾧ [τοὺς Ἕλληνας] μὴ καίειν τὰς οἰκίας. (Xenophon, *Anabasis* 4.2.19)

6 The prison was so badly (φαύλως) guarded that all the prisoners escaped.

7 He is so clever that he is never punished.

8 Helen is too beautiful not to find a new lover.

9 Helen is very beautiful; so she will find a new lover.

10 She forgave her daughter on condition that she would obey her in the future.

Verbs of fearing and precaution

| Fearing

- When English uses the infinitive after verbs of fearing, so does Greek:

  φοβοῦμαι τοῦτο ποιεῖν.
  I am afraid to do this.

  The subject of the two verbs will be the same.

- Fear for the <u>future</u> — Greek uses μή[1] (negative μὴ οὐ) with the subjunctive or optative depending on sequence of tenses (see pp. 152–3). As in purpose clauses, the subjunctive can be used in historic sequence for a more vivid effect (see p. 174).

  δέδοικα μὴ … ὥσπερ οἱ λωτοφάγοι ἐπιλαθώμεθα τῆς οἴκαδε ὁδοῦ. (Xenophon, *Anabasis* 3.2.25)
  I am afraid that like the lotus-eaters we may forget the way home.

  ἔδεισαν οἱ Ἕλληνες μὴ προσάγοιεν πρὸς τὸ κέρας. (Xenophon, *Anabasis* 1.10.9)
  The Greeks were afraid that they might advance against their flank.

  ἐφοβοῦντο μή τι παθῇ. (Xenophon, *Symposium* 2.11)
  They were afraid that something might happen to him.

  δέδιμεν μὴ οὐ βέβαιοι ἦτε. (Thucydides 3.57.4)
  We are afraid you may prove unreliable.

---

[1] Compare English 'lest'. If one fears that something may happen, one hopes that it will <u>not</u>.

- Fear for the <u>present</u> or <u>past</u> — Greek uses μή (negative μὴ οὐ) with the indicative:

  δέδοικα σ', ὦ πρεσβῦτα, μὴ πληγῶν δέει. (Aristophanes, *Clouds* 493)
  I fear, old man, that you need blows. (*literally*, I fear you, old man, that ...cf. p. 166)

  δείδω μὴ δὴ πάντα θεὰ νημερτέα εἶπεν. (Homer, *Odyssey* 5.300)
  I fear that all that the goddess said was true.

The commonest verbs of fearing are φοβοῦμαι and δέδοικα. Note also φόβος ἐστί (there is fear) and κίνδυνός ἐστι (there is danger). They are used with the same construction.

| Precaution

Verbs of precaution (e.g. I take care, I am on my guard, I see to it that) can be followed by μή (negative μὴ οὐ) with the same construction as verbs of fearing.

Their commonest construction, however, is ὅπως (negative ὅπως μή) with the future indicative:

  εὐλαβούμενοι ὅπως μὴ ... οἰχήσομαι. (Plato, *Phaedo* 91c)
  taking care that I do not go away.

Verbs used to introduce this construction:

ὁράω	
σκοπέω, σκοπέομαι	I see to something
σκεπτέον ἐστί	
εὐλαβέομαι	
φροντίζω	I am on my guard
φυλάττω, φυλάττομαι	

☑ For urgent exhortations, ὅπως or ὅπως μή can stand on their own without the introductory word meaning 'see to it' (e.g. σκόπει, ὁρᾶτε):

ὅπως δὲ τοῦτο μὴ διδάξεις μηδένα. (Aristophanes, *Clouds* 824)
But be careful not to teach anyone this.

Cf. p. 169.

| Practice sentences

Translate into English or Greek as appropriate:

1 ὥστε οὐ τοῦτο δέδοικα, μὴ οὐκ ἔχω ὅτι δῶ (I can give) ἑκάστῳ τῶν φίλων ... ἀλλὰ μὴ οὐκ ἔχω ἱκανοὺς οἷς δῶ. (Xenophon, *Anabasis* 1.7.7)

2 ἐφοβήθην ... καὶ ἔτι καὶ νῦν τεθορύβημαι (= I am agitated) μή τινες ὑμῶν ἀγνοήσωσί με. (Aeschines 2.4)

3 ὅπως τοίνυν περὶ τοῦ πολέμου μηδὲν ἐρεῖς. (Demosthenes 19.92)

4 φροντίζω (I am worried) μὴ κράτιστον ᾖ μοι σῖγᾶν. (Xenophon, *Memorabilia* 4.2.39)

5 I am afraid to die.

6 He was afraid that the doctor might not help him.

7 The girls took care to stay at home.

8 I am afraid that the enemy may defeat us. See that you fight bravely!

Conditional sentences

Conditional clauses in English are introduced by 'if', 'unless', 'if ... not', 'whether ... or'. You must be careful not to confuse them with indirect questions (see p. 164–6). Conditional sentences are made up of a conditional clause and a main clause which gives the consequence or implication of the conditional clause. In both English and Greek the conditional clause usually (but by no means always) comes first.

Here are some examples to illustrate them.

> If Penelope was ever angry, I was a wretched husband.
> If Penelope is unfaithful, I am a wretched husband.
> If Penelope proves unfaithful, I shall be a wretched husband.
> If Penelope were to be unfaithful, I would be a wretched husband.
> If Penelope had been unfaithful, I would have been a wretched husband.

In both English and Greek, conditional sentences can simply state facts, as in the first three above and in the axiomatic:

> If a triangle has two equal sides, it is an isosceles triangle.

In this grammar we call conditionals of this type **open (any time)**.

The fourth and fifth sentences above fall into the categories of **remote** (referring to the **future**) and **unfulfilled** (referring to the **present** or **past**) respectively. Comparison between the third and fourth sentences will show how the fourth is expressed in a doubtful or remote way in contrast with the third. The words 'were to' and 'would' signal this remoteness.

In the fifth sentence, we are in the area of the unreal or the impossible. Penelope was not unfaithful and the condition is unfulfilled. Here the words 'would have been' (or 'should have been') are the key.

Thus it is natural to call conditionals of these two kinds remote and unfulfilled.

We call the 'if' clause the **protasis** and the main clause the **apodosis**. (Protasis is the Greek for 'what is put forward', i.e. a premise; apodosis is the Greek for 'giving back, return', i.e. an answering clause.)

☑ The Greek for 'if' is εἰ, and for 'whether ... or' εἴτε ... εἴτε.

The negative in the protasis is μή. The negative in the apodosis is οὐ unless the clause has its own reasons for using μή.[1]

| Open conditionals

Past and present

In past and present time, the verbs in both the protasis and the apodosis go into the natural tense of the indicative:

εἰ ταῦτα λέγεις, καλῶς λέγεις.
If you are saying these things, you are talking sense.

εἰ ταῦτα ἔλεγες, καλῶς ἔλεγες.
If you were saying these things, you were talking sense.

εἰ ταῦτα εἶπες, καλῶς εἶπες.
If you said these things, you talked sense.

Future

An open conditional referring to the future <u>can</u> have its verb in the future indicative. However, Greek tends to take into account the fact that the future is uncertain and to use the indefinite construction (see pp. 195–6) in the protasis, i.e. ἐάν + the subjunctive (ἐάν is made up of εἰ and ἄν):[2]

ἐὰν ταῦτα λέγῃς, καλῶς ἐρεῖς.
If you say these things, you will be talking sense.

If the future indicative is used, it insists on the inevitability of the consequence. It is thus appropriate to emotional appeals, threats and

---

[1] In addition to being a statement, an apodosis may be a command, a wish or a question. μή may stand in these constructions.

[2] In Ionic, in Thucydides and in tragedy, ἤν appears in place of ἐάν. ἄν is also found in Attic Greek: Plato uses it more commonly than ἐάν.

warnings. In this case the word for 'if' is not ἐάν but εἰ:

εἰ ταῦτα ἐρεῖς, ἀποκτενῶ σε.
If you say these things, I shall kill you.

The future indicative is used in the apodosis whether the verb in the protasis is in the subjunctive or the indicative.

N.B. In the last two examples above, what looks like a present tense in English ('you say') in fact refers to the future. We call this a **concealed future**, and if you are translating from English into Greek, it is vital that you spot it.

 If the conditional clause begins with ἐάν and the verb in the main clause is in the <u>present</u> indicative, it is likely that ἐάν is introducing an indefinite conditional clause, where the rules relating to indefinite clauses affect those for conditional clauses. See pp. 195–6.

ἐὰν τοῦτο ποιῇς, σὲ ἐπαινῶ.
If (= whenever) you do this, I (always) praise you.

If the conditional clause had not been indefinite, the sentence would have read:

εἰ τοῦτο ποιεῖς, σὲ ἐπαινῶ.
If you are doing this, I praise you.

| Unfulfilled and remote conditionals

Present

To convey <u>present</u> time in unfulfilled conditionals, Greek uses the <u>imperfect</u> indicative in the protasis and the <u>imperfect</u> indicative with ἄν[1] in the apodosis.

---

[1] ἄν is often placed before or after the verb but it can be attached to negatives, to interrogatives or to any emphatic word. It never comes first word in a sentence or a clause.

εἰ ταῦτα ἔλεγες, καλῶς ἄν ἔλεγες.
If you were saying these things, you would be talking sense.

It is an interesting – and helpful – coincidence that 'you were saying', which is in fact an English subjunctive, is identical to the imperfect tense.

Past

To convey past time in unfulfilled conditionals, Greek uses the aorist indicative in the protasis and the aorist indicative with ἄν in the apodosis.

εἰ ταῦτα εἶπες, καλῶς ἄν εἶπες.
If you had said these things, you would have talked sense.

☑ ἦ or ἦν is usually considered to be the imperfect of εἰμί (I am). In this construction it may also convey the meaning of the aorist:

πολὺ ἄν θαυμαστότερον ἦν (imperfect meaning), εἰ ἐτιμῶντο. (Plato, *Republic* 489b)
It would be far more wonderful if they were being honoured.

Contrast:

ὥστ', εἰ παρῆσθα (aorist meaning), τὸν θεὸν τὸν νῦν ψέγεις
εὐχαῖσιν ἄν μετῆλθες εἰσιδὼν τάδε.
(Euripides, *Bacchae* 712-3)
And so, if you had been there, you would have sought with prayers the god whom now you criticize, after seeing these things.

The imperfect indicative is used to refer to an act as continuing or being repeated in the past. So

εἰ ταῦτα ἔλεγες, καλῶς ἄν ἔλεγες

could mean 'if you had been saying these things, you would have been talking sense' as well as 'if you were saying these things (now), you would be talking sense' (see the last example but one). The context should make the meaning clear.

Future

Remote conditionals referring to the <u>future</u> use εἰ + the <u>optative</u> in the protasis and the <u>optative</u> with ἄν in the apodosis.

> εἰ ταῦτα λέγοις, καλῶς ἂν λέγοις.
> If you were to say these things, you would talk sense.

Note that in English 'you said' could be substituted for 'you were to say'.

☑ The times at which the protasis and apodosis are set may be different. This is especially common with:

εἰ + aorist indicative, imperfect indicative + ἄν.
If I had done X, I would (now) be doing Y.

Greek uses the construction appropriate to each clause. So:

> εἰ μὴ ὑμεῖς ἤλθετε, ἐπορευόμεθα ἂν ἐπὶ βασιλέα. (Xenophon, *Anabasis* 2.1.4)
> If you had not come, we would now be marching against the king.

Examine the following sentences. To which of the categories described above does each belong?

> εἰ μὲν (Ἀσκληπιὸς) θεοῦ ἦν, οὐκ ἦν ... αἰσχροκερδής· εἰ δ' αἰσχροκερδής, οὐκ ἦν θεοῦ. (Plato, *Republic* 408c)
> If Asclepius was the son of a god, he was not greedy for profit; if he was greedy for profit, he was not the son of a god.

> ἐὰν οὖν ἴῃς νῦν, πότε ἔσει οἴκοι; (Xenophon, *Education of Cyrus* 5.3.27)
> So if you go now, when will you be at home?

> εἰ ταῦτα λέξεις, ἐχθαρῇ μὲν ἐξ ἐμοῦ. (Sophocles, *Antigone* 93)
> If you say these things, you will be hated by me.

εἰ μὲν περὶ ἄλλου τινὸς ἢ τοῦ σώματος ... Καλλίᾱς ἠγωνίζετο,
  ἐξήρκει ἄν μοι καὶ τὰ παρὰ τῶν ἄλλων εἰρημένα. (Lysias 5.1)
If Callias were fighting for anything apart from his life, even the things
  said by everybody else would be enough for me.

καὶ ἴσως ἄν ... ἀπέθανον εἰ μὴ ἡ ἀρχὴ διὰ ταχέων κατελύθη. (Plato,
  Apology 32d)
And perhaps I would have been killed, had not the government
  speedily been put down.

οὐ πολλὴ ἂν ἀλογίᾱ εἴη, εἰ φοβοῖτο τὸν θάνατον ὁ τοιοῦτος; (Plato,
  Phaedo 68b)
Would it not be a great absurdity if such a man were to fear death?

εἰ ἦσαν ἄνδρες ἀγαθοί, ὡς σὺ φής, οὐκ ἄν ποτε ταῦτα ἔπασχον.
  (Plato, *Gorgias* 516e)
If they had been good men, as you say, they would never have suffered
  these things (repeatedly).

| Conditional sentences in indirect statement

I said that if I made a mistake I would take responsibility for it.

Protasis

If the main verb (the verb of *saying*, etc.) is in a primary tense (see pp.
152–3), the verb in the protasis of the indirect statement is <u>unchanged</u>. If
the main verb is in a historic tense, the verb in the protasis can be put into
the optative, but only if it is in a primary tense. (It may, of course, be in the
optative already.) If the original subjunctive of the protasis is changed to
the optative, εἰ must replace ἐάν.

Apodosis

If the construction with ὅτι or ὡς is used, the rules on pp. 159–60 are
followed. If the infinitive or participle is used, this will be in the same
tense as the indicative or optative of the direct speech, with the present
infinitive and

participle standing in for the imperfect. If ἄν would have been used in the direct statement, it must remain.

ἐὰν τοῦτο ποιῆτε, πάντα καλῶς ἕξει.
If you do this, all will be well. (direct speech)

ἡγοῦμαι, ἐὰν τοῦτο ποιῆτε, πάντα καλῶς ἕξειν.
I consider that, if you do this, all will be well. (primary sequence)

ἡγούμην, εἰ τοῦτο ποίοιτε, πάντα καλῶς ἕξειν.
I considered that, if you did this, all would be well. (historic sequence)

In the last example ἐὰν τοῦτο ποιῆτε could have been kept from the direct speech.

εἰ τοῦτο ποιοίης, πάντα καλῶς ἂν ἔχοι.
If you were to do this, all would be well. (direct speech)

ἡγοῦμαι, εἰ τοῦτο ποιοίης, πάντα καλῶς ἂν ἔχειν.
I think that, if you were to do this, all would be well. (primary sequence)

| Practice sentences

Translate into English or Greek as appropriate:

1 ἐὰν δ' ἔχωμεν χρήμαθ', ἕξομεν φίλους. (Menander, *Sententiae* 165)

2 εἰ δ' ἀναγκαῖον εἴη ἀδικεῖν ἢ ἀδικεῖσθαι, ἑλοίμην ἂν μᾶλλον ἀδικεῖσθαι ἢ ἀδικεῖν. (Plato, *Gorgias* 469c)

3 εἰ μὴ καθέξεις γλῶσσαν, ἔσται σοι κακά. (Euripides, fragment 5.1)

4 ταῦτα δὲ οὐκ ἂν ἐδύναντο ποιεῖν, εἰ μὴ καὶ διαίτῃ μετρίᾳ ἐχρῶντο. (Xenophon, *Education of Cyrus* 1.2.16)

5 οὐκ ἂν ἐποίησεν Ἀγασίας ταῦτα εἰ μὴ ἐγὼ αὐτὸν ἐκέλευσα. (Xenophon, *Anabasis* 6.6.15)

6 εὖ ἴστε … ὅτι, ἐάν τις εἰς τὴν Ἑλλάδα μέλλῃ ἰέναι, πρὸς ἑσπέραν δεῖ πορεύεσθαι. (Xenophon, *Anabasis* 5.7.6)

7 If I were to become queen, I would be the happiest of women.

8 Whether she is queen or not, I still hate her.

9 If she sees me, she will choose me as (ὡς) her husband.

10 If you had not been stupid, you would have obeyed her.

11 If I were a rich man, I would be giving money to all the poor citizens.

12 If I'd known you were coming, I'd have baked (= ὀπτάω) a cake (= μᾶζα, f.).

Impersonal verbs

It's raining.	It's annoying.
It's pouring.	It hurts.
It's snowing.	It's a bore.
It's thundering.	It upsets me that …

In English, **impersonal verbs** (i.e. verbs used with 'it' as a sort of empty or dummy subject) are frequently used of the weather, and in other contexts too.

Greek has the following impersonal usages to describe the weather:

ὕει	νείφει
it's raining	it's snowing
βροντᾷ	ἀστράπτει
it's thundering	the lightning flashes
χειμάζει	ἔσεισε
it's stormy	there was an earthquake

The most common impersonal verbs are the following:

- with the accusative and the infinitive

  δεῖ με (τοῦτο πράττειν) it is necessary for me (to do this),
  I must do this

  χρή με … it is necessary for me …

  The imperfect of χρή is χρῆν or ἐχρῆν. English cannot say 'I oughted to do this', but Greek can:

  ἐχρῆν με τοῦτο πράττειν.
  I ought <u>to have done</u> this.

- with dative and the infinitive

  δοκεῖ μοι (τοῦτο ποιεῖν) it seems (a good idea) to me,
  I have decided (to do this)

  πρέπει μοι …
  προσήκει μοι … } it is fitting for me …

  συμφέρει μοι … it is of use to me …,
  it is advantageous for me …

  λῡσιτελεῖ μοι … it is profitable for me …

ἔξεστί μοι ...
πάρεστί μοι ... } it is possible/permitted for me, I can

- with the dative of the agent and the genitive of the thing
  μέτεστί μοι τούτου   I have a share in this
  μέλει μοι τούτου   I care for this
  μεταμέλει μοι τούτου   I am sorry about this

Note the following expressions:

ὄψε ἦν   it was late
καλῶς ἔχει   it's fine
δηλοῖ
δῆλόν ἐστι } it is evident (*i.e.*, the situation shows)
συμβαίνει   it happens
κηρύττει, ἐκήρυξε   (the herald) proclaims, the proclamation
               was made

☑ Impersonal verbs use the <u>accusative absolute</u> rather than the genitive absolute (see p. 141–2).

Note the following accusative neuter participles: δέον, ἐξόν, μετόν, παρόν, προσῆκον, μέλον, μεταμέλον, παρέχον (= it being possible), δοκοῦν, δόξαν.

Some examples:

ἀδελφεοκτόνος τε, οὐδὲν δέον, γέγονα. (Herodotus 3.65)
And I have become the killer of my brother when there was no need.

ἀλλὰ τί δή, ὑμᾶς ἐξὸν ἀπολέσαι, οὐκ ἐπὶ τοῦτο ἤλθομεν; (Xenophon, *Anabasis* 2.5.22)
But why then, when it was possible for us to destroy you, did we not proceed to do it?

| Practice sentences

Translate into English or Greek as appropriate:

1 ἡμέρᾱς ... ἐχείμαζε τρεῖς. (Herodotus 7.191)
2 δῆλον γὰρ ὅτι οἶσθα, μέλον γέ σοι. (Plato, *Apology* 24d)
3 οἱ δ' οὐ βοηθήσαντες, δέον, ὑγιεῖς ἀπῆλθον; (Plato, *Alcibiades 1* 115b)

4 ἀλλὰ τί ἡμῖν, ὦ μακάριε Κρίτων, οὕτω τῆς τῶν πολλῶν δόξης μέλει;
(Plato, *Crito* 44c)

5 παρέχον ... τῆς Ἀσίης πάσης ἄρχειν εὐπετέως, ἄλλο τι αἱρήσεσθε;
(Herodotus 5.49)

6 Since it is necessary to go away, let us go willing(ly).

7 It is of no advantage for us to kill the queen.

8 Though the men act bravely, Artemis decided (use ἔδοξε) to show herself better than them.

9 I am sorry about my bad deeds.

10 It was late; nevertheless it was possible for me to reach Athens.

The gerundive

This young man is by no means <u>to be despised</u>.
One word remains <u>to be said</u>.

As well as using χρή and δεῖ (see p. 190), Greek has another way of saying
'ought', 'must' or 'should'. This is the **gerundive**, a passive verbal
adjective (the equivalent of 'to be despised' and 'to be said' in the above
sentences). It expresses the necessity for the action of the verb to be
performed, and ends in -τέος, -τέα, -τέον, declining like φίλιος (see p. 32).
It usually adds the ending to the verb stem which has the same form as
that of the aorist passive (e.g. (ἐ)παύσ(θην)) with φ changing to π and
χ to κ:

παύω → παυστέος	to be stopped
ποιέω → ποιητέος	to be done
λαμβάνω → ληπτέος	to be taken (aor. ἐλήφθην)
πράττω → πρᾱκτέος	to be done (aor. ἐπράχθην)
πείθω → πειστέος	to be persuaded *or* to be obeyed[1]

Note the following less easily identifiable gerundives:

φέρω → οἰστέος	to be carried, endured (cf. fut. οἴσω)
εἶμι → ἰτέος	to be travelled (cf. 2 pl. ἴτε)

Gerundives are used in two ways:

- as straightforward adjectives. The agent is in the <u>dative</u>:

  ὠφελητέα σοι ἡ πόλις ἐστίν. (Xenophon, *Memorabilia* 3.6.3)
  The city must be helped (*literally,* is to be helped) by you.

- in the impersonal form -τέον (n. sg.) or -τέα (n. pl.), as the equivalent
  of χρή or δεῖ with the infinitive (this usage is essential for intransitive
  verbs), e.g.

  ποιητέον (*or* ποιητέα) (ἐστί) = ποιεῖν χρή *or* δεῖ
  It is necessary to do ...

---

[1] Note that verbs with different meaning in the active and middle have <u>both</u>
available in the gerundive.

σπευστέον (ἐστί) = σπεύδειν χρή *or* δεῖ
It is necessary to hurry.

The agent can be in the dative (as in the last example) or in the accusative (as if it were accompanying χρή or δεῖ).

ἡμῖν γ᾽ ὑπὲρ τῆς ἐλευθερίας ἀγωνιστέον. (Demosthenes 9.70)
We at any rate must struggle for freedom.

In this example, ἡμῖν could equally well have been ἡμᾶς.

Since the <u>sense</u> of the gerundive tends to be active, it can take an accusative object:

τὸν βουλόμενον ... εὐδαίμονα εἶναι σωφροσύνην διωκτέον καὶ ἀσκητέον. (Plato, *Gorgias* 507c)
It is necessary that the man who wishes to be happy should pursue and practise moderation.

οἰστέον τάδε. (Euripides, *Orestes* 769)
These things must be endured.

As can be seen from the above examples, ἐστί (the word for 'it is', or the equivalent) is frequently omitted.

| Practice sentences

Translate into English or Greek as appropriate:
1 ἐψηφίσαντο δὲ οἱ Λακεδαιμόνιοι τὰς σπονδὰς λελύσθαι καὶ πολεμητέα εἶναι. (Thucydides 1.88.1)
2 φημὶ δὴ διχῇ βοηθητέον εἶναι τοῖς πράγμασιν ὑμῖν. (Demosthenes 1.17)
3 οὐδὲ γὰρ τοῦτο φευκτέον ἀλλὰ πάντων μάλιστα διωκτέον τῷ νοῦν ἔχοντι. (Plato, *Theaetetus* 167d)
4 You must say one thing and do another. (Use gerundives.)
5 We must send the girls to a safe place. (Use the gerundive.)
6 The boys must go to the city and the girls to the fields. (Use the gerundive.)

Indefinite clauses

I like the books you write.	I like whatever books you write.
I welcomed her when she arrived.	I welcomed her whenever she arrived.

The word 'ever' added to 'what' and 'when' in the sentences in the second column above makes the clause in which it appears **indefinite**. In Greek, verbs in primary (i.e. present or future) time in an indefinite clause are in the subjunctive with ἄν.[1] Verbs in historic (i.e. past) time are in the optative without ἄν.

Negative μή.

 Since in most <u>other</u> constructions involving the subjunctive and optative, the subjunctive is not used with ἄν while the optative will have ἄν somewhere nearby, the indefinite construction is generally easy to recognize.

Some examples:

ἃ ἂν βούλωνται ἕξουσιν.
They will have whatever they want.

ὅτε βούλοιτο, τοῦτο ἔπρᾱττεν.
Whenever he wanted to, he used to do this.

Note these indefinite conditional clauses:

γελᾷ δ' ὁ μῶρος κἄν (= καὶ ἐάν) τι μὴ γελοῖον ᾖ. (Menander,
Sententiae 108)
The fool laughs (every time) even if something is not funny.

ἐάν is made up of εἰ and ἄν. (cf. p. 184.)

---

[1] ἄν never comes first word in a clause (or a sentence). In this construction it is likely to be closely attached to the word ('if', 'which', etc.) which begins the indefinite clause, often coalescing with it (e.g. ὅταν for ὅτε (when) ἄν, ἐπειδάν for ἐπειδὴ (when) ἄν, ἐάν for εἰ (if) ἄν).

ἐτίμα δ' εἴ τι καλὸν πράττοιεν, παρίστατο δ' εἴ τις συμφορὰ συμβαίνοι. (Xenophon, *Agesilaus* 7.3)
He honoured (them) if (ever) they performed a noble action and he stood by them if (ever) any misfortune befell them.

For this type of conditional, see pp. 184–5.

| Practice sentences

Translate into English or Greek as appropriate:

1 συμμαχεῖν καὶ προσέχειν τὸν νοῦν τούτοις ἐθέλουσιν ἅπαντες, οὓς ἂν ὁρῶσι παρεσκευασμένους καὶ πράττειν ἐθέλοντας ἃ χρή. (Demosthenes 4.6)

2 καὶ οὓς μὲν ἴδοι εὐτάκτως καὶ σιωπῇ ἰόντας (here = marching), προσελαύνων αὐτοῖς τίνες τε εἶεν ἠρώτα, καὶ ἐπεὶ πύθοιτο ἐπῄνει. (Xenophon, *Education of Cyrus* 5.3.55)

3 εἴ τίς γέ τι αὐτῷ προστάξαντι καλῶς ὑπηρετήσειεν, οὐδενὶ πώποτε ἀχάριστον εἴασε τὴν προθυμίαν. (Xenophon, *Anabasis* 1.9.18)

4 He praised whatever Penelope did.

5 Whenever I find out that she is in Athens, I leave the city as quickly as possible.

6 If ever I see my students struggling, I try to help them.

7 If ever I saw my students struggling, I tried to help them.

Time clauses

Time clauses referring to the present or the past have their verb in the appropriate tense of the indicative unless they are indefinite,[1] in which case they follow the indefinite construction (pp. 195–6).

ἕως ἐστὶ καιρός, ἀντιλάβεσθε τῶν πρᾱγμάτων. (Demosthenes 1.20)
While there is an opportunity, take matters in hand.

ἡνίκα δὲ δείλη ἐγίγνετο, ἐφάνη κονιορτός. (Xenophon, *Anabasis* 1.8.8)
When it was getting to be afternoon, a cloud of dust appeared.

ὅταν σπεύδῃ τις αὐτός, χὠ θεὸς συνάπτεται. (Aeschylus, *Persae* 742)
Whenever a man is eager himself, god too works with him.

Unlike English, the Greek language reflects the view that the future is inevitably indefinite. Therefore, in Greek, time clauses referring to the future are indefinite and therefore follow the indefinite construction for primary time, i.e. the verb is in the subjunctive with ἄν. This difference between the languages means that it is often better to translate words such as ὅταν not by 'whenever' but simply by 'when'.

ὅταν δὴ μὴ σθένω, πεπαύσομαι. (Sophocles, *Antigone* 91)
When my strength fails, I shall stop.

ἡνίκα δ' ἄν τις ὑμᾶς ἀδικῇ, ἡμεῖς ὑπὲρ ὑμῶν μαχούμεθα. Xenophon, *Education of Cyrus* 4.4.11)
But whenever anyone wrongs you, we shall fight for you.

---

[1] A time clause is indefinite:
  (a) when it refers to the future
  (b) when it happens an indefinite number of times
  (c) when it continues for an indefinite period.

Some temporal conjunctions:

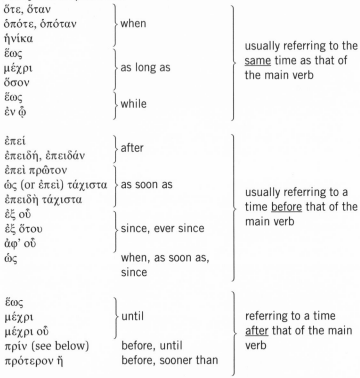

ὅτε, ὅταν ὁπότε, ὁπόταν ἡνίκα	when	usually referring to the <u>same</u> time as that of the main verb
ἕως μέχρι ὅσον	as long as	
ἕως ἐν ᾧ	while	

ἐπεί ἐπειδή, ἐπειδάν	after	usually referring to a time <u>before</u> that of the main verb
ἐπεὶ πρῶτον ὡς (or ἐπεὶ) τάχιστα ἐπειδὴ τάχιστα	as soon as	
ἐξ οὗ ἐξ ὅτου ἀφ' οὗ	since, ever since	
ὡς	when, as soon as, since	

ἕως μέχρι μέχρι οὗ	until	referring to a time <u>after</u> that of the main verb
πρίν (see below)	before, until	
πρότερον ἤ	before, sooner than	

πρότερον (before) can be used as an adverb looking forward to a temporal clause beginning with ἕως or πρίν (see below):

> καὶ *οὐ **πρότερον*** ἐπαύσαντο *ἕως* τὴν ... πόλιν εἰς στάσεις καὶ τὰς μεγίστας συμφορὰς κατέστησαν. (Lysias 25.26)
> They did not stop (before) until they divided the city into factions.

| πρίν

If πρίν is followed by the infinitive, it will mean 'before'. Otherwise translate it as 'until'.

For speakers of English, helpful rules for the use of πρίν are:

1 If πρίν can be translated <u>either</u> by 'before' <u>or</u> 'until' and the main verb is negative, its clause follows the rule of other temporal clauses (given above):

οὐ χρή με ἐνθένδε ἀπελθεῖν πρὶν ἂν δῶ δίκην. (Xenophon, *Anabasis* 5.7.5)
I must not go from here before (until) I pay the penalty.

οὐ πρόσθεν ἐπαύσαντο πρὶν ἐξεπολιόρκησαν τὸν Ὄλουρον.
(Xenophon, *Hellenica* 7.4.18)
They did not stop before (until) they had taken Olourus by siege.

2 If πρίν can be translated <u>only</u> by 'before', it is followed by the <u>infinitive</u> unless the main verb is negatived or contains a negative idea (e.g. ἀπαγορεύω (I forbid)). (In that case its clause follows the rule of other temporal clauses.)

οἱ καὶ πρὶν ἔμ᾽ εἰπεῖν ὁτιοῦν εἰδότες (Demosthenes 18.50)
those who know even before I say anything

λέγεται γὰρ Ἀλκιβιάδην, πρὶν εἴκοσιν ἐτῶν εἶναι, Περικλεῖ ... τοιάδε διαλεχθῆναι περὶ νόμων. (Xenophon, *Commentaries* 1.2.40)
For it is said that Alcibiades, before he was twenty years old, discussed such things about laws with Pericles.

πρότερον ἤ (sooner than, before) follows the same construction.

☑ The subject of the infinitive is regularly in the accusative unless it is the same as that of the main verb, in which case it is in the nominative.

| Practice sentences

Translate into English or Greek as appropriate:

1 ἦν γάρ ποτε χρόνος ὅτε θεοὶ μὲν ἦσαν, θνητὰ δὲ γένη οὐκ ἦν. (Plato, *Protagoras* 320c)

2 ἐπειδὴ δὲ ὀλιγαρχίᾱ ἐγένετο, οἱ τριάκοντα (= the Thirty (oligarchs)) αὖ μεταπεμψάμενοί με πέμπτον αὐτον (see p. 146) ... προσέταξαν ἀγαγεῖν ἐκ Σαλαμῖνος Λέοντα τὸν Σαλαμίνιον ἵνα ἀποθάνοι. (Plato, *Apology* 32c)

3 ἐχρῆν ... μὴ πρότερον περὶ τῶν ὁμολογουμένων συμβουλεύειν πρὶν περὶ τῶν ἀμφισβητουμένων ἡμᾶς ἐδίδαξαν. (Isocrates 4.19)

4 ἐπειδὰν ἅπαντ᾽ ἀκούσητε, κρίνατε. (Demosthenes 4.14)

5 ἐπὶ ... τὸ ἄκρον ἀναβαίνει Χειρίσοφος πρίν τινας αἰσθέσθαι τῶν πολεμίων (take τῶν πολεμίων with τινας). (Xenophon, *Anabasis* 4.1.7)

6 Go away before your wife sees you kissing the prostitute.

7 When you arrive in Athens, come to my house straight away.

8 I waited at home until the Thirty sent a man to arrest me. When he arrived, I was very frightened.

9 When you are angry with me, I am very unhappy.

10 Ever since you left Athens, she appears to be the happiest of women.

Verbs of preventing, hindering and denying

Minos tried to prevent Daedalus and Icarus from leaving Crete.
The mob in the street hindered his journey to the Pnyx.

In Greek, verbs of *preventing*, *hindering* and *denying* (all of which contain some sort of negative sense) are followed by the <u>infinitive</u>, which can often be preceded by μή.[1] When the verb of preventing is negated itself, or is part of a question expecting the answer <u>no</u>, Greek usually follows it with μή οὐ with the infinitive:

> καταρνῇ μὴ δεδρᾱκέναι τάδε; (Sophocles, *Antigone* 442)
> Do you deny that you did this?

> τίνα οἴει ἀπαρνήσεσθαι μὴ οὐχὶ (see p. 204) καὶ αὐτὸν ἐπίστασθαι τὰ δίκαια; (Plato, *Gorgias* 461c)
> Who do you think will deny that he too understands what is just?
> (The answer 'nobody' is implied.)

However, κωλύω (I hinder, prevent), whether negated or not, is usually followed by the infinitive without μή:

> τὸν μὲν Φίλιππον παρελθεῖν …οὐκ ἐδύναντο κωλῦσαι. (Demosthenes 5.20)
> They could not prevent Philip from passing through.

Other usages after these verbs:

- τὸ μή or τὸ μὴ οὐ with the infinitive:

> τὸν πλεῖστον ὅμιλον τῶν ψῑλῶν εἶργον τὸ μὴ … τὰ ἐγγὺς τῆς πόλεως κακουργεῖν. (Thucydides 3.1.2)
> They prevented the biggest company of the light-armed troops from ravaging the parts near the city.

---

[1] The μή is redundant, but strengthens the negative idea of the verb. Compare Shakespeare, *Comedy of Errors* 4.2.7: 'First he denied you had in him no right.'

οὐδὲν γὰρ αὐτῷ ταῦτ’ ἐπαρκέσει τὸ μὴ οὐ πεσεῖν. (Aeschylus, *Prometheus Bound* 918)
For in his case, these things will not be enough (to prevent him) from falling.

Contrast:

ἐπέσχον τὸ εὐθέως τοῖς Ἀθηναίοις ἐπιχειρεῖν. (Thucydides 7.33.3)
They refrained from immediately attacking the Athenians.

- τοῦ μή or τοῦ μὴ οὐ (or simply τοῦ) with the infinitive. This is the **genitive of separation**.

πᾶς γὰρ ἀσκὸς δύ’ ἄνδρας ἕξει τοῦ μὴ καταδῦναι. (Xenophon, *Anabasis* 3.5.11)
For each wine-skin will prevent two men from sinking.

Verbs and expressions of preventing, etc.:

εἴργω	
ἐμποδών εἰμι (+ dat.)[1]	} I prevent
κωλύω	I hinder, prevent
ἀπαγορεύω (+ dat.)	
ἀπεῖπον (+ dat.)	} I forbid
οὐκ ἐάω	
(ἀπ)ἀρνέομαι (and other compounds)	I deny
ἀπέχομαι	I refrain
φυλάττομαι	I guard against

| Practice sentences

Translate into English or Greek as appropriate:

1 ὦ Ἱππία, ἐγώ τοι οὐκ ἀμφισβητῶ μὴ οὐχὶ σὲ εἶναι σοφώτερον ἢ ἐμέ. (Plato, *Hippias Minor* 369d)

2 οἱ θεῶν ἡμᾶς ὅρκοι κωλύουσι πολεμίους εἶναι ἀλλήλοις. (Xenophon, *Anabasis* 2.5.7)

3 καὶ φημὶ δρᾶσαι κοὐκ ἀπαρνοῦμαι τὸ μὴ (δρᾶσαι). (Sophocles, *Antigone* 443)

4 καὶ ἐπὶ ἓξ ἔτη … καὶ δέκα μῆνας ἀπέσχοντο μὴ ἐπὶ τὴν ἑκατέρων γῆν στρατεῦσαι. (Thucydides 5.25.3)

---

[1] ἐμποδών is an adverb meaning 'in the way'. It does not change its form.

5 Minos tried to prevent Daedalus from flying from Crete.

6 I refrained from saying the terrible words which I had in mind.

7 Arachne could not stop herself from challenging Athene.

8 My mother forbade me to come to the theatre.

The negatives

Note the following commonly used compound negatives:

οὐ	μή	
οὐδείς, οὐδεμία, οὐδέν	μηδείς, μηδεμία, μηδέν	no one
οὐ ... ποτέ	μὴ ... ποτέ	
οὐδέποτε	μηδέποτε	never
οὔποτε	μήποτε	
οὐκέτι	μηκέτι	no longer
οὔπω	μήπω	not yet
οὐδέ	μηδέ	and not, not even[1]
οὔτε ... οὔτε ...	μήτε ... μήτε ...	neither ... nor
οὐδαμῶς	μηδαμῶς	in no way

☑ οὐ becomes οὐκ when the next word begins with a vowel with a smooth breathing, and οὐχ when the next word begins with a vowel with a rough breathing. οὐχί is a more emphatic denial than οὐ.

As a rule, compound negatives which follow another negative (simple or compound) confirm it rather than cancel it as in English:[2]

> μὴ ταῦτα λέγε μηδέποτε.
> Never say these things.

Two negatives cancel each other out – making a strong affirmative – only if a simple negative follows another negative:

> οὐδὲ τὸν Φορμίων᾽ ἐκεῖνος οὐχ ὁρᾷ. (Demosthenes 36.46)
> *literally,* nor does he not see Phormio, *i.e.* he sees Phormio plainly enough.

---

[1] When translating οὐδέ and μηδέ, note that these have both the weak meaning 'and not' and the strong meaning 'not even'.

[2] But compare colloquial 'I can't get no satisfaction'.

| The uses of οὐ and μή

οὐ is the negative of *facts* and *statements*. μή is the negative of *will* and *thought*.

οὐ is used in:	μή is used in:
statements, direct and indirect whether in the indicative, optative or infinitive	all commands, exhortations and wishes
direct questions that expect the answer 'yes', and in normal indirect questions	direct questions that expect the answer 'no', and in all deliberative questions
relative and temporal clauses unless indefinite	all indefinite clauses including temporal clauses
result clauses with the indicative	result clauses with the infinitive
	purpose clauses with the subjunctive, optative, future indicative or future participle; also relative purpose clauses
the normal apodosis (main clause) of conditional sentences	the protasis ('if ...' clause) of conditional or concessive sentences
the participle when it communicates a statement	the participle with conditional or generic force (see below)
	generic relative clauses (see below)
the infinitive in indirect statement (but see p. 156 for μή after verbs such as 'hope', 'promise', 'swear')	the infinitive except in indirect statement

Generic μή (indicating a *class* or *group*):

ταῦτα ἃ οὐ βούλεται πράττειν ἀποφεύγει.
He runs away from the (particular) things he doesn't want to do.

ταῦτα ἃ μὴ βούλεται πράττειν ἀποφεύγει.
He runs away from the sort of things he doesn't want to do.

ἐφ' οἷς γὰρ μὴ φρονῶ σῖγᾶν φιλῶ. (Sophocles, *Oedipus Tyrannus* 569)
For I am accustomed to be silent over (the kind of) matters I do not understand.

Also contrast:

ἐκεῖνοι οἱ οὐδὲν εἰδότες
those men who know nothing

οἱ μηδὲν εἰδότες
men who know nothing, the ignorant

τῶν οὐκ ὄντων (Thucydides 2.44.3)
of the dead (*literally*, of those who do not exist)

ὁ μηδὲν ἀδικῶν οὐδενὸς δεῖται νόμου. (Menander, fragment 845)
The (sort of) man who does no wrong needs no law.

| Double negatives

1 The uses of the double negative μὴ οὐ after verbs of *fearing* and *precaution* and of *preventing*, *hindering* and *denying* are explained on pp. 180–1 and pp. 201–2.

2 οὐ μή with the <u>aorist subjunctive</u> (less commonly the present subjunctive) or the <u>future indicative</u> expresses a strong negative statement:

οὐ μὴ παύσωμαι φιλοσοφῶν. (Plato, *Apology* 29d)
I will not cease from searching for wisdom.

οὔ τοι μήποτέ σ' ... ἄκοντά τις ἄξει. (Sophocles, *Oedipus at Colonus* 176)
No one shall ever take you against your will.

3 In Greek drama, οὐ μή may be used with the second person singular of the <u>future indicative</u> to express a strong prohibition:

οὐ μὴ προσοίσεις χεῖρα μηδ' ἄψῃ πέπλων. (Euripides, *Hippolytus* 606)
Don't lay your hand (on me) or touch my garment!

οὐ μὴ ληρήσεις. (Aristophanes, *Clouds* 367)
Don't talk rubbish!

Particles

Greek particles are short words which never change and serve one or more of the following functions:

1 They can connect one utterance to a preceding one.

2 They can qualify a word, phrase or clause ('even', 'also', 'anyway', etc.).

3 They can 'colour' a word, phrase or clause, conveying what is often expressed in spoken English by volume and tone of voice ('he <u>said</u> that', 'he said <u>that!</u>') and in written English by italics, exclamation marks, inverted commas, etc.

For reasons of convenience, a number of adverbs and conjunctions are included under this heading.

Those words marked * cannot stand first in a sentence.

ἀλλά	but; oh well
	ἀλλ' ἴωμεν (Plato, *Protagoras* 311a) Oh well, let's go!
ἀλλὰ γάρ	but in fact
οὐ μὴν ἀλλά	nevertheless, notwithstanding
οὐ μόνον ... ἀλλὰ καί ...	not only ... but also ...
ἄλλως τε καί	especially
ἄρα	then (logical), so then, after all (of realization)
	μάτην ἄρ', ὡς ἔοικεν, ἥκομεν. So it seems we have come in vain after all.
ἆρα	introduces a question (see pp. 162–3) ἆρ' οὐ; introducing a question expecting the answer 'yes' ἆρα μή; introducing a question expecting the answer 'no'
ἀτάρ	but , however (usually poetic, but found in Xenophon and Plato)

αὖ*   on the other hand, on the contrary, then again

οἱ Ἕλληνες ... ἐπῇσαν ... οἱ δ' αὖ βάρβαροι οὐκ
ἐδέχοντο. (Xenophon, *Anabasis* 1.10.11)
The Greeks came against them, but the barbarians for
their part did not wait to take them on.

γάρ*   for; in fact, indeed; yes, for ...; no, for ...

ὁμολογεῖς οὖν περὶ ἐμὲ ἄδικος γεγενῆσθαι; ἦ γὰρ
ἀνάγκη. (Xenophon, *Anabasis* 1.6.8)
So do you agree that you have been unjust towards me?
Indeed I have to.

φῂς τάδ' οὖν; ἃ μὴ φρονῶ γὰρ οὐ φιλῶ λέγειν μάτην.
(Sophocles, *Oedipus Tyrannus* 1520)
Do you agree to this? No, for I am not accustomed to
say pointlessly what I do not mean.

γάρ simply meaning 'for' is used very frequently in Greek.
There is often no need to translate it into English.

πῶς γὰρ οὔ;   for how could it not be? *i.e.,* how could it be otherwise?
thus, of course

γε* (enclitic) at least, anyway, at any rate, indeed

σὺ δ' οὐ λέγεις γε [αἰσχρά], δρᾷς δέ μ' εἰς ὅσον δύναι.
(Euripides, *Andromache* 239)
You're not (indeed) <u>saying</u> these disgraceful things
about me, but you're doing them as forcefully as you
can.

γε can correspond to an exclamation mark:

εὖ γε.   ἀμαθής γ' εἶ.
Well done! Why, you <u>are</u> stupid!

γοῦν*   at any rate, at all events (from γε οὖν)

δέ*   but, and

δ' οὖν*   but in fact; however that may be

δή*   this word puts an increased volume of voice on the
preceding word, or serves as an emphatic gesture to

sustain or revive the hearer's attention. It can convey scepticism or sarcasm:

> ἅπαντες δή ἴστε δή
> absolutely all   you know, of course
>
> Σωκράτης ὁ σοφὸς δή (Plato, *Apology* 27a)
> Socrates the wise (!)

δήπου*   doubtless, you will admit, I presume

δήπου often has a touch of irony or doubt in contexts where certainty would be expected:

> ὑμεῖς ... ἴστε δήπου ὅθεν ἥλιος ἀνίσχει. (Xenophon, *Anabasis* 5.7.6)
> You know, I presume, where the sun rises.

δῆτα   really, in truth

In answers, expressing agreement:

> γιγνώσκεθ᾽ ὑμεῖς ἥτις ἔσθ᾽ ἡδὶ ἡ γυνή; γιγνώσκομεν δῆτ[α]. (Aristophanes, *Thesmophoriazousae* 606)
> Do you know who this woman is? Yes, indeed we do.

οὐ δῆτα   certainly not (strong or indignant denial)

εἴτε ...   whether ... or ... (see p. 165 and p. 184)
  εἴτε ...

ἤ ... ἤ ...   either ... or ...

ἦ   in truth

> ἦ καλῶς λέγεις. (Plato, *Gorgias* 447c)
> In truth you speak well, *i.e.* what you say is truly splendid.

For ἦ introducing a question, see p. 162.

ἦ μήν   leads into strong assertions, threats and oaths:

> ὄμνυμι θεοὺς ... ἦ μὴν μήτε με Ξενοφῶντα κελεῦσαι ἀφελέσθαι τὸν ἄνδρα μήτε ἄλλον ὑμῶν μηδένα. (Xenophon, *Anabasis* 6.6.17)
> I swear by the gods that neither Xenophon nor anyone else among you told me to rescue the man.

καί   and, actually, also, even

καί ... καί ... both ... and ...

... τε* (...) καί ...	both ... and ... Note that as an enclitic τε must be translated into English in front of the word which it comes after in Greek: X τε καὶ Y = both X and Y.
καὶ γάρ	and in fact
καὶ δή	and above all (introducing a climax)
καὶ δὴ καί	and especially, and in particular, and what is more
καίτοι	and yet
μέν* ... δέ* ...	on the one hand ... but on the other hand ... Sometimes the δέ clause is missing and must be supplied in thought. To put the English word 'while' (expressing not time but contrast) between the μέν and δέ clauses may be a good way of translating these words, but should not be overused.

> ἡ μὲν ψυχὴ πολυχρόνιόν ἐστι, τὸ δὲ σῶμα
>   ἀσθενέστερον καὶ ὀλιγοχρονιώτερον. (Plato, *Phaedo* 87d)
> The soul lasts for a long time, while the body is weaker and lasts for a shorter time.

Remember that δέ means '<u>but</u> on the other hand', not simply 'on the other hand'. Thus the following sentence does not work:

> τῶν μὲν Λακεδαιμονίων ἐν τῇ Ἀττικῇ ὄντων, οἱ δὲ
>   Ἀθηναῖοι ἐν τῇ πόλει ἔμενον.
> When the Spartans on the one hand were in Attica, but the Athenians on the other hand stayed in the city.

μὲν οὖν*	certainly, in fact; no, on the contrary

> Crito: ἄτοπον τὸ ἐνύπνιον, ὦ Σώκρατες.
> Socrates: ἐναργὲς μὲν οὖν. (Plato, *Crito* 44b)
> The dream was strange, Socrates.
> No, on the contrary, it was clear.

The speaker corrects his own words or those of another speaker. μὲν οὖν can also signal transition to a new subject. In addition, it can also simply combine the usual sense of μέν and οὖν.

μέντοι*	however, certainly

> φιλοσόφῳ μὲν ἔοικας ... ἴσθι μέντοι ἀνόητος ὤν. (Xenophon, *Anabasis* 2.1.13)
> You are like a philosopher ... know however that you are stupid.

> ἀληθέστατα μέντοι λέγεις. (Plato, *Sophist* 245b)
> Certainly, what you say is very true.

μήν*	indeed, however (especially after a negative)
καὶ μήν	and indeed, and yet but here comes ... *i.e.* signalling the entry of a new character in tragedy:

> καὶ μὴν ἄναξ ὅδ[ε] ... πάρα. (Sophocles, *Oedipus at Colonus* 549–50)
> But look, here is the king

τί μήν;	(on its own) but of course (introducing a question) what indeed? but what?

> ἀλλὰ τί μὴν δοκεῖς; (Plato, *Theaetetus* 162b)
> But what is your opinion?

μήτε ... μήτε ...	neither ... nor ...
ὅμως	nevertheless
οὐδέ	and not, not even (also μηδέ – see pp. 204–6))
οὔτε ... οὔτε ...	neither ... nor ... (also μήτε ... μήτε ... – see pp. 204–6)
οὔκουν, οὐκοῦν	Give priority to the part of the word with the accent: οὔκουν means 'certainly not' οὐκοῦν means simply 'therefore', or alternatively 'not ... therefore?' (introducing a question expecting the answer 'yes', like ἆρ' οὐ (see above, p. 207)).
οὖν*	therefore, and so
δ' οὖν*	see under δέ

που* (enclitic)   που as an enclitic means 'I suppose' or 'somewhere'.

τε* (enclitic)   and (τε is translated into English <u>in front of</u> the word
which it comes <u>after</u>.)

> Ζεῦ ἄλλοι τε θεοί   (Homer, *Iliad* 6.476)
> O Zeus <u>and</u> the other gods

... τε* ... τε*
... καί ...   both ... and ... and ... (see under καί)

τοι* (enclitic)   you <u>do</u> realize (The speaker feels that the hearer's attitude
or behaviour should be affected by what is said.)

> τῶν τοι ματαίων ἀνδράσιν φρονημάτων
> ἡ γλῶσσ' ἀληθὴς γίγνεται κατήγορος.
>   (Aeschylus, *Seven Against Thebes* 438–9)
> So it is true that their tongue is the true accuser of
>   men's vain conceits.

τοίνυν*   further, therefore

ὡς   as, when, since, because
how!
that ..., e.g.

> ἔλεγον ὡς ...
> they said <u>that</u> ...

ὡς with the future participle is used to express purpose
(see p. 136).

Note that accented ὥς means 'thus, in this way'.

 Greek likes to have a connecting word at the beginning (usually first
or second word) of each sentence. δέ (and, but) will often be found at
the outset of a passage and throughout it (as second word). Often
there is no need to translate it into English.

| Practice exercise

What are the Greek connecting words you would use if you were translating this paragraph of *Mansfield Park* by Jane Austen? Fill in the gaps and give Greek equivalents for the words underlined. I have generally put the dots after the first word of their clause but you are welcome to use a connecting word that would in fact begin the clause.

> She ... was then taken into a parlour, so small that her first conviction was of its being only a passage-room to something better, and she stood for a moment expecting to be invited on; but when she saw there was no other door, and that there were signs of habitation before her, she ... called back her thoughts, reproved ... herself, and grieved lest they should have been suspected. Her mother, however, could not stay long enough to suspect anything. She ... was gone again to the street-door to welcome William. ... 'Oh! my dear William, [' she said, '] how glad I am to see you. But have you heard about the "Thrush"? She ... is gone out of the harbour already; three days before we had any thought of it; and I do not know what I am to do about Sam's things, they ... will never be ready in time; for she may have her orders tomorrow, perhaps. It ... takes me quite unawares. And now you must be off for Spithead too. Campbell ... has been here, quite in a worry about you; and now what shall we do? I ... thought to have had such a comfortable evening with you, and here everything comes upon me at once.'

Ψευδεῖς φίλοι

(Words easily confused)

ἀγείρω	I gather together
ἐγείρω	I wake (somebody) up, arouse
ἐπαινέω	I praise, commend
παραινέω + dat.	I advise
αἱρέω, αἱρήσω, εἷλον	I take
αἴρω, ἀρῶ, ἦρα	I raise
αὐλή f.	courtyard
αὐλός m. (poetic)	reed-pipe
αὐτός	himself
αὐτός = ὁ αὐτός	the same
αὐτή	she (herself) or same
αὐτή = ἡ αὐτή	the same
αὕτη (f. of οὗτος)	this woman
ἀϋτή f. (poetic)	battle-cry
αὐτήν = ἑαυτήν	herself
αὐτόν = ἑαυτόν	himself
βαθύς -εῖα -ύ	deep
βαρύς -εῖα -ύ	heavy
βραδύς -εῖα -ύ	slow
βραχύς -εῖα -ύ	short
βίος m.	life
βίᾱ f.	strength, force
δέω	I bind
δέω + gen.	I need, lack
δέομαι + gen.	I need; I beg
δεῖ	it is necessary

δέον	it being necessary
δέος, δέους n.	fear
εἰμί	I am
εἶμι	I shall go
ἔρις, -ιδος f.	strife, discord
ἔρως, -ωτος m.	love
ἐρῶ (άω)	I love passionately
ἐρῶ (έω)	*future of* λέγω (I say)
ἐρωτάω	I ask
θέᾱ f.	spectacle
θεά f. (poetic)	goddess
θεῶν	of the gods
θέων (participle)	running
ἴον n. (poetic)	violet
ἴός m. (poetic)	arrow
ἴός m. (poetic)	poison
ἴός m.	rust
ἴοις	you go (*2 sg. opt. of* εἶμι)
ἰών -οῦσα -όν	going (*participle of* εἶμι)
ἴσθι	be! (*sg. imperative*)
ἴσθι	know! (*sg. imperative*)
ἴθι	go! (*sg. imperative*)
καινός -ή -όν	new, strange
κεῖνος -η -ον (= ἐκεῖνος)	that
κενός -ή -όν	empty
κοῖλος -η -ον	hollow
κοινός -ή -όν	common
κιών -οῦσα -όν (Homeric)	going
κίων, -ονος usu. f.	pillar
χιών, -όνος f.	snow
μέλλω	I am likely to, intend to, am about to
μέλω	I am an object of care/thought

μέλε (ὦ μέλε)	my friend
μέλι, μέλιτος n.	honey
μέλος, -ους n.	limb
μέλος, -ους n.	song
μέλεος -ᾱ -ον (poetic)	miserable
μέλᾱς -αινα -αν	black
μόχθος m.	hardship, trouble
μοχλός m.	crowbar, bar
ὄχλος m.	crowd
νόμος m.	law
νομός m. (poetic)	pasture
νέμω	I distribute; I pasture
οἶμαι, οἴομαι	I think
οἴμοι (poetic)	alas!
οἰμώζω	I cry alas!
οἱ	to him, to her (usually reflexive); *nom. pl. of the definite article*
οἵ	who (*nom. pl. of the relative pronoun*)
οἷ	to where
οἶος -ᾱ -ον (poetic)	alone
οἷος -ᾱ -ον	of what sort, such as
ὄρος, -ους n.	mountain, boundary
ὅρος m.	boundary
οὗτοι (pl. of οὗτος)	these men
οὔτοι	indeed not
οὔτις	no one
μητίς (= μή + τις)	in case anyone, etc.
μῆτις, -ι(δ)ος f.	intelligence
ὀψέ	late
ὄψις, -εως f.	appearance
ὄψον n.	cooked food
ποῖος -ᾱ -ον	of what kind?
ποιεῖν	to do
ποίη f. (epic & Ionic)	grass, meadow

πόσις, πόσεως f.	drink
πόσις m. (acc. sg. πόσιν) (poetic)	husband
πούς, ποδός m. (dat. pl. ποσί(ν))	foot
πόσος -η -ον	how great?
στρατειᾶ f.	campaign, warfare
στράτευμα, -ατος n.	campaign, army
στρατεύω, στρατεύομαι	I wage war
στρατηγός m.	general
στρατηγέω + gen.	I command
στρατός m.	army
στρατιά f.	army
στρατόπεδον n.	camp, army
στρατιώτης, -ου m.	soldier
ταῦτα	these things
ταὐτά (= τὰ αὐτά)	the same things
τίσι(ν)	to whom? (*dat. pl. of* τίς)
τισί(ν)	(*dat. pl. of* τις = any, some)
τίσις, -εως f. (acc. sg. τίσιν)	retribution, punishment
τίνω	I pay a price
τείνω	I stretch
φοβέω (Homeric)	I put to flight
φοβέομαι	I am afraid
φόβος m.	fear
φόβη f. (poetic)	lock of hair, foliage
ὤμοι (poetic)	alas!
ὦμος	shoulder
ὠμός -ή -όν	raw, savage

Some tips

1 While almost all words of the second declension have their neuter nom. and acc. singular in -ov, the following words (which are or can be pronouns) have them in -o:

ὁ	τό	the
ὅδε	τόδε	this
ὅς	ὅ	who, which
οὗτος	τοῦτο	this
ἐκεῖνος	ἐκεῖνο	that
αὐτός	αὐτό	self, the same; it (acc.)
ἄλλος	ἄλλο	another, the other

2 Even if you do not learn the whole system of Greek accents, it is worthwhile noting:

   (a) τίς, τίνος (with an accent over the first syllable) means 'who? what?'

   τις, τινός (an enclitic, either with no accent or with an accent over the second syllable) means 'some, any, a'.

   (b) -έω verbs:

   ποιεῖ: the accent shows that this is in the present indicative active (3 sg.) or passive (2 sg.), 'he/she does', 'you are made ...'.

   ποίει: the accent shows that this is the singular present imperative: 'do!'.

   (c) ἡ, οἱ and αἱ do not have accents when they are definite articles, but <u>do</u> have them (ἥ, οἵ and αἵ) when they are relative pronouns.

   (d) ἄλλα = other things

   ἀλλά = but

3 <u>The historic present</u>: to convey excitement, vividness or immediacy, the present tense may be used of an action in the past:

   τηρήσας με ... παίει τε πὺξ καὶ ἁρπάζει μέσον καὶ ἐώθει με εἰς τὰς λιθοτομίας. (Demosthenes 53.17)

   after watching out for me, he hits me with his fist and grabs me round the middle and tried to shove me into the quarries.

In this example note also the shift into the imperfect. The historic present is rare in English and it is generally advisable to translate it into an English past tense.

4 The gnomic aorist: the aorist can be used in maxims and proverbs (γνῶμαι). (In English, as often in Greek also, these are usually expressed in the present tense, e.g. 'Too many cooks spoil the broth.' But compare 'Curiosity killed the cat.')

ῥώμη ... μετὰ μὲν φρονήσεως ὠφέλησεν, ἄνευ δὲ ταύτης πλείω τοὺς ἔχοντας ἔβλαψε. (Isocrates 1.6)
Strength joined with judgement does good, but without it, it does greater harm to those who have it.

5 The future tense:

(a) The Attic future of verbs with stems ending in ν is often a contracted form with the letter ε.

| μένω | μενῶ (έω) | I wait, wait for |
| φαίνω | φανῶ (έω) | I show |

This also happens with verbs with stems ending in λ, μ and ρ:

βάλλω	βαλῶ (έω)	I throw, hit
νέμω	νεμῶ (έω)	I distribute, pasture
ἐγείρω	ἐγερῶ (έω)	I wake (X) up

(b) The Attic future of verbs ending in -ίζω which have more than two syllables is also a contracted form with the letter ε as follows:

| νομίζω | νομιῶ (έω) | I consider |

6 Potential clauses: note how what is in effect the apodosis (main clause) of a conditional sentence containing ἄν is frequently found without the protasis ('if' clause), which is implied (see pp. 183–7). We call this usage 'potential':

τούτου τίς ἄν σοι τἀνδρὸς ... ἀμείνων ηὑρέθη; (Sophocles, *Ajax* 119–20)
Who could you have found better than this man [if you had looked *or similar*]?

δὶς ἐς τὸν αὐτὸν ποταμὸν οὐκ ἄν ἐμβαίης. (Heraclitus, quoted at Plato, *Cratinus* 402a)
You could not step twice into the same river [if you were trying to cross it *or similar*].

7 When the subjects of the verb are different persons, the verb is first person plural if one of the subjects is first person, second person if the subjects are second and third persons:

ὑμεῖς δὲ καὶ ἐγώ που τάδε λέγομεν. (Plato, *Laws* 661b)
But you and I, I suppose, say these things.

πάντες ἄν ὑμεῖς καὶ οἱ ἄλλοι Ἀθηναῖοι ἀναστάντες ἐπὶ τὸ βῆμ' ἐβαδίζετε. (Demosthenes 18.171)

All of you and the rest of the Athenians would stand up and go to the speaker's platform.

8 The verbal adjectives in -τέος and -τός:

For the use of the gerundive form in -τέος, see pp. 193–4.

The endings -τός -τή -τόν are added to verbs in the same way. These verbal adjectives <u>either</u> have the same meaning as a perfect passive participle, e.g. παιδευ-τός (educated), τακ-τός (ordered); <u>or</u> (more frequently) they convey *possibility*, e.g. ὁρᾱ-τός (visible, *i.e.* that can be seen), πρᾱκ-τός (that may be done). Many -τός forms fall into <u>both</u> categories. Some of them are active, e.g. ῥυτός (flowing).

9 The letter ν at the end of prefixes (ἐν, σύν) changes (is 'assimilated') before certain consonants to assist pronunciation:

before β, μ, π, φ, ψ it becomes μ — συμβαίνω (I come together)
before γ, κ, ξ, χ it becomes γ — συγχέω (I pour together)
before λ it becomes λ — ἐλλείπω (I leave out, undone; I fail)

10 ἀμΰνω (I defend) and θαυμάζω (I wonder at)

(a) ἀμΰνω basically means 'I keep [X (acc.)] away'. When it means 'I defend', the people (or whatever) defended go into the dative (of advantage). Thus:

ἀμΰνω τοῖς πολίταις.
I keep away (the danger) for the advantage of the citizens,
   i.e. I defend the citizens.

(b) θαυμάζω can be used with the genitive to mean 'I wonder at' as well as with the accusative in the sense 'I admire'.

11 καθίστημι: these two sentences, the first with a transitive form of the verb, the second with an intransitive form, will repay study:

κατέστησα ὑμᾶς εἰς ἀθῡμίᾱν.
I reduced you to despair (*literally,* I placed you into despair).

κατέστην εἰς ἀπορίᾱν.
I was reduced to helplessness (*literally,* I was placed into helplessness).

12 A vowel which is naturally short becomes 'heavy' when followed by two consonants. (More correctly, it is the syllable which is heavy.) However, it may remain short (i.e. the syllable remains 'light') if the vowel is followed by a pair of consonants in which the first is a *mute* (or *stop*) (π β φ τ δ θ κ γ χ) and the second a *liquid* or *nasal* (λ ρ μ ν).

13 If you are looking up a word beginning ξυν- or ξυμ- in a dictionary and cannot find it, look it up under συν- or συμ-. See p. 59.

Appendices

Accents

There are three accents in ancient Greek. These indicate the musical pitch of the syllable on which they are placed:

the acute	´	(high pitch)
the grave	`	(low pitch or possibly a falling of the voice)
the circumflex	^	(high pitch falling to low)

Almost all Greek words have their own accent. Among those which do <u>not</u> are:

- ὁ, ἡ, οἱ, αἱ (*nom. of the definite article*)

- οὐ, ὡς (= how)

- εἰ, ὡς (= when, as, that)

- εἰς, ἐν, ἐκ, ὡς (= to)

See also Enclitics below.

| The rules of accentuation

| The acute and the grave

The acute can fall on any of the last three syllables. If the last syllable contains a long vowel or a diphthong, it can fall only on one of the last two. So:

φίλιος ἀργύριον φιλίᾱ βασιλεύς τῑμή

If an acute falls on the last syllable, it becomes grave when followed by another word, unless it is immediately followed by a punctuation mark or the next word is an enclitic (see below). So:

ποίᾱ ἡ τῑμή; ἡ τῑμὴ ἣν οἱ θεοὶ διδόᾱσιν.
What sort of honour? The honour that the gods give.

Thus the grave can only stand on the last syllable not followed by a punctuation mark or an enclitic.

Note how in the example above τῑμή becomes τῑμὴ because of its different position in the sentence. θεοὶ would have appeared as θεοί if it had been the last word in its sentence.

| The circumflex

The circumflex can fall only on one of the last two syllables and only on a long vowel or a diphthong. If the last syllable contains a long vowel or a diphthong, a circumflex cannot stand on the second-last syllable. So:

ἐκεῖνος   ἐκείνη   ἐκεῖνο

 For the purposes of accentuation -αι and -οι of the nom. plural count as SHORT. So: φίλιοι, φίλιαι, γνῶμαι.

| Names of the accents

Each of the accents has a technical name:

	third-last	second-last	last
acute	proparoxytone	paroxytone	oxytone
grave			barytone
circumflex		properispōmenon	perispōmenon

| Enclitics

Enclitics are linked by accent to the previous word. They 'lean on' it (ἐγκλίνω (I lean on), hence 'enclitic'). They often have no accent of their own and are likely to throw an acute accent onto the final syllable of the previous word, if possible. So:

ἀνήρ *τις* ἔδωκέ *μοι* δῶρόν *τι*.
Some man gave me a gift.

The occasions when an enclitic cannot place an acute on the final syllable of the previous word are as follows:

1 The enclitic will cause a final grave accent on the previous word to revert to its natural accent, an acute, e.g. ἀνήρ τις.

2 If the accent of the previous word is a circumflex on the last syllable, the enclitic causes no change (βοῦς τις, cf. δῶρόν τι).

3 If the accent on the previous word is an acute on the second-last, again the enclitic causes no change to that previous word, e.g. ῥήτωρ τις.

4 Strings of enclitics throw their accents back onto each other. So:

εἴ τίς τί σοί φησιν ...
If anyone is saying anything to you ...

5 Note that a word can end up with two accents.

The principal enclitics are:

- indefinite τις (someone, anyone, some)
- the indefinite adverbs (που, ποι, etc. – see p. 52)
- the present indicative of εἰμί (I am) (except the 2 sg., but see p. 93)
- the present indicative of φημί (I say) (except the 2 sg.)
- the personal pronouns: με, μου, μοι; σε, σου, σοι (except when σέ, σοῦ, σοῖ are emphatic); ἑ, οὑ, οἱ
- τε (and), νυν ((logical) now, then), που (I suppose), γε, τοι (see pp. 208 & 212)

Enclitics of <u>more than one syllable</u> have an accent on their second syllable when the previous word has an acute on its penultimate (second-last) syllable (paroxytone), e.g. λόγοι τινές. Cf. **3** above.

| The position of the accent

| Nouns and adjectives

The accent on the nominative stays on the same syllable in the other cases as far as the general rules allow. Note the following:

1 Words of the first and second declensions with an acute on the last syllable of the nominative singular have a circumflex on the final syllable in the genitives and datives. So:

σοφός: σοφοῦ, σοφῷ; σοφῶν, σοφοῖς
σοφή: σοφῆς, σοφῇ; σοφῶν, σοφαῖς
σοφόν: σοφοῦ, σοφῷ; σοφῶν, σοφοῖς

2 All first declension nouns have a circumflex on the -ῶν of the genitive plural.

3 Monosyllables of the third declension have their accents on the final syllable of the genitive and dative. So:

βοῦς (cow): βοός, βοΐ; βοῶν, βουσί(ν)

4 Note πόλεως, πόλεων and ἄστεως, ἄστεων (and the declension of ἵλεως on p. 34). These are exceptions to the rule that if the last syllable is or contains a long vowel or diphthong, the accent can fall only on one of the last two syllables.

5 If a diphthong has an accent, it is placed over the second vowel. So βασιλεύς, σοφαῖς.

| Verbs

Generally the accent is placed as far back as possible. (This is almost always true of finite verbs.) The accent is nearly always acute. But note:

1 For the purposes of accentuation only, final -αι counts as short, except in the optative. Thus:

παῦσαι   aor. act. infinitive *or* 2 sg. aor. mid. imperative

παύεται   3 sg. pres. indic. mid./pass.

παύσαι   3 sg. aor. opt. act.

2 If the infinitive ends in -ναι, it will have its accent on the penultimate syllable and the nom. sg. masculine and neuter participles will be accented on the last syllable. Thus:

εἶναι – ὤν, οὖσα, ὄν (m. & n. gen. sg. ὄντος)

πεπαυκέναι – πεπαυκώς, πεπαυκυῖα, πεπαυκός
     (m. & n. gen. sg. πεπαυκότος)

παυσθῆναι – παυσθείς, παυσθεῖσα, παυσθέν
     (m. & n. gen. sg. παυσθέντος)

3 If the final syllable contains a short vowel, or is -αι (except in the optative), a circumflex is obligatory over a long penultimate vowel or diphthong when it is accented, e.g. εἶναι (to be) as opposed to διδόναι (to give).

4 In the 2nd aorist (see p. 69), verbs have their accents on the last syllable of the active infinitive, participle and 2 sg. imperative. Thus (from λαμβάνω (I take)):

λαβεῖν – λαβών, λαβοῦσα, λαβόν – λαβέ

5 Contracted verbs have a circumflex on the resulting contracted syllable when the <u>first</u> of the two contracted syllables was accented before contraction. Thus ποιέω → ποιῶ. They have the acute when the <u>second</u> of the syllables was accented, or when the last syllable is long. Thus ποιε-έτω → ποιείτω and τῑμα-οίην → τῑμῴην.

The contracted syllable is, of course, unaccented if neither of the two syllables was accented. Thus ποίε-ε → ποίει (2 sg. pres. imperative active).

What is the difference in meaning between φιλεῖ and φίλει?

Dialect

Some key features of Homeric dialect

The Greek after the equation marks is Attic.

1 The augment may be omitted – λῦσε = ἔλυσε (he loosed), βῆ = ἔβη (he went).

2 Nominative singular: Attic -ᾱ always appears as -η: θύρη (door), χώρη (country). But N.B. θεά (goddess): there is no Attic equivalent.

3 Genitive singular in -οιο: δώροιο = δώρου (of a gift); also in -αο, -εω: Ἀτρείδᾱο and Ἀτρείδεω = Ἀτρείδου (of the son of Atreus).

4 Dative plural:

(a) Where Attic has -αις we find -ῃς or -ῃσι: θύρῃσι = θύραις (doors), πύλῃσι = πύλαις (gates); τῆς and τῆσι = ταῖς (definite article, relative pronoun).

(b 2nd declension words can end -οισι: δώροισι = δώροις (gifts).

(c) 3rd declension words can end -(σ)σι or -εσσι: πόδεσσι and ποσσί = ποσί (feet); βελέεσσι, βέλεσσι and βέλεσι = βέλεσι (missiles). The moveable nu can be added to all of these.

5 The definite article:

(a) most commonly means 'he', 'she', 'it', 'they' or 'this', 'that'.

(b) οἱ and αἱ appear also as τοί and ταί.

(c) Forms identical with the definite article are used as the relative pronoun, though the masculine nominative singular of the relative is ὅς as in Attic.

6 The use of the enclitics οἱ (to him, to her) and τοι (to you (sg.)).

7 Active infinitives often end in -μεν or its extended form -μεναι: ἀκουέμεναι = ἀκούειν (to hear); τεθνάμεν(αι) = τεθνάναι (to be dead); ἔμεν, ἔμμεν, ἔμεναι, ἔμμεναι = εἶναι (to be).

8 Homer generally does not contract verbs ending in -έω, -άω and -όω which would contract in Attic.

9 κεν (κε, κ') can be used as well as ἄν, with the same force.

10 Tmesis, i.e. the separation of a preposition which is the prefix to a verb, from that verb: πρὸς μῦθον ἔειπεν = μῦθον προσεῖπεν (he addressed a word).

11 Particles frequently used in Homer:

ἄρα, ἄρ, ῥα	so, next (for transition)
δή	indeed (for emphasis, often of time)
ἦ	truly, certainly (for emphasis)
περ	just, even (for emphasis); although
τε	and; you know, let me tell you (to show that a comment is generalizing)
τοι	I tell you (for asssertion); can also = σοι (to you)

| Some key features of Herodotus' Ionic dialect

The Greek after the equation marks is Attic.

1 Herodotus often has η where Attic has ᾱ (especially after ε, ι, ρ): ἡμέρη = ἡμέρᾱ (day); πρῆγμα = πρᾶγμα (business, affair).

2 Herodotus uses -έω for the genitive singular of nouns like νεηνίης (= νεᾱνίᾱς, young man): νεηνίεω = νεᾱνίου.

3 Herodotus uses -έων for the genitive plural of nouns like τῑμή, θάλασσα, χώρη, κριτής: Περσέων = Περσῶν (of the Persians). (This is contracted in Attic.)

4 Dative plurals of the first and second declensions end in -σι: ἀγροῖσι (fields), τοῖσι (definite article), τούτοισι (these).

5 Herodotus uses σσ where Attic has ττ: θάλασσα = θάλαττα (sea), πρήσσω = πράττω (I do).

6 Herodotus can have:
ει for Attic ε: ξεῖνος = ξένος (foreigner, guest, host)
ου for Attic ο: μοῦνος = μόνος (alone)
ηϊ for Attic ει: οἰκήιος = οἰκεῖος (private, home-grown).

7 Herodotus often does not contract verbs ending in -έω which would contract in Attic: φιλέω = φιλῶ (I like), ποιέειν = ποιεῖν (to make). νόος (mind) does not contract.

8 Herodotus often does not contract nouns which have contracted forms in Attic (see p. 31), e.g. γένος (race): gen. sg. γένεος = γένους, nom. & acc. pl. γένεα = γένη. Compare σεο = σου (of you).

9 Herodotus can have ευ in place of Attic εο or ου: σευ (for σεο = σου, of you), μευ = μου (of me), ποιεύμενα (for ποιεόμενα = ποιούμενα, things being done), ποιεῦμεν = ποιοῦμεν (we do).

10 Herodotus uses forms identical with the definite article as the relative pronoun, though the masculine nom. singular of the relative is ὅς as in Attic.

11 With a few exceptions, there were no 'h' sounds in Ionic. Thus aspiration is often omitted: ἀπικνέομαι = ἀφικνέομαι (I arrive); μετίημι = μεθίημι (I let go).

12 The following Herodotean forms are well worth noting:

Herodotus		Attic
ἐμεωυτοῦ (gen.)	myself	ἐμαυτοῦ
ἑωυτοῦ (gen.)	himself	ἑαυτοῦ
ἐών, ἐοῦσα, ἐόν	being	ὤν, οὖσα, ὄν
κοῖος (ὁκοῖος)	of what kind	ποῖος (ὁποῖος)
κότε (ὁκότε)	when	πότε (ὁπότε)
κῶς (ὅκως)	how	πῶς (ὅπως)
μιν (acc. – enclitic)	him, her	no comparable form
οἱ (dat. – enclitic)	to him, to her, to it	rare in Attic[1]
ὦν	therefore	οὖν

| New Testament Greek

The Greek of the New Testament differs significantly from that of Plato or Xenophon. But it is not (as was once thought) a special variety of Greek used by Jews of the Near East, or by the Holy Spirit. On the whole, it reflects the everyday Greek of the first century AD.

[1] except as an indirect reflexive (see pp. 148-9).

Because of the political and commercial power of Athens, as well as the prestige of its literature, Attic became the dominant Greek dialect in the late fifth century BC. It gradually evolved (with an admixture of Ionic elements) into the so-called Koinē (ἡ κοινὴ διάλεκτος = the common dialect) of the Hellenistic period. The main catalyst was the fourth-century rise of Macedon under Philip the Second and his son Alexander the Great. The Macedonians were anxious to assert their Greekness (Demosthenes called them barbarians – 3.16, 3.24 etc.), but their own language (apparently unintelligible to other Greeks) lacked the cultural prestige to match their imperial ambitions. 'Great Attic', already dominant outside its region of origin, met the need. As Alexander moved eastwards through the former Persian empire to the borders of India, founding (according to tradition) seventy cities, this form of Greek was from the outset employed as the official language. It became the universal vernacular of the eastern Mediterranean, a form of Greek simplified and modified to be a suitable vehicle for ordinary people of many races.

The New Testament comes to us in Greek. However, the main language of Jesus and his disciples was Aramaic (a Semitic language related to Hebrew), and the gospel writers give several direct quotations of this. But the culture of Palestine was multi-lingual. Hebrew was widely spoken around Jerusalem. The inscription on the cross 'Jesus of Nazareth, the King of the Jews' was written in Hebrew, Latin and Greek (John 19.20).

Some key features of New Testament Greek:

1 There is a general simplification of both accidence and syntax.

2 In accidence, difficulties and irregularities are frequently ironed out: unusual forms of comparative adjectives are made regular; third declension adjectives are rare; monosyllabic nouns (irregular in declension) are replaced; verbs in -μι are given the endings of verbs in -ω; first (regular) aorist endings often replace 2nd aorists (see pp. 69–70); middle verbs are often replaced by active verbs with reflexive pronouns; the optative is rare; the dual number has disappeared.

3 ἵνα has acquired new rôles: it now introduces result clauses, indirect statements and third person direct commands.

4 Purpose is often expressed by the infinitive or by the genitive singular of the definite article with the infinitive (i.e. the gerund – see p. 124):

μέλλει γὰρ Ἡρώδης ζητεῖν τὸ παιδίον, τοῦ ἀπολέσαι αὐτό. (Matthew 2.13)
For Herod intends to seek the young child (in order) to destroy him.

5 Prepositions are used where the case alone would have sufficed in classical Attic. There are changes in the cases that prepositions take (the accusative advancing at the expense of others). Pronouns are used when the sense would be clear without them. Diminutive forms are used apparently with the same sense as the nouns of which they are diminutives, e.g. βιβλαρίδιον (book), diminutive of βίβλος.

6 There are about 900 words (about 10% of the total vocabulary) not found in classical authors.

7 There are numerous Semitic idioms, e.g. ἐγένετο introducing another verb (traditionally translated 'it came to pass that ...').

8 The narrative is generally without complication and clauses tend to follow one after another in a straightforward manner.

The dual

If a verb has two people or things as its subject, or if a noun or adjective denotes two people or things, Greek can use a form called the **dual**.

| Nouns and adjectives

The following endings are used:

	1st declension	2nd declension	3rd declension
dual			
nom./acc.	-ᾱ	-ω	-ε (sometimes -ει)
gen./dat.	-αιν	-οιν	-οιν

The dual of the definite article:

	m.	f.	n.
dual			
nom./acc.	τώ	τώ	τώ
gen./dat.	τοῖν	τοῖν	τοῖν

For example:

> τὼ καλὼ ἀνθρώπω
> the two handsome people
>
> τοῖν σοφαῖν θυγατέροιν
> of the two wise daughters

| Verbs

In verbs, duals are almost entirely limited to the second and third person. The following endings are attached to the stem + vowel-ending of the relevant tense (e.g. ε in the present tense of παύω):

	active	middle/passive
2	-τον	-σθον
3 (primary)[1]	-τον	-σθον
(historic)[1]	-την	-σθην

For example:

παύσετον	the two of you/them will stop
ἐπαυσάτην	the two of them stopped
παύσητον	the two of you/them stop (pres. subj. act.)
παυσαίσθην	the two of them stop themselves (aor. opt. mid.)

εἰμί (I am) has the following dual forms:

ἐστόν	(present indicative)
ἦστον, ἤστην	(imperfect indicative)
ἦτον	(subjunctive)
εἶτον or εἴητον, εἴτην or εἰήτην	(optative)
ἔστον, ἔστων	(imperatives, 2nd and 3rd persons)

[1] See pp. 152–3.

Some literary terms

alliteration the recurrence of the same or a similar consonant
(cf. *assonance*), especially at the beginning of words or syllables:

> τὸν δὲ ταύρῳ χαλκέῳ καυτῆρα νηλέα νόον
> ἐχθρὰ Φάλαριν κατέχει παντᾷ φάτις. (Pindar, *Pythians* 1.95–6)
> Universal condemnation seizes hold of Phalaris, the man of pitiless
> spirit who burned men in his bronze bull.

The use of alliteration imparts emphasis, and the effect this creates
depends on the meaning of the words emphasized.

anadiplosis the repetition (literally 'doubling') of one or several words, e.g.
Byron's 'The Isles of Greece, the Isles of Greece, Where burning Sappho
loved and sung' (*Don Juan*, Canto 3).

> Θῆβαι δέ, Θῆβαι πόλις ἀστυγείτων, μεθ' ἡμέρᾶν μίᾶν ἐκ μέσης τῆς
> Ἑλλάδος ἀνήρπασται. (Aeschines 3.133)
> Thebes, Thebes, a neighbouring city, has been uprooted from the
> midst of Greece in the course of a single day.

anaphora the repetition of a word or phrase in two or more successive
clauses:

> οὗτοι γὰρ πολλοὺς μὲν τῶν πολιτῶν εἰς τοὺς πολεμίους ἐξήλασαν,
> πολλοὺς δ' ἀδίκως ἀποκτείναντες ἀτάφους ἐποίησαν, πολλοὺς δ'
> ἐπιτίμους ὄντας ἀτίμους κατέστησαν. (Lysias 12.21)
> For these men drove many of the citizens out to the enemy, many they
> killed unjustly and left unburied, and many who had civic rights
> they deprived of them.

antithesis the contrasting of ideas emphasized by the arrangement of
words:

> ὡς τρὶς ἂν παρ' ἀσπίδα | στῆναι θέλοιμ' ἂν μᾶλλον ἢ τεκεῖν ἅπαξ.
> (Euripides, *Medea* 250–1)
> since I would rather stand three times in the battle line than give birth
> once.

aposiopesis a device in which the speaker breaks off before completing the sentence:

εἴπερ γάρ κ᾽ ἐθέλῃσιν Ὀλύμπιος ἀστεροπητής | ἐξ ἑδέων στυφελίξαι ... (Homer, *Iliad* 1.580–1)
for if the Olympian lightning-sender wishes to smash us from our seats ...

Here something like 'what can we do about it?' must be understood.

apostrophe the author 'turns away' (ἀποστρέφεται) from his narrative (told in the third person) to address one of his characters:

οὐδὲ σέθεν, Μενέλᾶε, θεοὶ μάκαρες λελάθοντο | ἀθάνατοι. (Homer, *Iliad* 4.127–8)
and you, Menelaus, the gods, the blessed immortals, did not forget.

Homer and other poets appear to use this device to express sympathy for their characters.

assonance the occurrence of similar vowel sounds in words close to each other (cf. *alliteration*):

κατῆγεν ἦγεν ἦγεν ἐς μέλαν πέδον. (Euripides, *Bacchae* 1065)
he pulled the branch down, down, down, to the black ground.

πάθει μάθος. (Aeschylus, *Agamemnon* 177)
through suffering (comes) knowledge.

asyndeton the omission of conjunctions (such as 'and' or 'but') where these would usually occur:

προσπεσόντες ἐμάχοντο, ἐώθουν ἐωθοῦντο, ἔπαιον ἐπαίοντο. (Xenophon, *Education of Cyrus* 7.1.38)
falling upon them, they fought, they pushed (and) were pushed, they struck (and) were struck.

bathos the juxtaposition of the intense or important and the trivial: in Aristophanes' *Birds*, Basileia (Royalty) is the keeper of the thunderbolt of Zeus, of good counsel, good sense, the dockyards, abuse, the paymaster and the three-obol bits (1538–41).

chiasmus (adjective **chiastic**) a pair of balanced phrases where the order of the elements of the second reverses that of the first:

> ἓν ... σῶμ' ἔχων καὶ ψῡχὴν μίαν (Demosthenes 19.227)
> having a single body and a single soul

This patterning can be represented with crossing diagonal lines like the Greek letter chi:

closure the sense of completion or resolution at the conclusion of a literary work or part of a literary work. Often conclusions deny us this sense of completion. For example, at the end of Homer's *Odyssey*, the peace that has been established by the hero on his island by his slaughter of the suitors is a disconcertingly uneasy one.

ellipsis the shortening of a sentence or phrase by the omission of words which can be understood:

> ἐξ ὀνύχων λέοντα (Alcaeus 113)
> (to judge) a lion by its claws

enallage and **hypallage** (in practice these terms cannot be distinguished) the use of the transferred epithet, i.e. transferring an adjective from the word to which it properly applies to another word in the same phrase:

> νεῖκος ἀνδρῶν ξύναιμον (Sophocles, *Antigone* 794)
> kindred strife of men (*for* strife of kindred men)

enjambement (single-word enjambement) running a sentence over the end of a line of verse and then ending it after the first word of the new line, lending emphasis to that word:

> πίπτει πρὸς οὖδας μῡρίοις οἰμώγμασιν | Πενθεύς. (Euripides, *Bacchae* 1112–13)
> He fell to the ground with innumerable cries of sorrow, did Pentheus.

euphemism the substitution of a mild or roundabout expression for one considered improper or too harsh or blunt: εὐφρόνη (the kindly time) for 'night', Εὐμενίδες (the kindly ones) for the Furies, ἀριστερός (better) for 'left', the unlucky side.

hendiadys a single idea expressed through two nouns or verbs:

    ἐν ἁλὶ κύμασί τε (Euripides, *Helen* 226)
    in the sea and the waves (*for* in the waves of the sea)

The word 'hendiadys' is Greek for 'one by means of two'.

hyperbaton the dislocation of normal word order, by way of displacing one part of one clause into another; the effect is often impossible to reproduce in a literal English translation of the Greek:

    σὺ δὲ αὐτός, ὦ πρὸς θέων, Μένων, τί φὴς ἀρετὴν εἶναι; (Plato, *Meno* 71d)
    but you yourself, by the gods, O Meno, what do you say that virtue is?

Here the hyperbaton seems to reflect the informality and emphasis of conversation: 'Now you yourself, Meno – come on – what's your opinion?'

hyperbole the use of exaggerated terms, not to be taken literally (cf. *litotes*). Thus μύριοι, which literally means 10,000, can (with the accentuation μῡρίοι) mean 'countless' or 'infinite'.

hysteron proteron the reversal of the normal (temporal) order of events:

    εἵματά τ' ἀμφιέσασα θυώδεα καὶ λούσασα (Homer, *Odyssey* 5.264)
    having dressed him in fragrant robes and washed him

Clearly he was washed first. By his order Homer lays emphasis on what he describes first, which seems to him to be the more important action.

irony the expression of one's meaning by using words of the opposite meaning in order to make one's remarks forceful.

    dramatic irony occurs when a character in a play uses words which have a different meaning for the speaker and for the audience, who know the truth of the situation. This is a device which is used with particular force by Sophocles. For example, in *Oedipus Tyrannus* he makes highly effective use of the fact that the blind seer Teiresias can see the truth while Oedipus, despite his gift of sight, cannot.

    Socratic irony the refusal to claim expertise, frequently employed by Socrates to provoke or confuse those in discussion with him.

juxtaposition the placing of words next to each other for effect (see also *oxymoron*):

    δημοβόρος βασιλεύς (Homer, *Iliad* 1.231)
    king who feeds on his people

liminality the use of location, especially involving passing through doors or gates, to make a symbolic point. In Euripides' play, Medea comes out of the house, to which her female rôle has confined her, to deliver the most assertive feminist manifesto in ancient literature (214).

litotes the use of understatement, involving a negative, to emphasize one's meaning (cf. *hyperbole*). Thus, οὐκ ὀλίγοι (not a few) can mean 'many' and οὐκ ἀφανής (not obscure) can mean 'famous'. Cf. οὐδ' οὕτω κακῶς (and not so badly), the words of a man who threw a tile at a dog but hit his stepmother (Plutarch, *Septem Sapientium Convivium* 147c).

metaphor the application of a word or phrase to something it does not apply to literally, indicating a comparison, for example 'a sea (κλύδων) of troubles':

> φωνῇ γὰρ *ὁρῶ*, τὸ φατιζόμενον. (Sophocles, *Oedipus at Colonus* 138)
> for I see by sound, as the saying is.

metonymy a form of expression by which people or things can take their name from something with which they are associated. Thus θέᾱτρον (a theatre) can be used of spectators, ἵππος (a horse) of cavalry, and ἰχθύες (fish) of a fish-market. In poetic texts, the names of gods are frequently used to denote their areas of control. Thus Dionysus (or Bacchus) can mean 'wine', Aphrodite 'love', etc.; cf. *synecdoche*.

onomatopoeia words or combinations of words, the sound of which suggests their sense, for example, βρεκεκεκέξ κοάξ κοάξ (the croaking of frogs) in Aristophanes' *Frogs* (209). In the following hexameter line, the rhythm, with its smoothly running light syllables, imitates the rolling of Sisyphus' stone:

> αὖτις ἔπειτα πέδονδε κυλίνδετο λᾶας ἀναιδής. (Homer, *Odyssey* 11.598)
> then down again to the plain rolled the shameless stone.

oxymoron the juxtaposition (see above) of two words of contradictory meaning to emphasize the contradiction:

> νόμον ἄνομον (Aeschylus, *Agamemnon* 1142)
> a discordant song

The word 'oxymoron' is Greek for 'sharp-blunt' and is an oxymoron itself.

paradox a statement which apparently contradicts itself but in fact makes a meaningful point:

> εἰ γὰρ ὤφελον, ὦ Κρίτων, οἷοί τ᾽ εἶναι οἱ πολλοὶ τὰ μέγιστα κακὰ ἐργάζεσθαι, ἵνα οἷοί τ᾽ ἦσαν καὶ ἀγαθὰ τὰ μέγιστα. (Plato, *Crito* 44d)
> if only, Crito, the majority were able to do the greatest evils, so that they might have been able to do the greatest good deeds as well.

paronomasia a punning play on words:

> οὐ γὰρ τὸν τρόπον ἀλλὰ τὸν τόπον μετήλλαξεν. (Aeschines 3.78)
> for he changed not his disposition but his position.

periphrasis a circumlocutory or roundabout way of saying things. Thus in verse, βλέπειν φάος can mean 'to see the light (of day)', i.e. 'to be alive'.

personification the representation of an idea or thing as having human characteristics. Death is frequently personified in Greek literature, and indeed appears as an actual character in Euripides' *Alcestis*.

pleonasm the use of words which are superfluous to the literal meaning:

> κεῖτο μέγας μεγαλωστί. (Homer, *Iliad* 16.776)
> he lay huge at his huge length.

prolepsis the use of an adjective to anticipate its result; i.e. the adjective will not be applicable until the action of the verb which controls it has been completed:

> τοῦτον τρέφειν τε καὶ αὔξειν μέγαν (Plato, *Republic* 565c)
> to rear and to exalt this man into greatness

> σὲ Θῆβαί γ᾽ οὐκ ἐπαίδευσαν κακόν. (Sophocles, *Oedipus at Colonus* 919)
> and yet, Thebes did not train you to be base.

simile a figure of speech in which one thing is compared explicitly with another; in English, the words 'like' or 'as' often indicate a simile. In Homer, for example, human beings are frequently compared to animals or birds. The simile is a notable feature of epic – hence the term 'epic simile'.

syllepsis an expression in which the same word is used in two phrases in two different ways but makes literal sense in both, e.g. 'she went home in a flood of tears and a sedan chair' (Charles Dickens, *The Pickwick Papers*) and 'Miss Nipper shook her head and a tin canister, and began unasked to make the tea' (Dickens, *Dombey and Son*):

χρήματα τελοῦντες τούτοις ... καὶ χάριτας (Plato, *Crito* 48c)
paying (*literally*) money and paying (*metaphorically*) thanks to his men

Cf. *zeugma*.

synecdoche a form of expression in which the part is used to imply the whole. Thus δόρυ (plank) can mean 'ship', while the other meaning of δόρυ (the shaft of a spear) can lead to 'spear' and 'war'. Cf. *metonymy*.

tautology repeating the same thing in different ways:

ἀγὼν μέγας, | πλήρης στεναγμῶν οὐδὲ δακρύων κενός. (Euripides, *Hecuba* 229–30)
a great contest, full of groans and not empty of tears.

zeugma a figure of speech in which a verb or adjective is applied to two nouns, though it is literally applicable to only one of them, e.g. 'with tearful eyes and mind' (cf. *syllepsis*):

οὔτε φωνὴν οὔτε του μορφὴν βροτῶν ὄψει. (Aeschylus, *Prometheus Bound* 21)
you will know (*literally,* see) neither voice nor form of any of mortals.

The Greek word ζεῦγμα means 'a yoking'.

Vocabulary

Throughout the following lists, the symbols † and ‡ indicate the verbs whose principal parts are given in the tables on pp. 98–109 and 110–19 respectively. The genitive is omitted for regular nouns of the first and second declensions ending in -η, -α, -ᾱ and -ος; for their endings, see pp. 25–6.

| Greek – English

ἀγαγ-	*aor. stem of* †ἄγω
ἀγαθός -ή -όν	good
Ἀγασίᾱς	Agasias
†ἀγγέλλω	I announce
ἄγε δή	come on now!
ἀγνοέω	I am ignorant of; I fail to understand
ἀγοράζω	I buy
†ἄγω	I lead, bring
ἀδικέω	I wrong
ἀεί	always
ἀείδω, ‡ᾄδω	I sing
Ἀθηναῖος -ᾱ -ον	Athenian
αἰεί	always
†αἱρέομαι	I choose
†αἰσθάνομαι	I perceive, realize, notice
†αἰσχύνω	I dishonour
αἰτέω	I ask (for)
αἴτιος -ᾱ -ον (+ gen.)	responsible (for), guilty (of)
†ἀκούω	I hear (+ gen. of person & acc. or gen. of thing)
ἄκρον n.	summit
ἀλλά	but; well then
ἀλλὰ καί	but also

ἀλλήλων (gen.)	one another, each other
ἄλλος, ἄλλη, ἄλλο	other, else
ἅμα	at the same time
ἅμαξα f.	wagon
†ἁμαρτάνω εἰς + acc.	I commit a wrong against
ἁμαρτίᾱ f.	wrong, fault
Ἄμᾱσις, Ἀμάσιος m.	Amasis
ἀμελέω	I am negligent
ἀμφισβητέω	I disagree, dispute
ἄν + indicative	*conditional* (pp. 184–5)
+ optative	*conditional* or *potential* (pp. 187 & 219)
+ subjunctive	*indefinite* (p. 195)
ἀναβαίνω	I go up
†ἀναγιγνώσκω	I read
ἀναγκαῖος -ᾱ -ον	necessary
†ἀνᾱλίσκω	I spend (money)
ἀνήρ, ἀνδρός m.	man; husband
ἄνθρωπος c.	human being, man, woman
ἄξιος -ᾱ -ον	worthy (of + gen.)
†ἀπάγω	I lead away
ἅπᾱς, ἅπᾱσα, ἅπᾶν	all
ἀπαρνέομαι	I deny
†ἀπελαύνω	I march off, ride off
†ἀπέρχομαι	I go away
†ἀπέχομαι + gen.	I refrain from
†ἀπέχω	I am distant
†ἀποβάλλω	I throw away
†ἀποδίδωμι	I give away, give back
†ἀποθνήσκω	I die; I am killed
ἀποκρύπτω	I hide, conceal
†ἀποκτείνω	I kill
Ἀπόλλων, -ωνος m.	Apollo
ἀπόλωλα	I am dead (*intr. pf. of* †ἀπόλλῡμι)
ἀπορέω	I am at a loss (for + gen.)
ἆρα	(see p. 207)
ἆρ' οὐ ...;	isn't ...? surely ...? (see p. 163)
ἀργύριον n.	silver, money
†ἄρχω	I rule, am in command (+ gen.); begin

Ἀσίη f. (Ionic spelling) — Asia
ἄτε — inasmuch as, seeing that
αὖ — again, further, moreover
αὐλέω — I play on the reed-pipe; I make music
αὐτόν, αὐτήν, αὐτό (acc.) — him, her, it
αὐτόν = ἑαυτόν (acc.) — himself
αὐτός, αὐτή, αὐτό — self (outside article + noun)
  ὁ αὐτός, ἡ αὐτή, τὸ αὐτό — the same (αὐτός inside article + noun)

αὐτοῦ = ἑαυτοῦ (gen.) — of himself, his own
†ἀφέλκω — I tow away
†ἀφικνέομαι — I arrive
ἀχάριστος -ον — unrewarded

βάρβαρος -ον — barbarian; foreigner
βαρύς -εῖα -ύ — heavy; annoying
βασιλεύς, -έως m. — king
βλάβη f. — damage, hurt
βοάω — I shout
βοηθέω (+ dat.) — I (run to) help
βουλεύομαι — I consider, make up my mind
†βούλομαι — I wish, want
βρέχω — I wet, drench

γάρ — for (second word)
γε — at least; at any rate (enclitic)
†γελάω — I laugh
γεν- — aor. stem of †γίγνομαι
γένος, -ους n. — race
γῆ f. — land
†γίγνομαι — I happen, become; I am born
γλῶσσα f. (Attic γλῶττα) — tongue

δέ — and, but (second word)
δέδοικα — I fear (pf. of δείδω)
†δεῖ — it is necessary for X (acc.) to Y (infin.)
δείδω — I fear
†δείκνῡμι — I show
δεινός -ή -όν — terrible; strange, clever

δειπνέω	I have dinner
δέκα	ten
‡δέω	I tie up, bind
δή	indeed (for emphasis)
δῆλος -η -ον	clear
δηλόω	I show
δῆτα	then (for emphasis)
διά + acc.	because of
διὰ τί;	why?
†διαβάλλω	I slander
δίαιτα f.	way of life
διασκευάζομαι	I prepare; I equip myself
†διαφέρομαι (+ dat.)	I am at variance with, am inconsistent with
†διδάσκω	I teach
†δίδωμι	I give
δικάζω	I judge
δικαστής, -οῦ m.	judge, juror
δίκη f.	justice
διότι	because
διχῇ	in two ways
‡διώκω	I pursue
δόξα f.	good repute, opinion
δόμος m. (often in pl.)	house, home
δουλόω, δουλόομαι	I enslave
‡δράω	I do
δρόμῳ	at a run, at speed
†δύναμαι	I am able
δύναμις, -εως f.	power
δυσμεταχείριστος -ον	hard to manage
δῶρον n.	gift
ἐάν	if
ἑαυτοῦ, ἑαυτῆς, ἑαυτοῦ	himself, herself, itself
†ἐάω	I allow
ἑβδομήκοντα	seventy
ἐγώ	I
†ἐθέλω	I wish, want; I am willing

εἰ	if
εἰ μή	unless, if … not
†εἰμί	I am (see p. 93)
†εἶμι	I shall go (*fut. of* †ἔρχομαι)
εἰς + acc.	into, to; with regard to
†εἴσειμι	I shall go into
†εἰσέρχομαι	I go into
εἰσηγέομαι	I propose
ἐκ + gen.	out of, from
ἕκαστος -η -ον	each
ἑκάτερος -ᾱ -ον	each (of two)
ἐκδέρω (aor. ἐξέδειρα)	I skin
†ἐκδιδάσκω	I teach (thoroughly)
ἐκεῖνος -η -ο	that
ἑλ-	*aor. stem of* †αἱρέω
Ἐλάτεια f.	Elateia
ἐλάττων -ον	smaller; less; fewer
ἐλευθερίᾱ f.	freedom
ἐλθ-	*aor. stem of* †ἔρχομαι, εἶμι
Ἑλλάς, -άδος f.	Greece
Ἕλλην, -ηνος m.	Greek
ἐμός -ή -όν	my
ἐν + dat.	in, on
ἐν φυλακῇ	under guard
ἕνεκα + gen. (usu. follows noun)	because of, for the sake of
ἐνταῦθα	here
ἕξ	six
†ἐξαιρέω (aor. ἐξεῖλον)	I take out, demolish
†ἐξελαύνω (aor. ἐξήλασα)	I drive out
ἔξεστι	it is possible for X (dat.) to Y (infin.)
†ἐπαινέω	I praise
ἐπεί	when, since
ἐπειδάν = ἐπειδὴ ἄν	
ἐπειδή	when, since, because
ἔπειτα	then, next
ἐπί + acc.	towards; against; for
ἐπί + gen.	on
†ἐπιπίπτω	I fall (up)on

ἐπιτήδεια n.pl.	provisions
ἐπιών -οῦσα -όν	following, succeeding
†ἕπομαι (+ dat.)	I follow
ἐρέω	I shall say (*fut. of* †λέγω)
ἐρίζω (+ dat.)	I quarrel with
†ἔρχομαι	I come, go
†ἐρωτάω	I ask
ἐς = εἰς	
ἔσομαι	I shall be (*fut. of* †εἰμί: see p. 93)
ἑσπέρᾱ f.	evening; west
ἐτετρώμην	I had been wounded (*plpf. pass. of* †τιτρώσκω)
ἔτι	still
ἔτος, -ους n.	year
εὖ	well
Εὔανδρος m.	Evander
εὐορκέω	I keep my oath
εὐπετέως	easily
εὐπρᾱξίᾱ f.	success
εὔτακτος -ον	orderly, well-disciplined
ἔφην	*impf. of* †φημί
ἐφ' ᾧ, ἐφ' ᾧτε	on condition that (see p. 179)
ἐχρῆν (also χρῆν)	*impf. of* †χρή
†ἔχω	I have, hold
†ἔχω + adverb	I am
Ζεύς, Διός m.	Zeus
ἤ	or; than
†ἥδομαι	I enjoy myself; I take pleasure in (+ dat.)
ἡδονή f.	pleasure
ἡδύς -εῖα -ύ	sweet, pleasant
ἦλθον	*aor. of* †ἔρχομαι, εἶμι
ἥκω	I have come (impf. ἧκον = I had come)
ἡμεῖς	we
ἡμέρᾱ f.	day
ἦν	*1 sg.* or *3 sg. impf. of* †εἰμί (I am)
ἡνίκα	when

ἡττάομαι	I am defeated
θαυμάζω	I wonder at, admire; I wonder (if, at the fact that …)
θεός m.	god
θέρος, -ους n.	summer
θέω	I run
Θῆβαι f.pl.	Thebes
θηρεύω	I hunt, seek
θηρίον	wild beast
Θησεύς, -έως m.	Theseus
θνητός -ή -όν	mortal
θυγάτηρ, θυγατρός f.	daughter
θῦμός m.	soul, heart; desire
ἰδ-	*aor. stem of* †ὁράω
ἰέναι	*pres. infin. of* †ἔρχομαι, εἶμι
ἱκανός -ή -όν	sufficient, enough
ἵνα + subjunctive *or* optative	in order that, to
ἵνα + indicative	where
ἴστε	*2 pl. indicative & imperative of* †οἶδα
ἴσως	perhaps
καθίζομαι	I sit down
καί	and; also; even
καί … καί	both … and …
καίπερ	although
†καίω	I burn (tr.)
κακόν n.	evil
κακός -ή -όν	bad, disloyal
καλός -ή -όν	beautiful, good; creditable
κατά + acc.	according to; in accordance with
†καταλαμβάνω	I seize, capture
†καταλέγω	I tell, recount
†καταμένω	I stay behind, remain
†καταφεύγω	I flee
καταχειροτονέω (+ gen.)	I vote against by a show of hands
κατείληπται	*3 sg. pf. pass. of* †καταλαμβάνω

†κατέχω	I check, stop; possess, keep
κεῖνος -η -ο = ἐκεῖνος -η -ο	
κελεύω	I order
κενός -ή -όν	empty
κινδῦνεύω	I am in danger, run a risk
†κλαίω	I weep (for)
Κλέαρχος m.	Clearchus
κλύω	I hear (+ gen. of person & acc. of thing)
κρατέω	I am strong; I control, defeat; I have power over, rule (+ gen.)
κράτιστος -η -ον	best
κείνω	I judge, decide
κρίνω	I judge, decide
†κτάομαι	I obtain, acquire, get; (pf.) I possess
Κῦρος m.	Cyrus (king of Lydia)
κωλύω	I hinder, prevent
Λακεδαιμόνιοι m.pl.	Lacedaimonians, *i.e.* Spartans
†λαμβάνω	I take
†λανθάνω	I escape (the) notice (of)
†λέγω	I speak, say
†λείπω	I leave
Λέων, -οντος m.	Leon
λῑμώττω	I am famished
λόφος m.	crest of a hill; a helmet
λοχᾱγός m.	captain
λῦπέομαι	I grieve, suffer distress
λύω	I loosen, untie; I break
μακάριος -ᾱ -ον	blessed, happy
μάλιστα	most, especially
μᾶλλον	more; rather
†μανθάνω	I learn, understand
Μαρσύᾱς, -ου m.	Marsyas (a satyr)
†μάχομαι	I fight
μεγαλοφροσύνη f.	greatness of spirit, arrogance
μέγας, μεγάλη, μέγα	great, big
μείζων -ον	greater (*comparative of* μέγας)
†μέλει	X (dat.) is concerned about Y (gen.)

†μέλλω	I am about to, intend to; I hesitate
μέν ... δέ ...	on the one hand ... but on the other hand ... (both second word in clause)
†μένω	I remain
μετά + acc.	after
μετά + gen.	with
†μεταδίδωμι	I give a share in X (gen.)
†μεταπέμπομαι	I send for, summon
μέτριος -ᾱ -ον	moderate
μή	not; in order that ... not, lest
μηδείς, μηδεμία, μηδέν	no one, nothing
μήν, μηνός m.	month
μήποτε	never
μήτηρ, μητρός f.	mother
μουσικός -ή -όν	musical, harmonious
μῦθος m.	word; story
μύρμηξ, -ηκος m.	ant
μῶν;	surely not?
νεᾱνίᾱς, -ου m.	young man
νεκρός m.	corpse
νέος -ᾱ -ον	young; new
νῑκάω	I conquer
νίκη f.	victory
νόμος m.	law
νοῦς m.	mind, sense
νῦν	now
νύξ, νυκτός f.	night
Ξενοφῶν, Ξενοφῶντος m.	Xenophon
Ξέρξης, -ου m.	Xerxes, a Persian king
ξυμφορά = συμφορά	
†ξύνειμι	I am with, live with
ὁ, ἡ, τό	the (definite article)
ὅδε, ἥδε, τόδε	this
Ὀδυσσεύς, -έως m.	Odysseus
οἱ = αὐτῷ	to him, to her (οἱ is enclitic)
οἱ μέν ... οἱ δέ ...	some ... others ...

†οἶδα	I know (see p. 95)
οἴκαδε	to home, homewards
οἰκέω οἶκον	I manage (my) household
οἰκίᾱ f.	house
οἰκονόμος m.	householder
οἶκος m.	house, household
†οἶμαι, οἴομαι	I think
οἴμοι	alas!
ὀλιγαρχίᾱ f.	oligarchy
ὄμμα, -ατος n.	eye
†ὄμνῡμι	I swear
ὅμοιος -ᾱ -ον + dat.	like, similar to
ὁμολογέω	I agree
ὅπλα n.pl.	arms, weapons
ὅποι	to where
ὅπως + subj. *or* opt.	in order that, to; that
ὅπως + fut. indic.	see to it that
†ὁράω	I see
ὀρθός -ή -όν	straight
ὅρκος m.	oath
ὀρχέομαι	I dance
ὅς, ἥ, ὅ	who, which
ὅστις, ἥτις, ὅτι	who(ever), which(ever), what(ever)
ὅτε	when; seeing that
ὅτι	that
οὐ (οὐκ, οὐχ)	not (see p. 204)
οὐδείς, οὐδεμία, οὐδέν	no, no one, nothing
οὐκοῦν	therefore; isn't it? (see p. 211)
οὖν	and so, therefore (second word)
οὖς, ὠτός n.	ear
οὐσίᾱ f.	property
οὔτε … οὔτε …	neither … nor …
οὗτος, αὕτη, τοῦτο	this
οὕτω(ς)	thus
παῖς, παιδός c.	boy, girl; child; slave
παρά + acc.	contrary to; alongside of
παρά + dat.	beside, in the presence of, with

παρασκευάζω	I prepare
†πάρειμι	I am present
†πάρεστι	it is possible for X (dat.) to Y (infin.)
†παρέχει	it is possible for X (dat.) to Y (infin.)
†παρέχω	I provide
πᾶς, πᾶσα, πᾶν	all
†πάσχω	I suffer, undergo
πατήρ, πατρός m.	father
πειράομαι	I try
πέμπτος -η -ον	fifth
†πέμπω	I send
πένης, -ητος m.	a poor man
πέπονθα	pf. of †πάσχω
Περδίκκᾱς, -ου m.	Perdiccas, king of Macedonia
περί + gen.	about, concerning
Πλάταια f.	Plataea
πλοῦς m.	sailing, voyage
πλούσιος -ᾱ -ον	rich
πόθεν;	from where?
ποῖ;	to where? where … to?
ποιέω	I do, make
πολεμέω (+ dat.)	I make war on
πολέμιος -ᾱ -ον	hostile
πολέμιοι m.pl.	the enemy
πόλεμος m.	war
πόλις, -εως f.	city
πολύς, πολλή, πολύ	much (pl. many)
οἱ πολλοί m.pl.	(the majority of) the people
πορεύομαι	I travel; I march
πόσος -η -ον;	how much? how great? (pl. how many?)
ποτέ	once, at some time, ever (enclitic)
πότερον/πότερα … ἤ …	whether … or …
ποῦ;	where?
πρᾶγμα, -ατος n.	thing; business, negotiation; matter, affair
†πράττω	I do; I get on
πρεσβείᾱ f.	deputation
πρέσβυς, -εως m.	old man; ambassador
πρίν	before
προθῡμίᾱ f.	eagerness, enthusiasm

πρόθῡμος -ον	ready, willing, eager
πρός + acc.	to, towards
†προσελαύνω	I ride towards
†προσέχω (+ dat.)	I bring near, apply to
†προσέχω τὸν νοῦν (+ dat.)	I pay attention to
προσήκει	it is fitting for X (dat.) to Y (infin.)
‡προστάττω	I position at; I order
πρότερον	before, earlier
†πυνθάνομαι	I find out
πώποτε	ever
πῶς;	how?
Σαλαμίνιος -ᾱ -ον	from Salamis
Σαλαμίς, -ῖνος f.	Salamis
σῑγάω	I keep quiet
σιωπή f.	silence
Σκῦρος, -ου f.	Scyrus (an island in the Aegean)
σοφός -ή -όν	wise, intelligent, clever
σός, σή, σόν	your, of you (sg.)
σπονδαί f.pl.	treaty, truce
στάδιον n.	stade (see p. 135)
στολή f.	dress, robe
στόλος m.	expedition
στρατεύω	I march
στρατηγός m.	general
στρατιᾱ́ f.	army
στρατιώτης m.	soldier
σύ	you (sg.)
συμβουλεύω (+ dat.)	I give advice, advise
συμμαχέω (+ dat.)	I am allied in war with
συμφορά f.	disaster
†συνάγω	I collect
συνακολουθέω (+ dat.)	I follow along with
σφῶν (gen.)	they (see p. 148–9)
σχολάζω	I have spare time
σωτηρίᾱ f.	safety, deliverance

τἆλλα = τὰ ἄλλα	
τάξις, -εως f.	rank, order
ταὐτά = τὰ αὐτά	
Ταφίοι m.pl.	Taphians
τέθνηκα	I am dead (*pf. of* †θνῄσκω)
τέττιξ, -ῑγος m.	grasshopper
τί;	why?
τίς; τί; (gen. τίνος)	who? what?
τις, τι (gen. τινός)	a certain, some, someone, something (enclitic)
†τιτρώσκω	wound
τοι	then (enclitic, drawing inference)
τοίνυν	well then; further (second word)
τράπονται = τρέπονται	
τρεῖς, τρία	three
†τρέπω	I cause to turn
†τρέπομαι	I turn (intr.)
τριήρης, -ους f.	trireme
Τροίᾱ f.	Troy
τροφή f.	food
†τυγχάνω	I happen; I meet (+ gen.)
τυφλός -ή -όν	blind
ὑβρίζω	I insult, treat violently
ὕβρις, -εως f.	wanton violence, outrage
ὑγιής -ές	healthy
ὑμεῖς	you (pl.)
ὑπέρ + gen.	on behalf of
ὑπηρετέω (+ dat.)	I serve
ὑπό + gen.	by; out of
ὑστεραίᾱ f.	the next day
(τῇ) ὑστεραίᾳ	on the next day
ὕστερον	later
†φέρω	I bring, carry
†φεύγω	I flee, run away from
†φημί, οὐ φημί	I say; I say … not, deny (see p. 156)
φιλέω	I love, like

φιλίᾱ f. friendship
φίλος m. friend
†φοβέομαι I fear
φροντίζω I think, worry; I take thought for (+ gen.)

Χαλκιδική f. Chalcidice
χειμάζει it's stormy
χειμών, -ῶνος m. winter; storm
χείρ, χειρός f. hand
  (poetic gen. χερός)

Χειρίσοφος m. Cheirisophus
χιών, -όνος f. snow
χράομαι + dat. I use
†χρή it is necessary for X (acc.) to Y (infin.)
χρήματα, -άτων n. money
χρῡσίον n. a piece of gold, gold
χρόνος m. time

ψευδής -ές false
ψηφίζομαι I vote
ψύχω I blow; I make cool; I dry out

ὦ O (addressing someone)
ὥρᾱ f. season
ὡς that; as
ὡς + acc. to (motion towards people, not places)

ὦτα ears (*nom. & acc. pl. of* οὖς)
ὠφελέω I help
ὤφελον + infin. if only!

| English – Greek

able, I am	†δύναμαι; οἷός τ’ εἰμί (see p. 93)
act	†πράττω
admire	θαυμάζω
advantage, it is of	λῡσιτελεῖ + dat. & infin.
advise	συμβουλεύω + dat. & infin.; †παραινέω + dat.
afraid, I am	†φοβέομαι; δέδοικα
Agathon	Ἀγάθων, -ωνος m.
all	πᾶς, πᾶσα, πᾶν
always	ἀεί
Amazon	Ἀμαζών, -όνος f.
and	καί
angry, I am ~ with	ὀργίζομαι + dat.
appear	†φαίνομαι + infin.
apple	μῆλον n.
Arachne	Ἀράχνη f.
arrest	†ἀπάγω; †συλλαμβάνω
arrive in, at	†ἀφικνέομαι εἰς + acc.
Artemis	Ἄρτεμις, -ιδος f.
ask (a question)	†ἐρωτάω
Athene	Ἀθήνη f.
Athenians, the	Ἀθηναῖοι m.pl.
Athens	Ἀθῆναι f.pl.
Athens, in	Ἀθήνησι
Athens, to	Ἀθήναζε
bad	κακός -ή -όν
be	†εἰμί (= I am)
beautiful	καλός -ή -όν
because	διότι (see p. 172); ἐπεί, ἐπειδή; ἅτε + participle (see p. 137)
become	†γίγνομαι
before	πρίν (see p. 199)
believe (that)	πιστεύω; †νομίζω
betray	†προδίδωμι

better	ἀμείνων -ον
book	βιβλίον n.; βίβλος f.
both ... and ...	τε (enclitic) ... καί ...; καί ... καί ...
boy	παῖς, παιδός m.
brave	ἀνδρεῖος -ᾱ -ον
bring	†φέρω; †ἄγω (= lead)
brother	ἀδελφός m.
build	οἰκοδομέω
bury	†θάπτω
but	ἀλλά; δέ (second word)
by (= at the hands of)	ὑπό + gen.
can (= I am able)	†δύναμαι; οἷός τ' εἰμί (see p. 93)
carefully	ἐπιμελῶς
celebrated	λαμπρός -ά -όν
challenge	†προκαλέομαι
choose	†αἱρέομαι
citizen	πολίτης, -ου m.
city	πόλις, -εως f.
Cleopatra	Κλεοπάτρᾱ f.
clever	σοφός -ή -όν
come	†προσέρχομαι
come on!	ἄγε
come to	†προσέρχομαι
companion	ἑταῖρος m.
condemn	†καταγιγνώσκω + gen. (*person condemned*) & acc. (*penalty*)
condition, on ~ that	ἐφ' ᾧ; ἐφ' ᾧτε (see p. 179)
continue	‡διατελέω + participle
converse	†διαλέγομαι
corrupt	†διαφθείρω
country (= land)	χώρᾱ f.
courage	ἀνδρείᾱ f.
cowardice	κακίᾱ f.
cowardly	κακός -ή -όν; δειλός -ή -όν
Crete	Κρήτη f.
Cyprus	Κύπρος f.
Cyrus	Κῦρος m.

Daedalus	Δαίδαλος m.
dark	σκοτεινός -ή -όν
daughter	θυγάτηρ, -τρός f.
dawn, at	ἅμα (τῇ) ἕῳ
death	θάνατος m.
deceive	ἐξαπατάω
deed	ἔργον n.
defeat	νῑκάω
desire	ἐράω + gen.
desperate, I am	ἀπορέω
die	†ἀποθνῄσκω
dispute	ἀγωνίζομαι
do	†πρᾱ́ττω; ποιέω
doctor	ῑ̓ᾱτρός m.
enemy	πολέμιοι m.pl.
escape	†φεύγω
escape (the) notice (of), I	†λανθάνω
ever since	ἐξ οὗ; ἐξ ὅτου; ἀφ᾽ οὗ
famous	ἀξιόλογος -ον
father	πατήρ, πατρός m.
field	ἀγρός m.
fight	μάχομαι
find	†εὑρίσκω
find out	†πυνθάνομαι
first	πρῶτος -η -ον
fly	πέτομαι
foot	πούς, ποδός m.
forbid	ἀπαγορεύω
forgive	†συγγιγνώσκω + dat.
former, the	ἐκεῖνος -η -ο
friend	φίλος m.
friendly	φίλιος -ᾱ -ον
frightened, I am	†φοβέομαι
from	ἐκ + gen.; ἀπό + gen.
future, in the	εἰς τὸν ἔπειτα χρόνον
girl	κόρη f.; παῖς, παιδός f.
give	†δίδωμι

give back	†ἀποδίδωμι
go	†ἔρχομαι; †βαίνω; χωρέω
go away	†ἀπέρχομαι; †ἄπειμι (fut. meaning in indicative, see p. 94)
go to	†προσέρχομαι
god, goddess	θεός c.
gone, ought to be	ἰτέος -ᾱ -ον (see pp. 193–4)
Greek	Ἕλλην, -ηνος m.
grounds, on the ~ that	ὡς + participle; ὅτι
guard	†φυλάττω
gymnasium	γυμνάσιον n.
hand, on the other	δέ (second word)
handsome	καλός -ή -όν
happen	†τυγχάνω
happy	μακάριος -ᾱ -ον
hate	μῑσέω
have	†ἔχω
hear	†ἀκούω (see p. 18)
Helen	Ἑλένη f.
help	ὠφελέω + acc.; βοηθέω + dat.
her	αὐτήν (acc.)
Heracles	Ἡρακλῆς, -έους m.
here	ἐνθάδε
here (= to here)	ἐνθάδε, δεῦρο
hero	ἥρως, ἥρωος m.
herself	ἑαυτήν or αὐτήν (acc.)
him	αὐτόν (acc.)
himself	αὐτός (see p. 146)
his own	ἑαυτοῦ (= of himself)
home, (to)	οἴκαδε
home, at	οἴκοι
hope	ἐλπίς, -ίδος f.
hope	ἐλπίζω
house	οἰκίᾱ f.
how (with adjectives & adverbs)	ὡς
how many	ὁπόσοι -αι -α
how?	πῶς;

hundred	ἑκατόν
hurry	σπεύδω
husband	ἀνήρ, ἀνδρός m.

I	ἐγώ
if	εἰ; ἐάν
if ever (indefinite)	ἐάν (with subj.); εἰ (with opt.)
if only	see pp. 169–70
impossible	ἀδύνατος -ον
in order to	ἵνα, ὅπως, ὡς, etc. (see pp. 174–5)
inasmuch as	ἅτε; οἷα; οἷον (all + participle)
intelligent	σοφός -ή -όν

kill	†ἀποκτείνω
king	βασιλεύς, -έως m.
kiss	κυνέω
know	†οἶδα; †γιγνώσκω

late	ὄψε
latter, the	οὗτος, αὕτη, τοῦτο
lead	†ἄγω
leave	†λείπω
like (= similar to)	ὅμοιος -ᾱ -ον + dat.
long (= in length)	τὸ μῆκος
loss, I am at a	ἀπορέω
love	φιλέω; ἐράω + gen.
lover	ἐραστής, -ου m.

make (= appoint)	ποιέω; †καθίστημι
man	ἀνήρ, ἀνδρός m.;
	ἄνθρωπος c. (= human being)
marry	†γαμέω; γαμέομαι (of the woman)
Medea	Μήδεια f.
meet with	†ἐντυγχάνω + dat.
messenger	ἄγγελος m.
mind, I have in	ἐν νῷ †ἔχω
Minos	Μίνως, -ω m.
mistake, I make a	†ἁμαρτάνω

money	χρήματα, -άτων n.pl.
more	μᾶλλον
mother	μήτηρ, -τρός f.
much (= by far) (with comparatives)	πολλῷ
my	ἐμός -ή -όν

necessary, it is	†δεῖ
never	οὐδέποτε; μηδέποτε
nevertheless	ὅμως
new	νέος -ᾱ -ον
next day, on the	τῇ ὑστεραίᾳ
night	νύξ, νυκτός f.
none, no one	οὐδείς, οὐδεμία, οὐδέν; μηδείς etc.
not	οὐ, οὐκ, οὐχ; μή (see pp. 204–6)
now(adays)	νῦν

obey	†πείθομαι + dat.
obviously (doing X), I am	†φαίνομαι; δῆλός εἰμι; φανερός εἰμι (all + participle)
of old	πάλαι
old man	γέρων, -οντος m.
one thing ... another ...	ἄλλο ... ἄλλο ...
opinion	γνώμη f.
or	ἤ
other	ἄλλος -η -ο

Penelope	Πηνελόπη f.
Pericles	Περικλῆς, -έους m.
philosopher	φιλόσοφος m.
place	τόπος m.
Plato	Πλάτων -ωνος m.
poor man	πένης, -ητος m.
possible, it is	ἔξεστι or πάρεστι (both + dat. & infin.)
praise	†ἐπαινέω
prevent	εἴργω; κωλύω
prison	δεσμωτήριον n.
prisoner	δεσμώτης, -ου m.

promise	†ὑπισχνέομαι
prostitute	πόρνη f.
punish	κολάζω
queen	βασίλεια f.
quickly, as ~ as possible	ὡς τάχιστα
reach	†ἀφικνέομαι εἰς (or πρός) + acc.
read	†ἀναγιγνώσκω
realize	†αἰσθάνομαι
refrain from	†ἀπέχομαι + gen.
remember	†μιμνήσκομαι usu. + gen.
responsible (for)	αἴτιος -ᾱ -ον + gen.
rich	πλούσιος -ᾱ -ον
road	ὁδός f.
safe	ἀσφαλής -ές
sail	†πλέω
same, the	ὁ αὐτός, ἡ αὐτή, τὸ αὐτό
save	†σῴζω
say	†λέγω; †φημί (see p. 96)
say … not	οὐ φημί (see p. 156)
see	†ὁράω
see that	ὅπως (see p. 169)
self	αὐτός -ή -ό
send	†πέμπω
set out	ἀφορμάομαι
she	αὕτη
show	†δείκνῡμι
since	ἐπεί; ἐπειδή
sister	ἀδελφή f.
slave	δοῦλος m.
snake	ὄφις, ὄφεως m.
so (= therefore)	οὖν (second word); ὥστε
so X (adj. or adv.) that	οὕτω(ς) … ὥστε (see pp. 177–8)
so (with adjectives & adverbs)	ὡς
Socrates	Σωκράτης, -ους m.
soldier	στρατιώτης, -ου m.

some ... others ...	ἄλλοι ... ἄλλοι ...;
	οἱ μέν ... οἱ δέ ...
sorry, I am	μεταμέλει + dat. (*person who is*
	sorry) & gen. (*cause of sorrow*)
soul	ψυχή f.
stade	στάδιον n. (but see p. 135)
stay	†μένω
still (of time)	ἔτι
still (= nevertheless)	ὅμως
stop (= prevent, hinder)	εἴργω; κωλύω
straight away	εὐθύς
struggle (= I am in difficulties)	ἀπορέω
student	μαθητής, -οῦ m.
stupid	μῶρος -ᾱ -ον
such	τοιοῦτος, τοιαύτη, τοιοῦτο
surely ... not ...?	ἆρα μή ... ; μῶν ... ;
surely ...?	ἆρ' οὐ ... ;
take care	εὐλαβέομαι
teach	†διδάσκω
tell (= inform)	†ἀγγέλλω + dat.
tell (= order, command)	κελεύω
terrible	δεινός -ή -όν
than	ἤ (or use genitive – see p. 16)
theatre	θέᾱτρον n.
them	αὐτούς -ᾱς -ά (acc.)
think	†νομίζω
Thirty, the	οἱ τριάκοντα
this	οὗτος, αὕτη, τοῦτο
though	καίπερ (+ participle)
thousand	χίλιοι -αι -α
thyself	σεαυτόν, σεαυτήν (acc.)
to	πρός + acc.; (to people) ὡς + acc.
to (= in order to, in order that)	ἵνα, ὅπως, ὡς, etc. (see pp. 174–5)
trick	μηχανή f.
try	πειράομαι
understand	†μανθάνω
unhappy	δυστυχής -ές
until	ἕως; μέχρι; μέχρι οὗ
use	χράομαι + dat.

very	μάλα
virtuous	ἀγαθός -ή -όν; σώφρων -ον
wait	†μένω
want	†βούλομαι; †ἐθέλω
we	ἡμεῖς
weak	ἀσθενής -ές
what?	τί; (in indirect question also ὅτι)
what (indirect question)	ὅτι
what sort of (indirect question)	ὁποῖος -ᾱ -ον
when	ἐπεί; ἐπειδή
whenever	ὅταν (with subj.); ὅτε (with opt.)
where ... from?	πόθεν;
where?	ποῦ;
whether ... or ... (indirect questions)	πότερον ... ἤ ...
whether ... or ... (in conditionals)	εἴτε ... εἴτε ...
which (relative pronoun)	ὅς, ἥ, ὅ
who?	τίς;
who (indirect question)	ὅστις, ἥτις, ὅτι
who (relative pronoun)	ὅς, ἥ, ὅ
wife	γυνή, γυναικός f.
willing	ἑκών -οῦσα -όν
willing, I am	†ἐθέλω
winter	χειμών, -ῶνος m.
wisdom	σοφίᾱ f.
wise	σοφός -ή -όν
with	μετά + gen.; σύν + dat.
woman	γυνή, γυναικός f.
word	λόγος m.
work	ἐργάζομαι
wound	†τιτρώσκω
wrong, do ~ to	ἀδικέω
you	σύ (sg.), ὑμεῖς (pl.)
young man	νεᾱνίᾱς, -ου m.
Zeus	Ζεύς, Διός m.

Index of Greek Words

Index